Africa: War and Conflict in the Twentieth Century

MW00995814

This book examines the causes, course and consequences of warfare in twentieth-century Africa, a period that spanned colonial rebellions, both world wars and the decolonization process. Timothy Stapleton contextualizes the essential debates and controversies surrounding African conflict in the twentieth century while providing insightful introductions to such conflicts as the following:

- African rebellions against colonial regimes in the early twentieth century, including the rebellion and infamous genocide of the Herero and Nama people in present-day Namibia;
- the African fronts of World War I and World War II, and the involvement of colonized African peoples in these global conflicts;
- conflict surrounding the widespread decolonization of Africa in the 1950s and 1960s;
- rebellion and civil war in Africa during the Cold War, when United States and Soviet elements often intervened in efforts to turn African battlegrounds into Cold War proxy conflicts;
- the Second Congo Civil War, which is arguably the bloodiest conflict in any region since World War II.

Supported by a glossary, a who's who of key figures, a timeline of major events, a rich bibliography and a set of documents that highlight the themes of the book, *Africa: War and Conflict in the Twentieth Century* is the best available resource for students and scholars seeking an introduction to violent conflict in recent African history.

Timothy Stapleton is a professor in the Department of History at the University of Calgary, Canada. He is the author of *A History of Genocide in Africa* (2017), the three-volume *A Military History of Africa* (2013) and *A Military History of South Africa: From the Dutch–Khoi Wars to the End of Apartheid* (2010).

Introduction to the series

History is the narrative constructed by historians from traces left by the past. Historical enquiry is often driven by contemporary issues and, in consequence, historical narratives are constantly reconsidered, reconstructed and reshaped. The fact that different historians have different perspectives on issues means that there is often controversy and no universally agreed version of past events. Seminar Studies was designed to bridge the gap between current research and debate, and the broad, popular, general surveys that often date rapidly.

The volumes in the series are written by historians who are not only familiar with the latest research and current debates concerning their topic, but who have themselves contributed to our understanding of the subject. The books are intended to provide the reader with a clear introduction to a major topic in history. They provide both a narrative of events and a critical analysis of contemporary interpretations. They include the kinds of tools generally omitted from specialist monographs: a chronology of events, a glossary of terms and brief biographies of 'who's who'. They also include bibliographical essays in order to guide students to the literature on various aspects of the subject. Students and teachers alike will find that the selection of documents will stimulate the discussion and offer insight into the raw materials used by historians in their attempt to understand the past.

Clive Emsley and Gordon Martel
Series Editors

Africa: War and Conflict in the Twentieth Century

Timothy Stapleton

Routledge
Taylor & Francis Group

LONDON AND NEW YORK

First published 2018
by Routledge
2 Park Square, Milton Park, Abingdon, Oxon OX14 4RN

and by Routledge
711 Third Avenue, New York, NY 10017

Routledge is an imprint of the Taylor & Francis Group, an informa business

© 2018 Timothy J. Stapleton

British Library Cataloguing-in-Publication Data
A catalogue record for this book is available from the British Library

Library of Congress Cataloging-in-Publication Data
A catalog record has been requested for this book

ISBN: 978-1-138-28195-0 (hbk)
ISBN: 978-1-138-28196-7 (pbk)
ISBN: 978-1-351-10468-5 (ebk)

Typeset in Sabon
by Florence Production Ltd, Stoodleigh, Devon, UK

Contents

Figures

Chronology

1899–1902	South African War (Second Anglo-Boer War) (South Africa)
1900	Asante Rebellion (Ghana)
1900–4	Rebellion in British Somaliland
1901–5	British conquest of the Igbo (Southeastern Nigeria)
1902–3	British conquest of the Sokoto Caliphate (Northern Nigeria)
1904–7	Genocide of the Herero and Nama in German South West Africa (Namibia)
1905	Maji Maji Rebellion in German East Africa (Tanzania)
1906	Zulu Rebellion (South Africa)
1907–11	French occupation of Morocco
1913	Rebellion in British Somaliland
1914	Togoland Campaign of World War I
1914–15	Afrikaner Rebellion in South Africa
1914–15	South West Africa Campaign of World War I
1914–16	Cameroon Campaign of World War I
1914–18	East Africa Campaign of World War I
1915	Chilembwe Rebellion in Nyasaland (Malawi)
1915–16	Rebellions in Gold Coast (Ghana) and Nigeria
1915–16	Ottoman/German offensives against the Suez Canal
1915–17	Sanussi attacks from Libya into Egypt
1916	British conquest of Darfur
1916	Tuareg Rebellion in French West Africa
1917	Volta–Bani War in French West Africa
1919–20	British use air power to defeat rebels in British Somaliland
1920–6	Spanish–Rif War (Morocco)
1931–4	French crush resistance in Morocco
1911–12	Italian occupation of Libya (Italo–Ottoman War)
1922–31	Italian counter-insurgency in Libya
1927–32	Rebellion in French Equatorial Africa (War of the Hoe Handles)
1935	Italian invasion of Ethiopia

1940	Battle of Dakar (Senegal)
1940	Free French forces seize Libreville (Gabon)
1940–1	East Africa Campaign of World War II
1940–3	North Africa Campaign of World War II
1942	South African and British forces occupy Madagascar
1947–8	Rebellion in Madagascar
1948	Arab–Israeli War
1952–60	Kenya Emergency
1954–62	Algerian War of Independence
1955–71	Insurgency in Cameroon
1955–72	First Sudan Civil War
1956	Suez Crisis
1960–3	Katanga Secession (Congo Crisis)
1960–74	Independence wars in Portuguese Africa (Angola, Mozambique and Guinea-Bissau)
1961–90	Anti-apartheid struggle in South Africa
1961–91	Independence war in Eritrea
1962	Tuareg Rebellion in Mali
1964–5	Rebellion in Eastern Congo and Kwilu
1965–80	Zimbabwe's independence war/Rhodesian Bush War
1966–7	Mutinies in Eastern Congo
1966–89	War of Independence in South West Africa (Namibia)
1967	Arab–Israeli War (Six Day War)
1967–70	Nigerian Civil War
1968–90	Civil war in Chad
1973	Arab–Israeli War (Yom Kippur War)
1975–89	Angolan Civil War (Involvement of South African, Cuban, Soviet forces)
1976–91	Western Sahara Conflict
1977–8	Ogaden War (Somalia–Ethiopia)
1977–8	Egypt–Libya War
1978–91	Insurgency in Tigray, Ethiopia
1978–9	Kagera War (Tanzania–Uganda)
1981	US Naval operations off Libya
1981–6	Insurgency in Southern Uganda
1981–present	Somalia Civil War
1983–2005	Second Sudan Civil War
1985	Mali–Burkina Faso (Christmas War)
1986	US Naval operations off Libya
1986–2006	Insurgency in Northern Uganda
1987	Libya–Chad War (Toyota War)
1989	US Naval operations off Libya
1989–97	Liberian Civil War
1990–5	Tuareg Rebellion in Mali and Niger
1990–3	Rwandan Patriotic Front (RPF) invasion of Rwanda

Who's who

Abd el-Karim el-Khattabi – Led resistance to Spanish colonialism in Morocco's Rif Mountains during the 1920s.

Afwerki, Isaias – A leader of the Eritrean People's Liberation Front (EPLF) during the independence war of the 1970s and 1980s and president of independent Eritrea from 1991 to the present.

Aguiyi-Ironsi, Johnson – A major-general in the Nigerian army who became head of state following the January 1966 coup but was then murdered during another coup in July of the same year.

Aidid, Mohamed Farrah – An officer of the Somali military who led a faction of the United Somali Congress (USC) during Somalia's civil war of the 1980s and 1990s. He opposed United Nations intervention in 1992, eluded captured by US forces the following year and passed away in 1996.

Al-Bashir, Umar Hasan Ahmad – Coming to power through a military coup in 1989, he led the Sudanese government during rebellions in the south (1983–2005) and west (2002+). His regime's violent campaign in the western region of Darfur from 2002 has resulted in his indictment for crimes against humanity and genocide by the International Criminal Court (ICC).

Al-Mahdi, Sadiq – The Islamist prime minister of Sudan from 1985 to 1989 during the Second Sudanese Civil War (1983–2005).

Amin, Idi – The commander of the Ugandan military who overthrew President Milton Obote in 1971. Amin imposed a brutal regime on Uganda until he was deposed by the Tanzanian invasion of 1979.

Badoglio, Pietro – As Italian governor of Libya from 1929 to 1933, he was instrumental in crushing local resistance. In 1935 he took over Italian forces that were invading Ethiopia.

Bambatha – A Zulu leader who led a rebellion against British colonial rule in Natal in 1906.

Barka Ngainoumbey – A Central African prophet who initiated resistance against French rule during the late 1920s.

Barre, Siad – Taking power in a 1969 military coup, he served as president of Somalia until he was overthrown in 1991 during the country's civil war.

Bemba, Jean-Pierre – Leader of the Ugandan-backed Movement for the Liberation of Congo (MLC) during the Second Congo War (1998–2002). In 2008 he was arrested and sent to the International Criminal Court in The Hague where, in 2016, he was convicted of crimes against humanity and war crimes.

Botha, Louis – Commander of Boer Transvaal forces during the Second Anglo-Boer War (1899–1902). He became the first prime minister of the Union of South Africa in 1910 and during World War I he led South African troops during the suppression of the Boer rebellion and the invasion of German South West Africa.

Bouteflika, Abdelaziz – A veteran of Algeria's independence movement, he was elected president in 1999 and pursued a policy of amnesty that eventually ended the country's civil war (1991–2002).

Buller, Redvers Henry – Commanded British forces in South Africa during the initial phase of the Second Anglo-Boer War (1899–1902) until he was replaced by Frederick Sleigh Roberts at the start of 1900. Buller was retained as commander of British troops in Natal.

Buyoya, Pierre – A Tutsi military officer who ruled Burundi from 1987 to 1993 and from 1996 to 2003.

Cabral, Amilcar – Leader of the African Party for the Independence of Guinea and Cape Verde (PAIGC) that fought Portuguese colonial forces during the 1960s and early 1970s. He was assassinated in 1973.

Chilembwe, John – A Baptist minister who played a central role in an African rebellion against British rule in Nyasaland (now Malawi) in 1915.

De Spinola, Antonio – Commander of Portuguese forces in Guinea-Bissau during the late 1960s and early 1970s. In 1974 he briefly served as president of Portugal following the military overthrow of the Marcello Caetano regime.

Deby, Idriss – Leader of the Patriotic Salvation Movement (MPS) that overthrew Chad's Hissene Habre in 1990. He became president of Chad the same year and continues in that role.

Denard, Bob – A French mercenary leader who worked for the separatist regime in Katanga during the early 1960s and then for the pro-Western Congolese government during its 1964–5 campaign against leftist rebels in eastern Congo. He was involved in a mercenary mutiny against the Congolese government in 1967.

Diagne, Blaise – In 1914 he became the first black Senegalese elected to the French National Assembly and during World War I was placed in charge of recruiting in French West Africa.

Dinuzulu – The legitimate Zulu king who stayed out of the Zulu Rebellion of 1906 yet was imprisoned in its wake.

Djamous, Hassan – A general who led Chadian forces to victory during the 1987 "Toyota War" with Libya. In 1989 he was killed on the orders of Chad's President Hissene Habre who suspected the general of plotting a coup.

Doe, Samuel – A master sergeant in the Liberian military who overthrew the last Americo-Liberian president in 1980. Doe ruled Liberia until 1990 when he was killed by rebels during the First Liberian Civil War (1989–96).

Dos Santos, Jose Eduardo – A veteran of the Angolan war of independence against Portugal, he became president of Angola in 1979 and led that country through most of its civil war (1975–2002). He retired from the presidency in 2017.

Eboue, Felix – The Black French governor of Chad who stuck with the Free French during World War II.

Gaddafi, Muammar – Coming to power in a 1969 military coup, he was the dictator of Libya until killed by rebels in 2011. Backed by the Soviet Union during the Cold War, his regime sponsored many rebel groups throughout Africa and sought the creation of an Islamic State of the Sahel.

Garang, John – Leader of the Sudan People's Liberation Army (SPLA) during the Second Sudanese Civil War of 1983–2005. He became president of the Government of South Sudan in July 2005 but died in a helicopter crash a few weeks later.

Gowon, Yakubu – A lieutenant colonel in the Nigerian army who became head of state following a military coup in July 1966 and led the federal military government during the Nigerian Civil War of 1967–70.

Guevara, Ernesto "Che" – Originally from Argentina, this leftist revolutionary led a contingent of Cuban troops to eastern Congo in 1965. He was killed while trying to lead an insurgency in Boliva in 1967.

Habre, Hissene – Founding leader of the Armed Forces of the North (FAN) in Chad during the civil war of the late 1970s. Between 1982 and 1990, he was president of Chad and was supported by France and the United States in a war against northern rebels and Libyan invaders. In 2016 an

African Union international court in Senegal convicted him of human rights abuses.

Habyarimana, Juvenal – The Hutu commander of the Rwandan military who took power in a coup in 1973. In April 1994 he was killed when his presidential jet was shot down which signaled the beginning of the genocide against the Tutsi.

Hoare, Mike – A South African-based mercenary leader who worked for the separatist regime in Katanga during the early 1960s and then for the pro-Western Congolese government during its 1964–5 campaign against leftist rebels in eastern Congo.

Itote, Waruhiu – Known as "General China," he was a leader of the Kenya Land and Freedom Army, called Mau Mau by the British, during the 1950s.

Kabila, Joseph – Inherited the presidency of the Democratic Republic of Congo (DRC) when his father Laurent Kabila was assassinated in 2001.

Kabila, Laurent – Led the Alliance of Democratic Forces for the Liberation of Congo (AFDL) during the First Congo War (1996–7). He became president in 1997, led the Congolese government during the first years of the Second Congo War (1998–2002) and was assassinated in 2001.

Kagame, Paul – A Rwandan Tutsi exile who grew up in Uganda and became prominent in the National Resistance Army (NRA) during the 1980s. After the death of Fred Rwigyima in 1990, Kagame took command of the Rwandan Patriotic Forces (RPF) that had invaded Rwanda. With the RPF takeover of the country following the 1994 genocide, Kagame became vice president and defence minister until 2000, when he became president.

Kalonji, Albert – Leader of the secessionist state of South Kasai during the Congo Crisis of the early 1960s.

Kasavubu, Joseph – In 1960, he became the first president of the Congo upon independence from Belgium. He was overthrown by Congolese military leader Joseph Mobutu in 1965.

Kenyatta, Jomo – A Kenyan nationalist leader who was jailed by the British during the Mau Mau Uprising of the 1950s and who became Kenya's first prime minister in 1963 and first president in 1964.

Kijikitile Ngwale – An African prophet involved in the Maji Maji rebellion against German rule in East Africa.

Kimathi, Dedan – A leader of the Kenya Land and Freedom Army, known to the British as Mau Mau, during the 1950s. He was captured by the British and executed in 1957.

Kitchener, Horatio Herbert – After leading British forces in Sudan during the 1890s, Kitchener became chief-of-staff to Frederick Sleigh Roberts in South Africa in 1900 and took over command of British forces there at the end of that year.

Kony, Joseph – Leader of the Lord's Resistance Army (LRA), which staged an insurgency in northern Uganda from 1987 until it was pushed out of the country in 2006. Still under Kony, the LRA operates in the remote borderlands of the Central African Republic and the Democratic Republic of Congo (DRC).

Kruger, Paul – President of the South African Republic (Transvaal) from 1883 until the Second Anglo-Boer War (1899–1902). In 1900 he escaped British occupation by fleeing to Europe, where he died in 1904.

Lagu, Joseph – Leader of the Southern Sudan Liberation Movement (SSLM) from the late 1960s to the end of the First Sudanese Civil War in 1972.

Lugard, Frederick – As the first commissioner of the British Protectorate of Northern Nigeria, he was responsible for the conquest of the Sokoto Caliphate during 1902 and 1903. Lugard also became instrumental in popularizing the British administrative system of indirect rule in colonial Africa. In 1914, he became the first British governor of Nigeria.

Lumumba, Patrice – An African nationalist political leader who, in June 1960, became the first prime minister of the Congo after independence from Belgium. In September 1960 he was deposed by the Congolese military and subsequently flown to the separatist territory of Katanga, where he was killed in January 1961.

Machar, Riek – In the 1990s he led an ethnic Nuer faction during violence within the Sudan People's Liberation Army (SPLA).

Machel, Samora – He took over leadership of Front for the Liberation of Mozamibque (FRELIMO) following the death of Eduardo Mondlane in 1969, continued the independence war against the Portuguese and became the first president of Mozambique in 1975. He died in a 1986 aircraft crash in South Africa.

Mandela, Nelson – A leading member of the African National Congress (ANC) during its passive resistance against apartheid in South Africa during the 1950s. In the early 1960s he became a founding leader of Umkhonto we Sizwe (MK), which embarked on an armed struggle to liberate South Africa. Following 27 years in prison, he became the first black president of South Africa in 1994.

Maherero, Samuel – Herero leader during the Herero and Nama rebellion that took place in German South West Africa (Namibia) from 1904 to 1907.

Massu, Jacques – A French officer who directed counterinsurgency operations in Algeria in the 1950s. In 1958 he led a group of officers who seized power in Algiers and were instrumental in bringing Charles de Gaulle to power in Paris.

Mathenge, Stanley – A leader of the Kenya Land and Freedom Army, known as Mau Mau by the British, during the 1950s.

Mengistu, Haile Mariam – Head of Ethiopia's Soviet backed military regime from 1977 to 1991.

Mobutu, Joseph (Mobutu Sese Seko) – Backed by the United States and France, he was the dictator of Zaire (Democratic Republic of Congo) from 1965 to 1997.

Mondlane, Eduardo – US-educated leader of the Front for the Liberation of Mozambique (FRELIMO) that fought Portuguese colonial forces during the 1960s. He was assassinated by Portuguese agents in 1969.

Montgomery, Bernard – A British officer who took over command of the British 8th Army in North Africa in 1942.

Moumie, Felix-Roland – Leader of the Cameroonian Army of National Liberation (ALNK) which opposed the pro-French government during the late 1950s and 1960. He was surreptitiously poisoned by French agents and died in Geneva in November 1960.

Mugabe, Robert – A leading figure in the Zimbabwe African National Union (ZANU) that opposed white minority rule in Rhodesia during the 1960s and 1970s. He became leader of ZANU in the early 1970s. After Zimbabwe's independence, he became prime minister in 1980 and president in 1987. In 2017, after 37 years in power, Mugabe was overthrown by a military coup.

Mulele, Pierre – Leader of a rebellion in the Kwilu region of the Democratic Republic of Congo during 1964.

Museveni, Yoweri – An exiled Ugandan rebel leader during the late 1970s, he participated in the 1979 Tanzanian invasion of Uganda that overthrew Idi Amin. From 1981–6, he led the National Resistance Army (NRA) that fought an insurgency in southern Uganda. He became president of Uganda after the NRA seized Kampala in 1986.

Mussolini, Benito – The fascist leader of Italy who ordered the invasion of Ethiopia in 1935.

Nassar, Gamal Abdel – Leader of the Free Officers Movement that took power in Egypt in 1952, he served as prime minster and president from 1954 to his death in 1970. A prominent Arab nationalist, he led Egypt during the Suez Crisis of 1956 and the Arab-Israeli War of 1967.

Ndadaye, Melchior – Burundi's first Hutu president who was elected to office in June 1993 and assassinated by Tutsi soldiers in October of the same year.

Neto, Agostinho – Leader of the Popular Movement for the Liberation of Angola (MPLA) that fought for independence against Portuguese colonial forces during the 1960s and early 1970s. With the MPLA victory in the 1975 civil war, he became the first president of Angola and served in that position until his death in 1979.

Nkomo, Joshua – Leader of the Zimbabwe African People's Union (ZAPU) that opposed white minority rule in Rhodesia during the 1960s and 1970s. Following the suppression of ZAPU by Robert Mugabe's ZANU-PF government during the early and middle 1980s, Nkomo served as vice-president of Zimbabwe from 1987 to his death in 1999.

Nkurunziza, Pierre – A Hutu leader of the National Council for the Defence of Democracy (CNDD) – Forces for Defence of Democracy (FDD) during Burundi's civil war (1993–2006). He was elected president in 2005.

Nujoma, Sam – Leader of the South West African People's Organization (SWAPO) which, from 1960–89, opposed the South African occupation of South West Africa. He became the first president of independent Namibia in 1990.

Numayri, Ja'afar Muhammad – Coming to power in Sudan in a 1969 military coup, he ended the First Sudanese Civil War by engaging in the 1972 Addis Ababa Agreement but started the Second Sudanese Civil War in 1983 by issuing "Republican Order Number One." In 1985 he was overthrown in another military coup.

Nyerere, Julius – President of Tanzania from 1964–85, he orchestrated his country's invasion of Uganda in 1979.

Nzeugwu, Kaduna – A major in the Nigerian military who led the country's first coup in January 1966. As an officer in the Biafran forces, he was killed in action in 1967 during the Nigerian Civil War.

Obasanjo, Olusegun – A Nigerian military officer who led federal forces, mostly famously the Third Marine Commando Division, during the Nigerian Civil War of 1967–70. Subsequently, he twice served as Nigeria's head of state; as leader of a military regime from 1976–9 and as a civilian president from 1999–2007.

Obote, Milton – The first prime minister of Uganda upon independence in 1962. He became president in 1966 but was overthrown by a military coup in 1971. Obote returned to the presidency in 1980 but was again deposed by a coup in 1985.

Ojukwu, Chukwuemeka Odumegwu – A Nigerian military officer who led the separatist state of Biafra during the Nigerian Civil War of 1967–70.

Omar Mukhtar – Led Libyan resistance to Italian colonialism during the early twentieth century and was captured and executed in 1931.

Oueddei, Goukouni – Led the Libyan sponsored People's Armed Forces (FAP) during Chad's late 1970s civil war. Oueddei seized power in Chad in 1979 but was toppled by Hissene Habre's Armed Forces of the North (FAN) in 1982.

Rhodes, Cecil John – An ardent British imperialist, mining tycoon and Cape Colony politician of the late nineteenth century. He orchestrated the colonial conquest of Southern Rhodesia (Zimbabwe) in the 1890s and his ambitions for Britain to take over the Boer republics led to the South African War (1899–1902).

Roberto, Holden – Leader of the Union of Peoples of Angola (UPA) and then the National Front for the Liberation of Angola (FNLA), which fought Portuguese forces in Angola during the 1960s and early 1970s. He also led the FNLA when it was decisively defeated during the Angolan civil war of 1975.

Roberts, Frederick Sleigh – During 1900 he commanded British forces in South Africa within the context of the Second Anglo-Boer War (1899–1902).

Rommel, Erwin – German general who commanded the German "Afrika Korps" that was sent to North Africa to assist allied Italian forces during World War II.

Rwigyima, Fred – A Rwandan Tutsi exile who grew up in Uganda and became a key leader within the National Resistance Army (NRA) during the 1980s. In October 1990 he led the Rwandan Patriotic Front (RPF) invasion of Rwanda but within several days he was killed by some of his officers during an argument over tactics.

Sadat, Anwar – Succeeded Nassar as president of Egypt in 1970 and continued in that role until his assassination in 1981. After Egypt's defeat during the Yom Kippur War of 1973, he made peace with Israel and shifted Egypt's alliance from the Soviet Union to the United States.

Salan, Raoul – Commander of French forces in Algeria in the late 1950s. He became head of a group of officers that staged a 1958 coup in Algeria that brought Charles de Gaulle to power in Paris. In 1960 he was involved in the right-wing "Secret Army Organization" that used terrorism in an ultimately failed effort to derail Algerian independence.

Salim Saleh – Brother of Yoweri Museveni and a key leader of the National Resistance Army (NRA) during the Ugandan civil war of 1981–6. After the NRA seized power in 1986, he served as a general in the Ugandan military and a cabinet minister in the Ugandan government.

Sankara, Thomas – A revolutionary military officer in Upper Volta who seized power in 1983 and renamed the country Burkina Faso (Land of Upright Men). In 1987 he was overthrown and killed during another coup.

Sankoh, Foday – Leader of the Revolutionary United Front (RUF) during the Sierra Leone Civil War of 1991–2002. He was arrested in 2000 and died of a stroke in 2003 while awaiting trial by a UN-backed court.

Savimbi, Jonas – Leader of the National Union for the Total Independence of Angola (UNITA) that fought the Portuguese during the late 1960s and early 1970s. He continued to lead UNITA throughout the long Angolan civil war until he was killed by government forces in 2002.

Sayyid Mohammed Abdullah Hassan – Led Somali resistance to British colonization during the early twentieth century. The British derisively called him the "Mad Mullah."

Selassie, Haile – The emperor of Ethiopia who was driven to exile by the 1935 Italian invasion and returned to power by the British in 1940. In 1974 he was overthrown by a military coup and he died the following year.

Smith, Ian – Prime Minister of Rhodesia from 1964–79. He issued Rhodesia's Unilateral Declaration of Independence from Britain in 1965 and led the white minority government through the war of the late 1960s and 1970s.

Smuts, Jan Christiaan – As state attorney for the Transvaal Republic, Smuts played a central role in planning Boer strategy during the Second Anglo-Boer War (1899–1902) during which he led a commando. In 1910 he became the minister of the interior, mines and defense for the Union of South Africa and during World War I he commanded British imperial troops in East Africa.

Soumialot, Gaston – Leader of a leftist insurgency, often called the Simba Rebellion, in eastern Congo during 1964–6.

Taylor, Charles – He led the National Patriotic Front of Liberia (NPFL) during the country's first civil war of 1989–96. While he was elected president at the end of the conflict, he fled to Nigeria in 2003 during the country's second civil war (1999–2003) and was subsequently transferred to the International Criminal Court in The Hague where he was eventually convicted of war crimes and crimes against humanity with reference to his involvement in the Sierra Leone Civil War (1991–2002).

Tongogara, Josiah – Commanded the Zimbabwe African National Liberation Army (ZANLA), the military wing of ZANU, during the 1970s war against Rhodesia's white minority state.

Traore, Moussa – A military officer who took power in Mali in 1968, his regime was supported by France and pursued a brutal campaign against a Tuareg rebellion that broke out in the north in 1990. Although Traore's government negotiated a settlement with the Tuareg rebels in January 1991, he was overthrown by a military coup in March of the same year and the insurgency in the north continued.

Tshombe, Moise – Leader of the secessionist state of Katanga from 1960–3 during the Congo Crisis and prime minister of the Congo from 1964–5.

Um Nyobe, Ruben – Leader of the Union of the Peoples of Cameroon (UPC), which demanded immediate independence from France during the late 1940s and 1950s. He was killed by French forces in 1958.

Von Lettow-Vorbeck, Paul – Commander of German military forces in East Africa during World War I.

Von Trotha, Lothar – As commander of German forces in South West Africa (today's Namibia) during the Herero and Nama rebellion of 1904–7, he issued an "extermination order" against the Herero.

Witbooi, Hendrik – Led the Nama resistance to German colonization in South West Africa (now Namibia) in the 1890s and from October 1904 to his death in October 1905.

Zenawi, Meles – A member of the Tigray People's Liberation Front (TPLF), which fought Ethiopia's Mengistu regime during the 1980s, he served as president of Ethiopia from 1991–5 and prime minister from 1995 to his death in 2012.

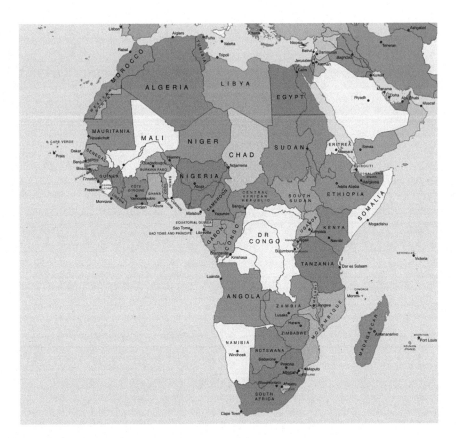

Figure 0.1 Map of Africa

Part I
Introduction

Introduction
Background and context

Although knowledge of pre-colonial African history is somewhat limited given that most African languages did not utilize a written script until the late nineteenth century, sources such as oral tradition, archaeology and a few documentary records authored by literate visitors have revealed some important trends. Most of Sub-Saharan Africa was inhabited by settled agricultural, pastoral and iron-using societies over 2000 years ago. These African communities were involved in intercontinental trading systems for a very long time. During the first millennium, the camel caravans of the Trans-Sahara network connected West Africa with the Mediterranean milieu of North Africa, the Middle East and Europe and Arab ships in the Indian Ocean traded between the coasts of East Africa, Arabia and Asia. Beginning in the early 1500s CE, European and colonial American oceanic slave traders began to acquire captives from African powers along the West African coast and shipped them across the Atlantic where they worked (often to death) the plantation economy of the "New World." As West African states became dependent on imported firearms that could only be obtained through exporting captives, the Atlantic slave trade resulted in increased warfare in the region. Around the same time, seafaring Portuguese pushed into the Indian Ocean where they displaced Arab merchant sailors as carriers of regional goods and dominated parts of the East African coast. During the early 1800s, abolitionist Britain used its naval supremacy to suppress the Trans-Atlantic slave trade and, in turn, West Africa became an important source of raw materials such as palm oil and rubber for the rising industries of Western Europe and North America. Ironically, this meant an increased use of slaves to produce these commodities within West Africa, which also became the scene of a series of Islamic holy wars resulting in the rise of large interior empires such as Sokoto and Tukolor. With the demise of the oceanic slave trade out of West Africa, international slaving expanded to East Africa during the nineteenth century with firearm equipped Swahili-Arab caravans securing captives and ivory from interior warlords and then transporting these to the coast for export. As happened earlier on the west side of the continent, the growth of the slave trade caused much suffering and displacement among East African people.

Before around 1880, most African people lived in independent and diverse societies ranging from highly centralized kingdoms such as Buganda in East Africa to decentralized communities such as those of the Igbo in West Africa. By the late nineteenth century there was already a long history of European intrusion in Africa but it had been limited by tropical disease and the existence of powerful African societies. Up to around 1880, the European colonial presence in Africa amounted to a series of coastal enclaves in the West and East, and to some settler colonies such as those of the British and Boers in the far south and the French in Algeria in the north. The African societies of the interior were completely independent and had little direct contact with Europeans.

During the 1880s and 1890s, in a process called the "Scramble for Africa," almost all the continent came under the colonial rule of European powers such as Britain, France, Germany, Italy and Portugal. This rapid conquest was impelled by a mix of strategic and economic motives, informed by extreme racism, nationalism and evangelical Christianity, and facilitated by new Western technologies such as steam-powered ships and trains, medical treatments for tropical disease and rapid-firing guns such as the Maxim. The first European invasions of the "scramble" period included the 1881 French seizure of Tunisia, which was justified as protecting the neighboring colony of Algeria, and the 1882 British occupation of Egypt, which secured the Suez Canal – vital for British shipping to and from India. At the 1884 Berlin Conference, European officials planned the partition of Africa and agreed on a principle of "effect occupation," which meant that territorial claims had to be ratified by agents on the ground. While some African communities came under European rule through negotiation and treaty, many were invaded and defeated by European-led armies, mainly composed of African troops. To some extent, the sudden arrival of colonizers from a newly unified Germany in parts of Africa prompted the older colonial powers such as Britain and France quickly to formalize control over hitherto vaguely understood spheres of influence. In southern Africa, the discovery of precious minerals – diamonds in the late 1860s and gold in the late 1880s – stimulated the rapid growth of established settler states at the expense of African kingdoms such as the Zulu and Pedi, and caused conflict between Britain and local Boer republics. In central Africa, Belgian king Leopold II used the abolition of the slave trade and scientific exploration as excuses to orchestrate the private colonization of the Congo River Basin, which he called the Congo Free State and from which his locally recruited Force Publique brutally extorted rubber. Beginning in Senegal in the mid-1800s, French colonialism in West Africa gradually pushed eastward across the interior Sahel and Sahara during the 1880s and 1890s defeating the large Tukolor and Mandinka empires. Along the West African coast, British, French and German traders and agents responded to a worldwide depression in the 1870s by seeking to seize sources of raw materials so as to cut costs. Although the British and Egyptians had been expelled from Sudan by an Islamist movement led by the Mahdi in the 1880s, the British reconquered Sudan in the 1890s as control of this territory was seen as important in securing Egypt. In East Africa, British and German agents raced inland toward the agriculturally rich Buganda Kingdom, which was taken by the former at the start of the 1890s.

In much of Africa, the colonial conquest of the late nineteenth century was initiated by chartered companies formed by wealthy European businessmen with established economic interests in parts of the continent and who gained permission to rule territory on behalf of their home governments. The Cape-based British mining magnate Cecil Rhodes formed the British South Africa Company, which, during the 1890s, took control of what became the settler territory of Southern Rhodesia (now Zimbabwe) and the copper-mining colony of Northern Rhodesia (now Zambia). Around the same time, parts of East Africa were similarly conquered by Carl Peters' German East Africa Company and William Mackinnon's Imperial British East Africa Company. In West Africa, George Goldie's Royal Niger Company brought part of what became Nigeria under British rule. While these chartered companies arranged the military invasions of parts of Africa and built the first colonial economic infrastructure, they found it difficult to survive financially and the colonies they founded were eventually all taken over by the governments of the colonial powers.

After the "scramble," the only parts of Africa that remained outside European colonial rule were Ethiopia and Liberia. Although the Italians took possession of Eritrea on the strategically important Red Sea coast in 1889, their invasion of the hinterland empire of Ethiopia ended in disaster at the 1896 Battle of Adowa. Ethiopia was arguably Africa's most powerful independent state and Italy was among the weakest of the European invaders. In West Africa the Republic of Liberia, established by freed black slaves from the United States earlier in the nineteenth century and under US protection, remained outside European control and during the "Scramble" era it formalized its frontiers with neighboring French and British colonies. Liberia was similar to neighboring European colonies as it developed a colonial economy based on the extraction of raw materials and mistreatment of indigenous people.

Although warfare was certainly nothing new in African history, the continent experienced protracted and intense violence throughout the twentieth century with very few areas remaining unaffected. The first four decades of the century, the 1900s to 1930s, were characterized by continued wars of colonial conquest and suppression of widespread African rebellions incited by colonial taxation, exploitation and oppression. Within this period, the German reaction to African uprisings in South West Africa (now Namibia) can be understood as the first genocide of the twentieth century. Both world wars (1914–18 and 1939–45) dominated the colonial era, involving military campaigns fought throughout parts of Africa by rival European powers, and more broadly the mobilization of African military manpower and the extraction of African resources that supported the global struggles of the combatants. While World War I generally strengthened colonial rule in Africa and finalized the colonial division of the continent, World War II informed the rise of African nationalism and demands for independence in the 1950s. From the 1950s to 1980s, African insurgents fought a series of wars against the colonial rulers such as the British in Kenya and the French in Algeria, and against white minority settler regimes in Southern Africa. Most African colonies became independent states through negotiation between outgoing colonial powers and emerging African politicians but a few key wars shaped the process. The optimism of the 1960s that post-colonial Africa would become a peaceful and prosperous continent was quickly disappointed by a wave of military coups and the outbreak of different types of wars. Civil wars began as separatist movements challenged the new African states that had inherited problematic borders and stark regional disparities created during the colonial era. Adopting the practices of late colonial counterinsurgency campaigns, many post-colonial African states responded to insurgency by herding civilians into squalid concentration camps euphemistically termed "protected villages." Direct state-versus-state conflicts occurred less frequently given that most African governments wished to maintain the existing state structures. That said, it became sadly common for post-colonial African governments to fight each other indirectly through backing rebel groups in each other's territories.

From around 1960 to 1990, the global Cold War was superimposed on Africa's civil and inter-state conflicts as the two superpowers, the United States and the Soviet Union, tried to undermine each other by arming rival African forces, whether governments or insurgents. Africa became the venue for a number of major proxy conflicts of the larger Cold War. The superpowers and their allies shipped many billions of dollars'-worth of weapons to Africa, which increased the destructiveness and deadliness of conflict. At the start of the 1990s, with the collapse of the Soviet Union and the end of the Cold War, authoritarian African regimes lost their superpower support and therefore dissolved, which led to a rash of civil wars between factions that sustained themselves by exporting valuable resources to the world market and pressganging child soldiers. This post-Cold War era also saw the rise of Islamist militancy as an increasingly important, though certainly not entirely new, factor in African conflicts in the Maghreb, West Africa and the Horn of Africa. Direct international military intervention represented an important theme in Cold War and post-Cold War Africa as, for example, France sought to uphold its neocolonial influence and international governmental organizations, including African regional groupings and the United Nations, dispatched peacekeeping forces to conflict zones. As the twentieth century came to a close, Africa experienced the world's deadliest genocide since the end of World War II, which took place in Rwanda, and the largest single armed conflict in the continent's history, as the Democratic Republic of Congo was invaded by neighboring countries that backed local warring groups and looted resources in what became called "Africa's World War" (1998–2002).

In studying the many wars of twentieth-century Africa, it is important to consider several stereotypes of the continent and its people. There is an unfortunate tendency in the popular media to explain conflicts in Africa as resulting from what is seen as the inherent violence of African society and by allegedly primordial conflicts between African ethnic groups, which are often described as "tribal warfare." Such views are unhelpful in understanding armed conflict in Africa as they offer no specific or accurate explanations. While ethnic identity has been used to mobilize people during African wars, the causes of such conflicts are generally the same as in other parts of the world and are related to struggles over political power and resources. As this book demonstrates, war in twentieth-century Africa can be explained in terms of the overused Clausewitzian phrase "politics by other means." The equally inaccurate reverse of the stereotype of innate African violence is the myth that Africa was a peaceful and idyllic place before the arrival of Europeans, upon whom all Africa's subsequent problems can be blamed. It is well established that warfare was as common in pre-colonial Africa as it was among similarly complex societies elsewhere in the world. While colonial rule was established and maintained through violence and created the framework for future conflict, post-colonial African leaders were (are) autonomous agents and many of them made decisions based on incredibly selfish motives and caused considerable misery. Of course, not all African leaders have been bad, and the continent has produced a few visionaries, such as Nelson Mandela. Lastly, some might say that examining warfare in twentieth-century Africa will reinforce the previously mentioned and inaccurate image of Africans as inherently violent. For many years, this myopic view caused many historians and other scholars of Africa to neglect the study of warfare, which has meant that the continent's military history has been generally underdeveloped until fairly recently. No one can deny that twentieth-century Africa witnessed very many destructive and deadly wars, with some large countries, for example Angola and Sudan, experiencing five consecutive decades of armed strife. For too long, far too many African people have experienced the horrific effects of war – such as violence, displacement, food insecurity, psychological trauma and lack of education and basic health care. Ignoring the historical causes, conduct and consequences of wars in modern Africa will only contribute to similar tragedies continuing well into the twenty-first century.

Part II

War and conflict in Africa (1900–45)

War and conflict in Africa (1900–45)

1 Wars of colonial conquest (1900–36)

Introduction

African resistance to European conquest did not end with the loss of African sovereignty in the 1880s and 1890s. Africans were forced to build infrastructure, taxation compelled them to become wage-workers or cash-crop producers, and in some areas they lost their land to white settlers. This oppression incited African rebellions. The first of these conflicts happened in the late 1890s in Southern Rhodesia (now Zimbabwe) and Sierra Leone but similar events continued into the early twentieth century, including in German South West Africa (now Namibia) in 1904–7, German East Africa (mostly now Tanzania) in 1905 and Natal (now part of South Africa) in 1906; and some rebellions happened as late as the 1930s. In Southern Africa's Boer Republics, northern Nigeria, Morocco and Libya, the initial European invasion was delayed until the early twentieth century. Ethiopia, the only African state to have successfully defended itself during the "Scramble for Africa," was occupied by Italy in 1935–6. While new military technology such as the machine-gun enabled the European conquests of the 1880s and 1890s, it was even more important during the colonial wars of the early twentieth century when motor vehicles, aircraft and poison gas were used to suppress African resistance. The guerrilla nature of some of these conflicts meant that civilians in South Africa, Namibia, French Equatorial Africa and Libya were confined to concentration camps, which foreshadowed the atrocities of the War II and late twentieth-century counter-insurgency campaigns.

The South African War or Second Anglo-Boer War (1899–1902)

Compared to the rest of Africa, what is now South Africa experienced much earlier European colonial conquest and a different type of colonialism which, given the favorable non-tropical environment, was characterized by a European settler society that expanded at the expense of African communities. By the 1880s most of this area consisted of the two coastal British colonies of the Cape and Natal, and the interior Boer republics of the Orange

Free State and Transvaal. The 1880–1 rebellion of the Transvaal, the First Anglo-Boer War, had undermined a British imperial attempt to impose a pro-British confederation on these territories that had been inspired by diamond discoveries in the Northern Cape. For a time, Britain contented itself with control of the strategically important coastline. However, the discovery of gold in the Transvaal in the late 1880s rejuvenated British ambitions to dominate the Southern African interior. Cecil Rhodes, premier of the Cape, mining magnate and ardent British imperialist, orchestrated the colonization of the area immediately north of the Transvaal during the early 1890s but his agents failed to discover new sources of gold in what became Southern Rhodesia. In 1895, Rhodes, with tacit agreement from London, arranged an unsuccessful armed incursion into the Transvaal that failed to stimulate the expected uprising by foreign mine-workers (uitlanders). This Jameson Raid resulted in the fall of Rhodes' government at the Cape and escalated tensions between Britain and the Boer republics. Britain demanded that the uitlanders, many of whom were British subjects, gain voting rights so as to elect a pro-British regime in the Transvaal that would then join a regional union under Britain. This was resisted by Transvaal President Paul Kruger, who wanted to maintain Boer independence. British officials also worried that the growing wealth of the Transvaal would enable it to form a republican regional grouping that would pull in the Cape, Natal and the Orange Free State, and potentially ally with imperial rivals such as Germany, which had established the neighboring colony of South West Africa. The purchase of German weapons by the newly enriched Boer republics seemed to confirm these anxieties. In October 1899, with negotiations over the uitlander matter going nowhere, the Boer republics launched a pre-emptive military strike on the British territories. The Boers hoped to seize the railway centers of the Northern Cape and occupy all of Natal to make it difficult for the British to land large military forces and therefore compel London to offer a favorable settlement.

In October 1899, the Boer republics had 55,000–60,000 available men and deployed around 35,000–42,000 in the war's opening campaign. Lacking standing militaries, the republics raised commandos consisting of Boers, who brought along their own horses and guns, called up for unpaid obligatory military service. Commando leaders were elected from among local elites, and battle plans discussed and voted on in councils of war. Though motivated by ideas of manhood, Calvinist Christianity and national freedom, Boer absenteeism became a severe problem for the commandos. Boer forces lacked a formal logistical system and relied on the Boers' wives and black servants, who tended horses, transported and cooked rations, and treated the wounded. Numbering around 10,000 at the war's start, black auxiliaries (agterryers) also worked as scouts and sentries. In addition, the Boers were assisted by around 2000 foreign volunteers including Dutch, French, Germans, Russians, Irish, Americans and Italians. The Boers were armed with recently purchased and up-to-date German-made Mauser rifles and around

100 artillery pieces, though given their lack of capability to manufacture artillery ammunition, they were limited to around 100,000 shells.

Although the British garrison in South Africa at the start of the war was small, they mobilized quickly, and from October 1899 to the end of January 1900, some 112,000 regular soldiers were shipped to the area with reinforcements to follow. Notwithstanding their numerical superiority, the British army in South Africa suffered from many problems, mostly resulting from the recent experience of fighting poorly armed indigenous forces and the failure to learn from their 1881 defeat by the Boers. The British had more artillery than the Boers but the British standard practice of firing from forward positions to shock the enemy was not suited to modern warfare and exposed gun crews to Boer rifle fire. While British soldiers had replaced their red coats with less conspicuous khaki uniforms in the 1880s and their new Lee series of rifles were equal to Boer weapons, many British infantry were physically unfit and lacked experience moving at night or over rough terrain. While the Boers had developed an intelligence network in the neighboring British territories, the British were almost entirely ignorant about the strength and location of Boer forces and lacked accurate maps. Most significantly, British officers were not familiar with commanding or supplying the massive forces they deployed to South Africa.

Fighting a two-front war in the Cape and Natal, the Boers became bogged down in sieges unfavorable to their highly mobile forces, which gave the British time to ship in reinforcements. The war began on October 12, 1899, with a skirmish at the Northern Cape railway siding of Kraaipan, where 800 Boers under Koos de la Rey ambushed a British train on its way to Mafeking, 50 km to the north. The Boers concentrated their efforts on Natal, which was invaded by 14,000 Transvaal Boers under Piet Joubert and 6,000 Free State Boers under Marthinus Prinsloo. While the Boer invasion force was ultimately pushed back around the town of Dundee during October 19–21, the British suffered heavy casualties including Major General Sir William Penn Symons, commander of British forces in Natal, who was killed. British troops withdrew to Ladysmith, which the Boers besieged for the next four months, abandoning the goal of reaching the Natal coast. In the Northern Cape, Transvaal General Piet Cronje led around 9,000 Boers towards the large rail depot of Mafeking where, beginning on October 14 and lasting for the next seven months, they besieged a small British garrison led by R.S.S. Baden-Powell. Similarly, on October 15, 4,800 Boers under the Free State's Christian Wessels began a four-month siege of Kimberley, during which Rhodes redirected the resources of his De Beers Diamond Company into defending the town. Free State commandos raided into the Cape in November but an anticipated Cape Boer uprising did not happen.

At the end of October, General Redvers Buller, the new British military commander in South Africa, arrived in Cape Town with the initial expeditionary contingents. Buller discarded the original British plan for a concerted offensive up the Cape railway to Bloemfontein, Johannesburg and Pretoria, and divided his troops so as to also confront the largest Boer force, which was in Natal. While Lieutenant General Lord Methuen would lead 20,000 men up the western railway to relieve Kimberley and then invade the Free State, detachments under Lieutenant Generals William Gatacre and William French would drive the Boers out of the Cape Colony. Under Buller, the remaining 27,000 men went to Natal to relieve Ladysmith.

In mid-December 1899, the advancing British forces across South Africa suffered three critical battlefield defeats collectively known as "Black Week." At Magersfontein, near the Northern Cape's border with the Free State, some 8,500 Boers under De la Rey occupied trenches in low ground, from where they avoided the British bombardment of the unoccupied high ground and then halted the march of Methuen's 13,000-strong British force toward Kimberley. The British suffered 1,000 casualties, compared to 250 Boers. At Stormberg Junction in the Cape Midlands, British troops under Gatacre attempted a night assault but became lost; and in the morning they attempted a disastrous uphill attack on Boer positions. A confused Gatacre forgot to order the withdrawal of a 600-man unit, which surrendered. At Colenso, on route to Ladysmith in Natal, Buller's frontal attack on Boer positions turned disastrous, with the British suffering 1,130 casualties to the Boers' casualty of 40. Dubbed "Reverse Buller" by British troops, Redvers Buller was relieved of overall command in South Africa.

On January 10, 1900, Field Marshall Lord Frederick Sleigh Roberts and Lord Horatio Herbert Kitchener, the new British commander and chief-of-staff, respectively, arrived at Cape Town. Immediately following "Black Week," 47,000 British soldiers reached South Africa and by the end of 1899 another 40,000 were on ships. In early 1900, the British had 180,000 men in South Africa, including contingents from Canada, Australia and New Zealand. Favoring mobility and encirclement, Roberts created a new cavalry division and local settlers were formed into irregular mounted units. The British imported 0.5 million horses from around the world into South Africa, of which two-thirds died. Intelligence was improved with African spies and better maps. Logistically, the British military commandeered the rail system and established an integrated transport network.

In Natal, Buller continued his offensive against Boer defenses blocking the way to Ladysmith including at Spion Kop, which British troops captured on January 23, 1900, only to be exposed to deadly Boer rifle and artillery fire from surrounding positions. Some 1,100 British soldiers were killed or wounded, compared to just over 300 Boers. In mid-February, Buller mounted a series of well-planned attacks on hills east of Colenso, to which he committed his entire 25,000 troops. As the Boer defenses along the Tugela River collapsed, British troops crossing a pontoon bridge were ambushed and took 1,400 casualties before retiring. On February 27, the British renewed their offensive supported by heavy shelling, which prompted Boer commander Louis Botha to gradually withdraw from Natal. The next day British troops entered Ladysmith.

Figure 1.1 Boer railway scouts guarding the Natal to Transvaal railway line

In February 1900, Roberts initiated a British offensive in the Cape with a huge force moving west along the railway towards Kimberley but then shifting east to threaten the Free State capital of Bloemfontein. Repeatedly changing directions, the British kept the Boers guessing on their objective, which led to the abandonment of Kimberley and Magersfontein. British cavalry overtook 5,000 retreating Boers at Paardeberg on February 17, and the next day 15,000 British infantry under Kitchener arrived and immediately attacked but suffered 1,300 casualties. On February 19, Roberts arrived and ordered a sustained bombardment of Boer positions, which Boer commander Cronje, against the wishes of his subordinate officers, had decided not to abandon. On February 27 an aggressive British attack resulted in the surrender of 4,000 Boers, including Cronje. This Battle of Paardeberg represented a decisive loss for the Boers as 10% of their total force had capitulated and they had incurred 4,000 casualties. Boer fighters withdrew from the Cape Midlands, republican home-front morale sank and many Boers deserted the commandos.

While Roberts focused on occupying the republics' capitals, rural Boer society placed little value on them. In early March, the Boers tried to establish a defensive line straddling the Modder River but a massive British encirclement caused their retreat. Robert's 40,000 men marched toward Bloemfontein pillaging and burning farms. Though briefly delayed at Driefontein, the British seized Bloemfontein on March 13. As Roberts demanded that Boers surrender and take a loyalty oath or face confiscation of property, 12,000–14,000 capitulated between March and July.

After the fall of Bloemfontein, a Boer war council decided to adopt mobile harassing tactics to make the unstoppable British campaign very costly. In late March and April, Boers under Christiaan De Wet began raiding British posts around Bloemfontein and besieged Wepener, a town on the Free State–Basutoland (now Lesotho) border, for two weeks. These successes encouraged many surrendered Boers to return to the fight.

At the start of May 1900, Roberts resumed the British advance to Pretoria some 480 km to the north. Around the same time, Buller's force marched through Natal towards the mountain pass into the Transvaal while Botha moved his commandos west to the Sand River where they demolished bridges and waited for the arrival of Roberts' troops. On May 10 Roberts' force crossed the Sand River despite Boer resistance and two days later occupied Kroonstad. The British halted to allow supplies to catch up and bridges to be repaired but they suffered more casualties from typhoid during May than they had during the fighting of "Black Week." On May 17, Mafeking was relieved by a 2,000-strong flying column from Roberts' force and troops from Southern Rhodesia.

The British invaded the Transvaal from several directions. Contingents from Bechuanaland (Botswana) and Southern Rhodesia advanced from the west and more troops from Rhodesia pushed down from the north. As Buller's force from Natal marched into the south-eastern Transvaal, Roberts' main body advanced from the south and crossed the Vaal River by the end of May. The seizure of the Vereeniging coal fields, which the Boers left intact, in the southern Transvaal eased British transportation problems as coal for trains no longer had to be brought up from the south. Although some radical Boers and Irish volunteers suggested demolishing the Witwatersrand gold mines, conservative Boer leaders refused as they knew these would be needed after the war and some were connected to the mining industry. As Botha led most remaining Transvaal forces north, British soldiers overwhelmed limited resistance at Doornkop and given the mutual desire to control African workers, both sides agreed to a peaceful handover of Johannesburg at the end of May.

On June 5, British forces entered Pretoria without a fight. While President Kruger left for Portuguese territory, many Boers who wanted to continue the war moved east toward the Magaliesberg Mountains. Roberts abolished the Boer republics by declaring British authority over the Orange River Colony and Transvaal Colony, and extended the neutrality oath to the Transvaal. Some 14,000 Boers from both territories surrendered and were derisively called "Hensoppers" (Hands Uppers) by their fellows. Those who intended to continue the struggle to the bitter end were called "bittereinders."

The Boers began a transition from conventional to guerrilla warfare. In early June, 8,000 Free State Boers under De Wet raided British railway garrisons north of Kroonstad and then escaped a large British force under Kitchener sent in pursuit. At the Battle of Diamond Hill or Donkerhoek, fought on June 10 and 11 east of Pretoria, 12,000 British soldiers outflanked 5,000 Boers under Botha, who then withdrew east towards Machadodorp. From the Boer perspective, this was the war's last conventional battle. In mid-July a large Free State Boer force was trapped by the British at Brandwater Basin where, despite the escape of De Wet, 4,500 Boers surrendered. This was a disaster on the same level as Paardeberg. In August the Boer rail link to Portuguese East Africa (Mozambique) was cut by both Roberts' main force and Buller's Natal contingent. With 7,000 Boers in the western Transvaal, De la Rey directed attacks on British posts within 160 km of Pretoria.

By the end of August 1900, three prominent Boer leaders remained in the field; De Wet in the Free State, De la Rey in the western Transvaal and Botha in the eastern Transvaal. They attacked trains, cut telegraph wires, burnt stores, bombarded outposts and temporarily seized small towns. Responding to De Wet's northern movement to support De la Rey, which had prompted the temporary evacuation of Potchefstroom, 30,000 British troops under Methuen pursued De Wet for six weeks and over 800 km but failed to catch him. At the Battle of Dalmanutha or Bergendal, the last large engagement of the war fought in late August, Buller's force of 20,000 men dispersed Botha's 5,000 Boers, who had been defending a 60-km line near Machadodorp. This enabled Roberts to occupy other towns in the eastern Transvaal. As Kruger went to Europe where he died in 1904, Roberts declared the war over and returned to Britain, leaving Kitchener in charge.

Many Boers returned to the commandos, as the British destruction of farms meant they had nothing to lose. The guerrilla war continued as Boer leaders hoped to inflict enough damage on the British to convince them to negotiate. In December 1900, as the British in the Free State again pursued De Wet, some 2,000 Boers ventured into the Cape Colony. British casualties began to grow. In early December, Boers under De la Rey and Jan Smuts attacked a British convoy outside Rustenburg where 120 British soldiers were killed, wounded or captured, and 115 wagons destroyed. On December 13, Smuts, De la Rey, Christiaan Beyers and Jacobus Kemp combined forces for an attack on a British camp in Nooitgedacht Gorge in the Magaliesberg that inflicted 640 British casualties. In the northeast Free State, in January 1901, a Boer attack annihilated an entire 150-strong British company. De Wet led his men into the Cape, where they eluded fifteen British columns for six weeks and then returned to the Free State. In August, Smuts led 300 Boers into the Cape in a final but unsuccessful bid to provoke a Boer uprising. Botha and 1,000 Boers made for Natal in September but were blocked by 21,000 British troops and 10,000–12,000 armed Zulus. During the second half of 1901, the Boers divided into smaller groups that continued hit-and-run attacks.

By the start of 1902, Kitchener had developed an effective counter-insurgency program. The 220,000 British troops in South Africa were divided into 100 mobile columns, each with around 1,200–2,000 men, that traversed the countryside searching for Boer fighters, burning farms and confiscating livestock. The former republics were divided into small sections demarcated by lines of fortified block houses and barbed-wire fences, and these were patrolled by flying columns and armored trains with searchlights. The Boer fighters responded by forming even smaller groups that were difficult to find but had little firepower. Furthermore, the British recruited around 5,500 Boers, angrily called "joiners" by their former comrades, who knew the local terrain and Boer tactics. Manipulated by the British, the conflict developed into a Boer civil war, with the "bittereinders" tending to be formerly rich property owners who had lost everything and the "hensoppers" and "joiners," who often originated from the landless and resentful poor. Given that Boer farms served as insurgent logistical bases, the British began to move Boer non-combatants and their African servants into concentration camps. Squalid camp conditions resulted in the deaths of 25,000 Boers and 20,000 Africans. Boer fighters became alarmed when formerly subject African communities began to resist their attempts to confiscate supplies and in some areas Africans began to occupy abandoned Boer farms. An important incident took place in early May 1902 when a Zulu raiding party attacked a Boer camp at Holkrantz in Natal, killing fifty-six Boers. In all, some 15,000–17,000 Boer fighters eluded 250,000 British troops.

Both sides wished to end the costly war. While the British government faced criticism at home for its handling of the war and wanted to avoid further destruction which would lessen the chances of installing a friendly local government, the Boers remained divided, with some such as Botha and Smuts favoring negotiations and others such as De la Rey wanting to fight indefinitely. The war ended with negotiations held in late May 1902 at Vereeniging in the southern Transvaal. Boer delegates voted 54:6 to concede independence. British concessions included the return of prisoners, general amnesty, non-punitive taxation, protection of property rights, generous funds for reconstruction, assurance of eventual self-government, guarantees that black voting rights would not extend north of the Cape and safe-guarding of Dutch language. The Transvaal and Orange River Colony were granted responsible government in 1907 and the Cape Colony, Natal and the two former republics became the Union of South Africa, a self-governing British dominion, in 1910. Former republican Boer military leaders Botha and Smuts became the first and second prime ministers of South Africa, inspiring the saying that "the Boers lost the war but won the peace." Nevertheless, many Boers had been horrified by the loss of independence and the memory of farm burning and concentration camps became a powerful grievance and an important factor in the rise of Afrikaner nationalism during the twentieth century. A total of around 75,000 people died during the conflict. This included some 22,000 out of 450,000 British imperial troops and 7,000 out of 70,000 Boer fighters (Pakenham, 1979; Smith, 1996; Nasson, 1999; Pretorius, 1999, 2009; Van Der Waag, 2015, pp. 9–58).

British campaigns in West Africa (1900–5)

Although the West African state of Asante had been defeated by the British in 1873–4, it recovered under the reign of Prempeh and rejected a British offer to become a protectorate in 1890. In 1894, Prempeh dismissed a British proposal to pay him a stipend in exchange for accepting a British resident and an Asante delegation to London the next year failed to prevent British invasion. In January 1896, fearing that the French to the west or the Germans to the east would intervene; British forces, including West Indian troops and African auxiliaries moved up from Britain's established Gold Coast territory and occupied Asante without a fight. The British declared a protectorate, and exiled Prempeh and his family to the Seychelles Islands in the Indian Ocean.

In late March 1900, after Gold Coast Governor Sir Frederic Hodgson refused to repatriate the exiles and insisted on claiming the sacred golden stool, the Asante rebelled under the leadership of Queen Mother Yaa Asantewa and besieged the British fort at Kumasi. The organization of a relief force from the coast was delayed by British operations in South Africa. Two small relief forces reached the fort in April and May but they only put more pressure on the rapidly diminishing supplies. Within the fort, two or three dozen people a day died of hunger and smallpox. In late June the governor and most of the fort's inhabitants broke out of the siege, abandoning about 100 men too ill to march. On July 15, the main relief force from the coast, consisting of 1,000 African soldiers and 1,600 porters, arrived at Kumasi and rescued the fort's desperate defenders. By September, with 2,000 troops at Kumasi, the British attacked nearby Asante towns and in October some Asante leaders accepted amnesty. On September 30, 1900, the last battle between the British and Asante was fought at Aboasu, northwest of Kumasi. With artillery and machine guns, the British colonial force of 1,200 men slowly drove the Asante up a hill where they were outflanked and fled into the forest. Kobina Chere, a defiant rebel leader, was later captured and brought to Kumasi, where he was hanged. Yaa Asantewa and fifteen other captured rebel leaders joined Prempeh in the Seychelles. The British administration dropped the demand for the golden stool. In this last Anglo-Asante war, the British lost 692 soldiers and carriers, while the Asante estimated their dead at more than 1,000. In 1902, Asante became part of the Gold Coast Protectorate (today's Ghana). In 1925, Prempeh was returned home as a private citizen, and in 1935, the monarchy was restored under Prempeh II, who ruled within a British colonial context. Under the British, the Gold Coast became a major supplier of cocoa for the international chocolate industry. The nature of

African resistance changed during the 1930s as cocoa farmers engaged in boycotts of the colonial marketing board, which set artificially low prices for their product.

At the start of 1900, the Royal Niger Company (RNC) territory south of the Niger and Benue rivers was added to the Niger Coast Protectorate to form the larger Protectorate of Southern Nigeria. Former RNC territory in the north, plus Ilorin on the south side of the Niger became the Protectorate of Northern Nigeria with Frederick Lugard as its first commissioner. The independent Sokoto Caliphate, established by a jihad in the early nineteenth century, presented the British in Northern Nigeria with two problems: its tributary relations with small neighboring states such as Ilorin could inspire resistance, and it could serve as a route for French intrusion from the north. Consequently, the British embarked on the conquest of the caliphate. Sokoto's decentralized administration and lack of a standing army meant that the caliphate's subordinate rulers or emirs responded individually to British invasion. The caliphate's military comprised traditional cavalry with few modern weapons. The British justified their invasion of Sokoto as abolishing the slave trade and removing a threat to regional stability. At first, Lugard directed the occupation of the emirates of Bida and Kontagora on the Niger, and Yola on the Benue, where he installed pro-British rulers. Lugard's locally recruited West African Frontier Force (WAFF) then took Bauchi and Gombe, and had seized Zaria by 1902.

In February 1903, 750 WAFF troops stormed Kano, where British artillery breached the 40-foot thick city walls. Lugard's next objective was Sokoto, where Caliph Attahiru II and his army, perhaps seeking to prevent the capital's bombardment, confronted the British outside the gates. In mid-March, the 700 WAFF soldiers arrived and repelled a series of Sokoto cavalry and infantry changes, compelling the caliph to withdraw east. At the end of July, with Lugard having proclaimed victory and appointed a new caliph, Attahiru fought a desperate but unsuccessful last stand on the sacred ground of Bima Hill near the town of Burmi some 320 km southeast of Kano. Some 600 Sokoto fighters, including Attahiru and his two sons, were killed. The Sokoto Caliphate was absorbed into the Northern Nigeria Protectorate, as was Bornu the following year. In northern Nigeria, Lugard developed the indirect-rule system whereby the Muslim emirs would rule their communities on behalf of a few British officials who kept out destabilizing influences such as Christian missionaries. While this made it seem that colonialism had not really changed anything and thus reduced the chance of African resistance, it meant that northern Nigeria became a comparatively marginalized region, with few educational or economic opportunities.

During the late 1880s and 1890s, Britain established the Niger Coast Protectorate in what is now southeastern Nigeria by signing treaties with local Igbo rulers and arresting and exiling Jaja, the powerful ruler of the town of Opobo. Further British expansion inland was blocked by the powerful Aro confederation between the Niger and Cross rivers. In September 1899, Sir Ralph Moor, the Niger Coast Protectorate commissioner, recommended to the Colonial Office that a military expedition subjugate the Aro confederacy but this was delayed by the South African War (1899–1902) and the Asante rebellion of 1900. Meanwhile, the Niger Coast Protectorate and the RNC territory were amalgamated into the Protectorate of Southern Nigeria.

The November 1901 Aro attack on the pro-British town of Obegu provided the British with an excuse for war. The Aro Field Force was assembled and consisted of 1,700 colonial troops, 2,300 supply carriers, several mountain guns and machine guns and gunboats on the waterways. Sometimes travelling on boats and sometimes marching overland, four British columns invaded Aro territory at different points at the end of November. For the next few weeks the British were harassed by sniping and skirmishing, and overcame entrenched defensive positions. On December 24, British forces fought their way into the Aro capital of Arochukwu where they faced several more days of resistance and destroyed the oracle's shrine. Throughout January and February 1902, the British columns deployed across Aro territory and defeated further opposition. Some Aro leaders were hanged. In December 1902, a 300-strong British force subdued the Igbo town of Afigbo where it used machine guns to cut down courageous attacks. From March to June 1905, another British force of 300 colonial troops left Calabar near the coast and proceeded north to pacify Abakaliki district. Over the next several years, British colonial forces mounted small patrols to crush local resistance and confirm their domination of Igboland. Since the Igbo did not have a tradition of centralized states, the British administrative method of indirect rule did not work well in this area, where appointed "warrant chiefs" lacked legitimacy and were seen as glorified tax collectors. Tensions over this issue, together with economic problems, led to riots by Igbo women in 1929. In 1914, the protectorates of Southern Nigeria and Northern Nigeria were amalgamated to form Nigeria with Lugard as governor. However, the British continued to use different methods to govern the different parts of Nigeria, which contributed to regional disparities and regionalism (Lloyd, 1964; Nwabara, 1978; Afigbo, 2006; Falola and Heaton, 2008).

Genocide of the Herero and Nama (1904–7)

By the late nineteenth century, the arid grassland between the Kalahari and Namib deserts along Southern Africa's Atlantic coast was the scene of conflict between Khoisan-speaking Nama who had moved north from the Cape and Bantu-speaking Herero communities. While the Nama initially enjoyed the military advantage of horses and guns acquired from European settlers in the Cape Colony to the south, the Herero eventually obtained firearms through work in the diamond fields of the Northern Cape. Encouraged by Herero appeals for protection against Nama attacks, the British government annexed the Atlantic trading enclave of Walvis Bay in 1878. Hendrik Witbooi, a prophetic Christian convert, emerged as a Nama leader during the 1880s and 1890s and sought to unite the disparate Nama groups and directed them north, which led to more fighting with the Herero.

In 1884, Germany reversed its policy of focusing on empire-building in Europe by claiming colonial territories in West, East and Southern Africa. This inspired older colonial powers such as Britain and France to formalize control of parts of Africa, which contributed to the unfolding "scramble." Germany's colonial claims included part of southern Africa's Atlantic coast and hinterland from the Orange River in the south to the Cunene River in the north, with the exception of Walvis Bay. Although Herero leader Maherero initially accepted German protection, he renounced it in 1888 as Nama raids continued. In 1889 and 1890, the German military occupied the port of Swakopmund and advanced inland to found Windhoek, which became the capital of German South West Africa (SWA). Maherero renewed his agreement with the Germans just before his death in 1890, but Witbooi obstinately rejected German authority. During the German-Nama War of 1893–4, Witbooi fought a guerrilla campaign against the colonizers, who responded by making local alliances that isolated the Nama and importing reinforcements from Germany. In September 1894, Witbooi surrendered and acknowledged German rule.

Since German support had helped Samuel Maherero to become the primary Herero leader in 1896, he agreed to German settlement in Herero territory. With limited tropical disease, SWA was seen by Berlin as a venue for European settlement comparable to the neighboring British territories and the Boer republics, where Africans generally provided cheap labor to the colonial settler economy. By 1897, SWA was home to some 2,600 European settlers and unlike in Germany's other African colonies the local colonial military consisted almost entirely of white German troops. Governor Theodore Leutwein, responding to settler criticism about his reluctance to acquire more land for them, cautioned against an aggressive approach which he thought would lead to a "war of extermination against the Herero" that would denude the colony of African labor.

The Herero and Nama came under intense pressure at the turn of the nineteenth and twentieth century. The European population of SWA grew with the arrival of Boers escaping the South African War (1899–1902) and colonial recruiters sought African migrant workers for the region's mines. In 1903, the German government released plans to promote white settlement by building a railway though Herero territory and confining the Herero to reserves. Rendered destitute by the Rinderpest epizootic of 1896–7, many Herero and Nama sold land to settlers and incurred debts with European merchants. In 1903, the colonial administration announced that it would cancel African debts in an effort to ease tensions. However, European traders hired off-duty German soldiers to collect the debts all at once, which involved mass confiscation of Herero livestock and other property. This provoked the Herero uprising, which was launched in mid-January 1904 with a surprise attack on European settlers that killed 150 white men. Seeing the German colonial state as his enemy, Samuel Maherero banned the killing of Boer and British men, and any European women and children.

At the start of 1904, there were about 7,000–8,000 Herero combatants, half of whom possessed guns, and the German force in SWA consisted of 800 regular soldiers, the same number of reservists, 400 armed settlers, 250 African scouts and a few machine guns and cannon. When the rebellion began, Governor Leutwein and most of his soldiers were in the south suppressing another uprising by the small Bondelswart community. Nevertheless, Herero inexperience in assaulting fortified positions defended by rifles and machine guns gave the Germans time to organize. In late January and early February the Germans relieved the besieged towns of Okahandja and Windhoek, and some German marines landed on the coast. During February and March an expeditionary force of 1,500 men with 1,000 horses, along with more machine guns and artillery arrived from Germany. With 2,500 troops, Leutwein organized two columns that attempted to surround the Herero during March and April. These were withdrawn, however, given Herero attacks and the outbreak of disease among German soldiers.

In June 1904, Lothar von Trotha, one of Germany's few generals with colonial experience, landed in SWA with further reinforcements. Supplanting Leutwein as governor, von Trotha dismissed negotiation with the rebels and embarked on their complete military subjugation. With a now 10,000-strong colonial army supported by more than thirty artillery pieces, von Trotha mounted an offensive against the Herero who withdrew northeast to the Waterberg Plateau on the western edge of the Omaheke section of the Kalahari Desert. German forces took three months to reach the Waterberg as the railway had not yet extended that far inland. In mid-August, six German columns converged on the Herero position which was occupied by 4,000–6,000 armed men and thousands more non-combatants. The main German column under von Trotha marched from the south, overpowered Herero resistance to secure important waterholes and bombarded Herero positions on the Waterberg. The next day Samuel Maherero guided his people east through an opening in the German lines and into the Omaheke Desert. It is conceivable that this gap was intentionally created by von Trotha to channel the Herero into the desert but it could have been the unwitting result of a late movement of a German unit. The Herero, nonetheless, were driven into the desert and began a 320-km trek to the British territory of Bechuanaland.

Two important factors informed subsequent German actions. German authorities, including von Trotha, conceived of the conflict in SWA as a "race war" that would lead to the extinction of one side or the other, and the German military in general had developed an organizational culture of extreme violence. On October 2, 1904, von Trotha issued an "extermination order" for his soldiers to kill any Herero men, women and children remaining in the German colony. A military cordon was established to block the Herero from accessing water sources and German soldiers were told to shoot all Herero men and drive women and children into the desert to die of thirst.

Witbooi's Nama rebelled the day after von Trotha issued the "extermination order." The Nama were impelled by German cruelty against the Herero, the advance of German troops into Nama lands, rumors that Nama firearms would be confiscated and Christian-based prophecies. In turn, the German army in SWA disarmed its Nama scouts and extended the "extermination order" to the Nama. Avoiding a conventional battle such as the Herero had fought at Waterberg, some 1,000–2,000 Nama horsemen conducted a guerrilla war against 15,000 German troops, who replied with a scorched earth campaign. Although Nama resistance declined after the octogenarian Witbooi was killed in October 1905, the Germans continued operations until March 1907. The imperial German government, given concerns about African labor in SWA and the damage to Germany's international reputation caused by atrocity stories, annulled von Trotha's "extermination order" at the end of 1904, though the confinement of the Herero to the desert remained in effect until the end of 1905.

Now taking prisoners, the Germans in SWA copied the concentration-camp system that had been adopted by the British in South Africa a few years earlier, but added horrific elements. Starting in 1905, Herero and Nama prisoners were placed in camps where they became slaves on railway building or victims of medical experiments. By March 1907, around 7,600 Herero and 2,000 Nama out of 17,000 camp inmates had died. On Shark Island, labelled "Death Island," in Luderitz Bay, between 1,000 and 3,000 Herero and Nama perished from exposure, hunger, disease, violence and exhaustion. Shark Island may have been the world's first extermination camp.

While the number of fatalities caused by the German campaign of 1904–7 has been debated, it is likely that around 60,000 Herero, which amounted to perhaps 80% of their population, and 10,000 Nama, which comprised about 60% of their population, died. As such, and given the obvious intent illustrated by von Trotha's "extermination order," many historians regard this as the first genocide of the twentieth century. The post-rebellion labor shortage, called "the peace of the graveyard," prompted the Germans to extend colonial rule north over the Ovambo, which shaped what would become the border of modern Namibia and Angola (Bley, 1971; Drechler, 1980; Gewald, 1999; Hull, 2005; Sarkin, 2010).

The Maji Maji Rebellion in German East Africa (1905)

In February 1885, Germany declared a protectorate over the mainland of what is now Tanzania, which became German East Africa. This inspired the British to drop their support for the sultan of Zanzibar's authority over the East African mainland and London made colonial claims over present-day Kenya and Uganda. The 1889 rebellion of Swahili-Arab leaders on the coast against German East Africa Company rule was suppressed but inspired the German imperial government to take over administration of its East African territory. Absorbing company forces, the Germans founded a colonial military in East Africa with a few European officers leading an African rank-and-file. Throughout most of the 1890s, the German colonial military pushed inland and subjugated the Hehe of the territory's central region.

In July 1905, a rebellion against colonial rule began in the Matumbi Hills, northwest of the port of Kilwa, and spread rapidly throughout the southern part of German East Africa. The uprising was caused by the German imposition of cotton growing, which threatened food production, along with other grievances including taxation, hunting regulations and abuse by colonial soldiers. The subsequent war was dubbed the "Maji Maji" Rebellion, given that local spiritual leader Kijikitile Ngwale claimed that a magical water (called Maji in Kiswahili) would protect against German bullets. Consisting of only 1,100 African troops, German forces in the south were insufficient to contain rebel attacks on German officials, soldiers, traders and missionaries. On August 30, 1905, the German garrison at Mahenge, using several machine guns, repelled an assault by several thousand Pogoro, Ngindo and Mbunga rebels who then besieged the post for a month until the arrival of a relief force. In late October a German detachment from Mahenge moved south, where it dispersed 5,000 Ngoni fighters who had joined the rebellion.

The ongoing rebellion in German SWA meant that Berlin could initially dispatch only two warships with 200 marines, which arrived in East Africa in October. Three German columns then marched into the south, where they destroyed food resources, pardoned ordinary rebels and hanged their leaders. The Hehe sided with the colonizers, as they did not want to repeat their defeat of the 1890s. The uprising ended in June 1906 following months of prolonged guerrilla fighting. While the Germans claimed to have killed 26,000 rebels, it appears that between 250,000 and 300,000 people died in the resulting famine. Most of the southern highlands, once well populated and cultivated, had been turned into wilderness in which the Germans created a vast game park. Tanzanian nationalist historians of the 1960s claimed that Maji Maji represented the advent of proto-nationalism among the country's diverse peoples. More recent scholars, however, suggest it was a series of rebellions that happened for different reasons and was part of a series of wars that had begun before German colonialism (Iliffe, 1967; Monson, 1998; Sunseri, 2000; Becker, 2004; Giblin and Monson, 2010).

The Zulu Rebellion (1906)

In the British colony of Natal, located in Southern Africa, 100,000 Europeans and a similar number of Indians dominated around 1 million

Africans who were governed indirectly by their chiefs. The neighboring Zulu Kingdom had been subjugated by the British in 1879, plagued by civil war in the 1880s and then annexed to Natal in 1898. Granted responsible government in 1893, Natal organized a volunteer settler militia. The region's late nineteenth-century mineral revolution caused an expansion of settler commercial farming in Natal, but the mines also drained away African labor. After the South African War (1899–1902), confident Natal settlers wanted to complete the unfinished conquest of the local African population. In 1905, the entirely white Natal legislature tried to compel more young African men to undertake wage labor by imposing a poll tax on adult male Africans on top of the existing hut tax paid by homestead heads.

In early February 1906, two white policemen were killed when their patrol clashed with Africans protesting the poll tax south of Pietermaritzburg, the colonial capital. With the declaration of martial law, a colonial army under Colonel Duncan McKenzie marched through southern Natal flogging people, burning homesteads and confiscating livestock. Seventeen African men were executed because of their alleged participation in the policemen's deaths. To the north, chief Bambatha's subjects, who were mostly tenants on white farms, suffered crop failure, increased rents and the new poll tax. Deposed by colonial officials in early March, Bambatha fled to the bush where he gathered several hundred men and kidnapped his state-appointed replacement. In early April his supporters shot at a white magistrate sent to investigate and ambushed some police, killing three Europeans. Crossing east of the Thukela River into the former Zulu Kingdom, the rebels hid in the Nkandla Forest. Chiefs from the sheltered valleys to the north and west of Nkandla joined Bambatha, while those of the southern grassland rejected his struggle as their communities would be vulnerable to colonial firepower. A colonial force was formed, including a contingent of 500 mounted men from the Transvaal, a machine gun and crew funded by Castle Beer Company, and Sergeant Major Gandhi's Indian stretcher bearers. On May 3, this Natal Field Force, with 5,000 armed men and 150 wagons, left Dundee and advanced toward the Nkandla Forest in pursuit of Bambatha. The force destroyed Zulu settlements and skirmished with rebels. On the night of June 9–10 the militia discovered Bambatha's camp on the Mome River, artillery was positioned on high ground and the volunteers attacked at dawn. Bambatha's rebels were defeated and the chief's severed head exhibited around the colony. Among Bambatha's 12,000 supporters, 2,300 were killed and 4,700 captured during the rebellion.

Another scene of rebellion emerged in June 1906 when armed Africans attacked European stores and militia 50 km south of the Nkandla Forest in the densely populated Maphumulo area. Fighting then spread east to the settler farms near the coast and south through the sugar estates close to Durban. The rebels hid in densely forested valleys. By the end of June, with colonial soldiers returning from the fight against Bambatha, the colonial force in Maphumulo grew from a few hundred to 2,500 troops. In early

July, McKenzie's militia ravaged the Mvoti Valley, pillaging, burning, stealing livestock and indiscriminately shooting Africans who ran away. Discovering that a large rebel force was camped in the Izinsimba Valley, Mckenzie used the cover of darkness to position artillery and machine guns on the high ground to support a dawn attack. Some 450 Zulu, including key leaders, were killed, with no militia deaths. Colonial scorched-earth operations continued throughout July and ended the rebellion. Hundreds of Africans were convicted of treason and sentenced to flogging and two years of hard labor. Dinuzulu, the legitimate, though officially unrecognized Zulu king, had avoided fighting but was given a four-year prison sentence for sheltering Bambatha's family (Stuart, 1913; Marks, 1970; Thompson, 2003, 2004; Guy, 2005).

British Somaliland (1901–20)

In 1888, through signing treaties with Somali leaders, the British established a protectorate called British Somaliland to supply beef to the nearby British port of Aden, which controlled access to the Red Sea and Suez Canal. Beginning in 1899, Sayyid Mohammed Abdullah Hassan, nicknamed the "Mad Mullah" by the British, established a Muslim Sunni state in the interior of British Somaliland, mobilized an army of mounted Somali gunmen and urged his people to expel infidels such as the Ethiopians, Italians, French and British. In March 1900, Hassan began his struggle by directing an attack on the Ethiopian garrison at Jijiga, which led to a joint Anglo-Ethiopian operation against the Somali rebels in May of the next year. A British colonial expedition of 1,500 Somali soldiers and a 15,000-strong Ethiopian force converged on Hassan's army, which withdrew into Italian Somaliland. The British and Ethiopians then left the inhospitable region. The Italians did not assist in the campaign as they feared a repeat of their terrible 1896 defeat at Adowa. In 1903, another British offensive, which included an amphibious landing in Italian Somaliland, failed and resulted in Hassan's followers occupying both sides of the British and Italian Somaliland border up to the coast. In 1904, another British expedition, supported by British and Italian warships, drove Hassan's rebels inland.

By 1913, the rebels, mostly horsemen with guns, had constructed a network of stone forts that controlled the interior of the Somali Peninsula. At the August 1913 Battle of Dul Madoba in northwestern Somalia, some 2,700 of Hassan's men overcame a 110-man detachment of the British Somali Camel Constabulary. Subsequently, Hassan's army attacked and looted the British-controlled port of Berbera. The British quickly expanded the constabulary into the Somaliland Camel Corps but the outbreak of World War I delayed operations.

By 1919, the British had established posts in the mountain passes of British Somaliland but Hassan's rebels continued raids and ambushes. After the British imperial general staff recommended that it would take two army divisions and millions of pounds to subjugate the rebels, the Colonial Office turned to the newly formed Royal Air Force (RAF) which sought to prove itself by crushing the rebellion with aircraft supported by local colonial forces. By the start of 1920, the RAF based in Egypt had assembled "Z Force" at temporary air fields in British Somaliland. It included twelve biplane bombers, fourteen motorized logistical vehicles and 200 personnel. In late January and early February, the RAF bombed Hassan's forts, which were then easily seized by ground forces from the Camel Corps and King's African Rifles. Hassan's rebels were terrorized by the aircraft and scattered into the Ogaden Desert where their leader died in December. In what the British termed "the cheapest war in history," the Somaliland rebellion had been suppressed and colonial secretary Winston Churchill strategized that air power could be used as an inexpensive method to control the empire (Abdi Abdulqadir Sheik-Abdi, 1983; Omissi, 1990).

Resistance in Morocco (1903–34)

During the early twentieth century, Morocco in northwest Africa experienced civil war and gradually succumbed to French domination. In 1903, France withdrew claims to Egypt in exchange for Britain agreeing to not interfere in Morocco. In 1907, anti-European violence led to French forces landing in Casablanca on the Atlantic coast and French soldiers from Algeria occupying Oujda, and in 1911, the French took the Moroccan capital of Fez. While a German gunboat arrived on the Atlantic coast in 1911 to support Moroccan independence, this was recalled when Paris granted Berlin territory in Sub-Saharan Africa. The next year, the French forced the new Moroccan ruler Mawlay Abd al-Hafiz to sign the Treaty of Fez that imposed a protectorate on the core of his territory. Subsequently, France and Spain concluded that the latter should control Morocco's far north and south. Rebellions in Fez and Marrakech were suppressed by French firepower.

Resistance to Spanish intrusion in northeastern Morocco's Rif Mountains had begun in 1909 and was suppressed by a large Spanish force the next year. In 1920, local leader Abd el-Karim el-Khattabi, inspired by Muslim concepts of social and religious reform, established the core of a modern army to drive out the Spanish. In January 1921, a Spanish force of 20,000 men from the coastal city of Melilla advanced into the Rif Mountains where they established outposts. On July 22, after a five-day siege, some 4,000 Riffian insurgents overran the poorly located Spanish base at Annual where the Spanish soldiers dropped their weapons and ran away and between 8,000 and 15,000 were killed. This was the greatest African battlefield defeat of a European army during the twentieth century. The Spanish survivors of Annual escaped to Monte Arruit but were surrounded and in early August surrendered to the Riffians who executed many and took 600 prisoners. El-Karim decided against attacking vulnerable Melilla given fear of international disapproval. By the beginning of 1922, the Spanish army in Morocco had grown to 150,000 men and they had recovered most of the outposts lost during the Annual campaign.

With many captured weapons and a large ransom gained from the return of Spanish prisoners, el-Karim expanded his army and established an administration over the Riffian groups who declared him Amir of the Rif in 1924. The "Disaster at Annual," as the Spanish called it, provoked a political crisis in Madrid and the rise of General Miguel Primo de Rivera as dictator, who decided to abandon the interior of Morocco. From October to December 1924, some 7,000 Riffian rebels killed thousands of Spanish soldiers as they were withdrawing from the area.

From April to June 1925, el-Karim's Riffians invaded the French protectorate to the south, captured outposts and halted just 30 km from Fez. Marshal Henri Philippe Petain, World War I hero of Verdun, took over French forces in Morocco and the Spanish agreed to a massive joint campaign against the Riffians. In early September, 8,000 Spanish troops, including future dictator Francisco Franco, landed on Morocco's Mediterranean coast at Alhucemas Bay near the heart of Riffian territory. The Spanish expeditionary force took a month to advance 8 km to seize el-Karim's capital of Ajdir. In early October, el-Karim's forces departed French territory and moved north. The Riffians, with perhaps 5,000 fighters, were trapped, as another Spanish force marched from the east and a large French army under Petain pushed up from the south. Some 200,000 Spanish and 300,000 French troops imposed a blockade on the Rif mountains during which many inhabitants starved. In early May 1926, the Spanish and French launched an offensive and late in the month el-Karim, who thought the Spanish would kill him, surrendered to the French who sent him to the Indian Ocean island of Reunion and eventually allowed him to settle in Egypt. By early July 1927, Spanish pacification of the Rif was complete (Alvarez, 2001; Bowen and Alvarez, 2007, pp. 37–52; Pennell, 2009, pp. 142–7).

At the start of World War I much of the interior of French Morocco was not under colonial control. While greater wartime manpower demands limited French operations in Morocco, this changed in 1917 when an ambitious French offensive established new colonial outposts and divided the large zone of Berber resistance into three separate pockets. In August 1918, the French suffered a significant defeat when one of their columns dispatched to the southeast Tafilalet area was defeated by rebels. In 1919, the number of French troops in Morocco was reduced because of post-war demobilization and military commitments elsewhere. The occupation force returned to its pre-demobilization strength of 85,000–90,000 men in mid-1920, but by 1924 it had again shrunk to 62,000 and Paris planned a further reduction to 46,000 regulars and 10,000 reserves. Over the next decade, the French, under Resident-General Marshal Louis-Hubert Lyautey, defended the economically and militarily important parts of Morocco, and abandoned the central and high Atlas Mountains.

While the French in Morocco initially saw the Spanish-Rif conflict as improving their own position, this changed in the early 1920s as France became concerned that an independent Rif state would try to liberate all of Morocco. In April and May 1925, Riffian forces seized French border defences as the defection of 20,000 Moroccans prompted the French to abandon the frontier. After the French sustained heavy losses defending Fez from Riffian advance, French reinforcements arrived in late July and decisively changed the course of the war. In September the French under Petain launched two offensives, a limited one in the central area to recover territory and the main push in the east to distract Riffian forces from the Spanish landing at Alhucemas Bay. Postponed for the rainy season, Spanish and French operations recommenced in May 1926 and resulted in el-Karim's surrender. In late May and June, as the French occupied new areas, 3,000 Moroccan fighters and their families fled to the Atlas Mountains, which became a haven for dissidents who raided French forces.

In the late 1920s, war-weary France returned to the policy of only defending useful territory in Morocco while conducting minor operations against the dissident areas. This changed in 1930 when events in Germany prompted French military authorities to end resistance in Morocco so as to bring home regular troops who could defend the motherland. In July 1931, a French colonial force with air support advanced 15 km along a 100-km-wide front into the northern dissident territory, and a more daring operation in November advanced another 45 km. In a mid-January 1932 night operation, French forces captured the important oasis of Tafilalet, which they had abandoned in 1918. In turn, the road between Marrakech and Bou-Denib was usable by the French and the rebel controlled upper central Atlas was isolated. A series of huge French operations from May to July dramatically reduced the insurgent areas, which created a false sense of confidence among the French. Difficulties began when the French penetrated the Tazigzaout area where many dissidents had assembled under the Muslim religious leader Sidi el-Mekki, who refused to surrender. In late August, 1,000 colonial irregulars assaulted Tazigzaout Ridge where they met stiff resistance that took three weeks to overcome. The rebels were fragmented into four isolated pockets in the Great Atlas, and the blocks of Jabal Sarhro in the south and the Anti-Atlas in the southwest.

Based in the nearly inaccessible Sarhro, some 1,000 fighters began descending from the mountains to ambush French convoys moving between the Atlantic coast and Algeria as well as Moroccan communities that had accepted colonial rule. Consequently, the French shifted their focus from the Grand Atlas toward the south. In mid-February 1933, thousands of French-led irregulars stormed the Sarhro from east and west but communication difficulties, resistance and the refusal of some irregulars to fight resulted in heavy colonial casualties. This prompted the French to commit regular troops to an assault on the last dissident position on the cliff of Bou Gafer, which again led to substantial colonial losses. Unable to seize the area, the French then besieged the rebels, who negotiated favorable surrender terms which included amnesty, continued possession of firearms, exemption from forced labor and excessive taxation, and recognition of the authority of local leaders under French supervision. The capitulation at Bou Gafer demoralized rebels in other enclaves in the south, who then also surrendered. The French then concentrated on the Great Atlas and during a two-week operation in June, in which 200 colonial troops were killed, occupied the ridges of the Assif Melloul. This split the surviving insurgent zone into two pockets, which the French occupied during operations in July and August, giving them control of the highest points in the Atlas. With a force of 25,000 regulars and 18,000 irregulars, the French overwhelmed the Anti-Atlas in the southwest, which was the last dissident stronghold. During late February and early March 1934, a final offensive completed French control of Morocco and most regular troops were sent home (Gershovich, 2000, pp. 94–190).

Italian expansion in Libya (1911–31)

In 1911, Italian public demands for colonial expansion propelled Rome into war with the Ottoman Empire. In early October Italian warships bombarded Tripoli, which was occupied by a naval landing party as the Turkish garrison withdrew inland. During the rest of the month, a 30,000-strong Italian invasion force, with 100 artillery pieces, 800 trucks and four airplanes, secured the other coastal cities of Tobruk, Derna, Khoms and Benghazi. Since the Italian navy dominated the Mediterranean, Turkish soldiers and supplies were smuggled overland from Tunisia and Egypt, which remained neutral. Enver Bey, a Turkish officer who would lead his country during World War I, composed a plan to lure the Italians into the desert where they would be ambushed. Arab and Turk Muslim solidarity was promoted when the leader of the Arab Sanussi group, Ahmed Serif, declared holy war (jihad) against the Christian Italians. In November and December units under Mustafa Kemal, who later founded the Republic of Turkey, effectively fought the Italians at Tobruk and Derna, as did those under Neset Bey and Enver Bey at Tripoli and Benghazi, respectively. Although the 100,000 Italian troops in Libya outnumbered the 20,000–30,000 Arabs and several thousand Turks, a stalemate developed as the poorly trained Italians could not move more than 5 or 6 km inland away from naval gunfire, and the lightly equipped Arab–Turkish forces could not retake the coast. In Libya, the Italians performed the first aerial reconnaissance and bombing in the history of warfare. The start of another war in the Balkans meant that Istanbul had to make peace with Rome to redeploy military resources. In the October 1912 Treaty of Ouchy, the Ottoman Empire accepted Italian control of Libya for the return of captured Aegean islands.

In 1922, given the rise of Italian fascist Benito Mussolini, the Italians in coastal Libya extended their authority inland. The province of Tripolitania, around the capital of Tripoli, was quickly subdued while in the eastern province of Cyrenaica prolonged guerrilla resistance was directed by Omar Mukhtar. A veteran of the 1911–12 war, Mukhtar returned from exile in Egypt in 1923 to command 6,000 insurgents who mostly originated from nomadic Sanussi Arab communities and attacked Italian supply lines. The Italians responded by poisoning or destroying wells and slaughtering the nomads' livestock. In March 1923, an 8,000-strong Italian colonial force, supported by trucks and aircraft, easily seized towns and dispersed rebel camps in the open terrain of Cyrenaica. The rebels then fled to the forested and mountainous Jebel Akhdar. During the next four years Italian forces staged numerous forays into the mountains, killing 1,500 men – many of whom were unarmed – and some 100,000 animals. The rebels tenaciously clung to parts of the Jebel Akhdar and inflicted some serious reverses on the Italians. From July to September 1927, a highly mobile Italian force of 10,000 men, supported by armored cars, conducted a major sweep of the Jebel Akhdar. Mukhtar's remaining 2,000 rebels were dispersed and his main stronghold of Kuf overrun. The Italians killed 1,500 men, women and children and lost very few of their own troops. Afterward, the Italians built forts in the Jebel Akhdar to restrict rebel movement.

Despite this disaster, Mukhtar began orchestrating guerrilla attacks on Italian communication lines. The Italians used radio-equipped trucks, armored cars, aircraft and allied Arab cavalry to hunt down the mounted insurgents. When the rebels were detected they would disperse among the local population. By the close of 1928, the insurgents still controlled parts of the country and moved freely at night. In January 1929, Marshal Pietro Badoglio became governor of Libya and after the rebels rejected negotiation, he launched another major offensive. The next year, Italian forces, after the subjugation of southern Fezzan and Tripolitania, built a 300-km-long barbed-wire fence along the Egyptian border, which was patrolled by aircraft and armored vehicles. This blocked the rebels from moving back and forth across the frontier and stopped supplies coming from Egypt. Some 80,000 nomads, almost their entire population in Cyrenaica, were forcibly relocated to concentration camps to stop them from assisting the insurgents. Italian forces were accused of bombing civilians, killing children and the elderly, raping and disembowelling women, and executing prisoners by dropping them from flying aircraft or crushing them with tanks. Contact with the rebels became a capital offense and it is believed that the Italians executed 12,000 people during 1930–1. Mukhtar was captured in September 1931 when a group of rebel horsemen was intercepted and dispersed by Italian aircraft and ground forces. He was sentenced to death after a half-hour-long trial and went to the gallows with incredible composure before an audience of 20,000 concentration camp prisoners. The rebellion dissolved and during the rest of the 1930s the Italians combined the provinces of Tripolitania, Cyrenaica and Fezzan into a single Libya and about 40,000 Italian settlers arrived in what Mussolini called Italy's "fourth shore" (Childs, 1990; Simons, 1993; Vandervort, 2012).

French Equatorial Africa (1927–32)

The most extensive colonial pacification campaign in Sub-Saharan Africa between the world wars took place in French Equatorial Africa in present-day western Central African Republic and eastern Cameroon near the Congo-Brazzaville border. In the 1800s the area had been a sanctuary for people fleeing slave raids connected with the Atlantic and Trans-Saharan trades, and at the end of the century part of it became a German sphere of influence. Following World War I the entire area fell under the French, who contracted it to concessionary companies that extorted rubber and ivory from locals. Grievances mounted during the 1920s as the French imposed forced labor to build the Congo-Ocean railway and increased taxes. Around 1927 local prophet Barka Ngainoumbey, called Karnu or "roller up of earth," began to encourage his Gbaya people to refuse taxation and labor. He also issued magical hoe handles as protection from bullets and predicted that the French would turn into gorillas. Three colonial detachments were dispatched to the prophet's village but these were suddenly withdrawn on orders from the governor-general, who believed violence would worsen the situation. This had the opposite result as local people, who believed Karnu had defeated the French, attacked colonial officials and traders.

In October 1928, the French launched a total war against the people of this region with a column of 300 soldiers marching northwest from Bangui, and imposing a scorched-earth campaign on the Gbaya in which they were relocated to "protected villages." On December 11, French colonial infantry attacked Nahing, where Karnu was killed and his body exhibited as proof that he did not possess magic. A 1,000-strong colonial force mopped up pockets of resistance and by October 1929 the Lobaye and Haute Sangha areas had been pacified. During the campaign the Pana and Karre people around Bocarango, south of Bangui, hid in caves and conducted guerrilla warfare against the French as they had done against Fulbe (or Fulani) slavers in earlier times. French colonial forces used pepper-laden fires to drive the rebels out of caves so as to kill them with machine guns. The fighting lasted until late 1931 and early 1932. Concerned by anti-colonial criticism at home, French officials withheld reports about the rebellion from the French press. While later Central-African nationalists would see the Kongo Wara War (War of the Hoe Handle) as a broad attempt by a new prophetic leadership to oust the French, others understand it as a series of separate disturbances incited by French oppression (O'Toole, 1984; Thomas, 2005, pp. 232–4, 238).

The Italian invasion of Ethiopia (1935)

By the late 1920s, Italy's fascist regime talked of avenging the defeat by Ethiopia at the 1896 Battle of Adowa. In the early 1930s Italy built up military forces in its Horn of Africa colonies of Eritrea and Italian Somaliland

, and after 1933 Britain and France tried to keep Italy from siding with Nazi Germany by accepting Rome's ambitions in Ethiopia. In November 1934, at Wal Wal, some 100 km inside Ethiopia, an Italian force from Somaliland clashed with an Anglo-Ethiopian surveying expedition. While Mussolini demanded an apology and damages, Ethiopian Emperor Haile Selassie submitted the dispute to the League of Nations, which discussed it for eleven months. France and Britain declared an arms embargo on Italy and Ethiopia, which impacted the latter more significantly as it lacked the capacity to manufacture modern weapons. Eager to thwart Italian objections to its occupation of Austria, Nazi Germany secretly sent military aid to Ethiopia including three airplanes, 10,000 rifles and millions of rounds of ammunition. The military situation had changed considerably since 1896. In 1935, Ethiopia's army, which had just begun to modernize, consisted of between 350,000 and 750,000 men, of which only a quarter were trained, and they were equipped with 400,000 mostly outdated rifles, 200 obsolete artillery pieces, fifty anti-aircraft guns and a few light tanks. Ethiopian military transport relied on horse-drawn wagons and the new Ethiopian Air Force had a dozen airplanes and four pilots. Conversely, the Italian army in East Africa comprised around 500,000 Italian, Eritrean, Somali and Libyan soldiers with 6,000 machine guns, 2,000 modern artillery pieces, 800 tanks and 600 aircraft.

On October 3, 1935, without a declaration of war, nine Italian divisions based in Eritrea invaded Ethiopia, while two divisions from Italian Somaliland opened a diversionary southern front. Throughout the campaign, Italy dominated the air and on the first day symbolically bombed Adowa. The League of Nations imposed weak economic sanctions on Italy, which did not stop the campaign. Britain neglected to close the Suez Canal, which could have halted Italy's war effort. On October 15, the Italians captured Aksum, about 40 km inside Ethiopia, but poor roads meant that it was not until November 8 that they took Mekele, some 60 km south. In mid-November, Mussolini replaced the cautious commander General Emilio De Bono with Marshal Pietro Badoglio, who was told to complete the conquest before the onset of the rains in June 1936, and he was authorized to use poison gas, in contravention of the Geneva Convention. Haile Selassie first flew to Jijiga on the southern front to organize resistance and then moved to Dessie in the north which, despite heavy bombing, served as his headquarters for the rest of the war.

During Christmas 1935, the Ethiopians, with 190,000 men organized into four armies, launched an energetic counter-offensive aimed at isolating Italian forces around Mekele. The Italians lost most of the territory they had occupied and in places were driven back to the Eritrean border. Ethiopian troops swarmed the small Italian tanks and rolled boulders down from high ground to block their movement. At the First Battle of Tamben, fought between January 20 and 24, 1936, the Italians used tanks, aerial bombing and mustard gas to stop the Ethiopian advance. The Italians then mounted their own offensive, which began with an attack on Amba Aradam, south of Mekele, with mustard gas and a mass bombardment by 170 airplanes and 280 artillery pieces. At the Second Battle of Tamben, from February 27 to 29, the Italians inflicted heavy casualties on the Ethiopian central army, which retreated, thus prompting the other Ethiopian formations to withdraw. The Italian Air Force dropped explosives and gas on the retreating Ethiopians, set the countryside on fire with incendiary devices, and bombed Red- Cross hospitals and ambulances overwhelmed with civilian casualties. Deciding against guerrilla warfare, the emperor led an Ethiopian army in a determined attack on the Italians at May Chaw in southern Tigray at the end of March, which was thwarted by Italian aerial bombing and gas. As the emperor's men retreated south, they were further bombed and gassed, and harassed by local rebels sponsored by the Italians. The Italian advance continued and on May 5 Badoglio led the mechanized "Iron Will Column" into the capital of Addis Ababa without a fight. Haile Selassie had left for Britain a few days earlier and Mussolini declared Ethiopia part of Italian East Africa. In the south, the Italians overcame stubborn resistance to take Qorahe on November 7, 1935, and they captured Harar after the northern forces had taken Addis Ababa. The war claimed the lives of around 10,000 Italian and 275,000 Ethiopian soldiers and many more Ethiopian civilians.

Sanctions against Italy were lifted within days of Haile Selassie's futile address to the League of Nations in Geneva. Emerging nationalists across Africa were outraged by Italian aggression against the last independent African country, which had come to symbolize hopes of future African autonomy. Ethiopian resistance continued, and during July and August 1936, there were two attempts by Ethiopian forces to recapture Addis Ababa but they were both repelled by Italian airpower. Hopeful that an imminent war in Europe would work to their benefit, some Ethiopians fought a guerrilla war against Italian occupation. The Italians responded with a reign of terror that included massacres and the indiscriminate use of gas. By 1939, the military situation had reached a stalemate, with Ethiopian insurgents dominating the countryside and Italian troops defending towns and forts (Pankhurst, 2001, pp. 218–45; Marcus, 2002, pp. 147–63).

2 Africa and the World Wars (1914–18 and 1939–45)

Introduction

Africa's colonial period, roughly 1880 to 1960, was dominated by the two world wars. During both the global conflicts, the European colonial powers took different sides, which meant that military campaigns were fought in Africa and the continent became a wartime reservoir of manpower and resources. However, the two world wars had profoundly different impacts on colonial Africa. World War I (1914–18) resulted in the final reconfiguration of the colonial map of Africa and a general strengthening of the colonial system that stabilized during the inter-war years of the 1920s and 1930s. Conversely, World War II (1939–45) served to weaken the colonial powers, inspired African nationalist movements and broadly set the stage for the decolonization of Africa during the 1950s and 1960s.

World War I in Africa (1914–18)

World War I was fought in every region of Africa. The first British soldier to fire a shot in the entire war did so in German Togoland (now Togo) on August 12, 1914, and the last active German force capitulated in British-ruled Northern Rhodesia (now Zambia) on November 25, 1918, two weeks after the Armistice. All four German colonies in Africa were surrounded by enemy territories and eventually invaded. There were military campaigns in Togoland, Cameroon, South West Africa (today's Namibia) and German East Africa (the mainland part of today's Tanzania plus Rwanda and Burundi). From the Allied perspective, these invasions usually aimed at an initial strategic objective such as denying German naval raiders coastal sanctuary, but they eventually turned into a race for German territory. Some German colonial officials thought that Africa should remain neutral to avoid destroying new colonial infrastructure and provoking African resistance, but military officers felt obliged to tie down Allied resources that might be deployed in Europe and to retain a German presence in Africa as a bargaining chip in anticipated negotiations. The war was also fought in North Africa where the Ottoman Empire supported Sanussi Rebellion against the Italians in Libya and the British in Egypt, and Ottoman forces directly attacked the Suez Canal. Across Africa, global war presented recently colonized people with opportunities to reassert independence or ingratiate themselves to the colonial powers. In areas without fighting, African communities were often forced to supply recruits, laborers and agricultural products for the war effort all of which caused varying degrees of hardship.

Togoland

The shortest African campaign of World War I was fought in the small West African German colony of Togoland – a thin sliver between Britain's Gold Coast (now Ghana) and France's Dahomey (now Benin). The main Allied objective was Kamina, which was the location of Germany's most important overseas wireless transmitter that enabled Berlin to communicate with its other African territories, ships in the South Atlantic and South America. With just 700 police and border guards to defend Togoland, acting Governor Major Hans Georg Von Doering proposed that the West African territories stay neutral, but the Allies ignored him. In mid-August 1914, the Gold Coast Regiment seized the port of Lome, Togoland's capital which was only 1 km from the Gold Coast border. The Germans withdrew 110 km north along the road and railway; blew up the Chra River Bridge, the last major obstacle on the way to Kamina; and established a defensive position on its northern bank. Converging on Kamina, the British pursued the Germans north from Lome, another British force advanced east from the Gold Coast and French troops marched west from Dahomey. While the Gold Coast Regiment was repelled when it attempted to cross the Chra in late August, the German forces withdrew to Kamina, destroyed the wireless station and surrendered a few days later. A reluctant fighter, Doering, neglected to defend the two other rivers on the way to Kamina, did not mobilize reserves and still had plenty of ammunition when he surrendered (Strachan, 2004, pp. 13–18).

Cameroon

With French Equatorial Africa to the east and south, and British Nigeria to the west, the German territory of Cameroon was encircled by enemies, except the small Spanish possessions of Equatorial Guinea in the south and the island of Fernando Po off the Atlantic coast. While the Germans in Cameroon, led by General Karl Zimmerman, knew that they faced overwhelming enemy forces, their aim was to retain a physical presence in Africa until the end of the war. They planned to abandon the unfortified coast, let the swamps and tropical disease of the south hamper invaders and defend the northern grassland plateau. German forces in Cameroon numbered 205 European officers and 1650 African soldiers in 1914, which increased to a height of 1460 Europeans and 6550 Africans, but they lacked ammunition.

The Allied forces that invaded Cameroon in August 1914 had different agendas. Interested in territorial expansion, the French quickly seized German posts on the Ubangi and Congo rivers which had been under French control until ceded to Germany in 1911. Subsequently, and without orders from Paris, four French columns pressed into southeastern Cameroon. Although the Belgians had initially intended to remain neutral in Africa, events in Europe prompted them to facilitate the French invasion and 600 Belgian colonial troops joined a French column. British operations focused on denying the port of Douala to German cruisers. In late August, five columns of the Nigeria Regiment crossed into Cameroon at different points. When the northern columns inadvertently stumbled into the main German defenses around Mora, this revealed that the coast was undefended, which prompted the Royal Navy to land an Anglo-French expedition that seized Douala in late September. Up to early 1915, the Germans imported ammunition and supplies through Equatorial Guinea. In the interior, during early 1915, the Germans mounted counter-offensives against the British and French and raided into Nigeria and Gabon. In May and June, Anglo-French forces from Douala undertook a torturously slow advance toward the trading center of Jaunde (today's Yaounde). In June, French forces in the east regrouped and captured several centers, and British forces from Nigeria and French forces from Chad took Garua and other parts of the north. This incited a German shift toward the south. In November, after a pause in fighting caused by the rains, the Anglo-French force resumed their advance on Jaunde which was captured on January 1, 1916. By mid-February, despite the efforts of a French column from Gabon to block the border, 1,000 Germans, 6,000 African soldiers and 7,000 family members and followers had crossed into Spanish territory. The last German force in Cameroon, the garrison of Mora in the north, surrendered on February 18. The German forces in Equatorial Guinea moved to Fernando Po to vainly await a return to Cameroon (Strachan, 2004, pp. 19–60).

South West Africa

The South African invasion of German South West Africa (SWA) was motivated by several factors; the British imperial government requested Pretoria to secure German ports and radio facilities, while the South African government wanted more territory. Since the region was a venue for European settlement, both South Africa and German SWA restricted armed military services to whites. Although the Germans in SWA had around 2,000 mounted European infantry and a reserve of 3,000 volunteers supported by machine guns, artillery and three aircraft, these forces were dispersed and later formed into four composite battalions. Food supplies were limited as the settlers focused on cattle ranching and drought had disrupted farming by the recently colonized Ovambo in the north. German leadership was inconsistent as the military commander Joachim von Heydebreck was accidentally killed in November 1914; his obvious successor was killed in action in late September 1914 and the new commander, Viktor Francke, was a reservist and his chief-of-staff died after falling from a horse. In 1915, the South African invasion force numbered 45,000 European soldiers supported by 33,000 African, Colored and Indian unarmed transport drivers and labor. In the vast SWA, horse transportation and water resources became central to military operations.

The attack on SWA began on September 14, 1914, when the Royal Navy shelled German installations at the port of Swakopmund. The Germans withdrew from the coast because of British naval guns and concentrated on defending the Orange River border in the south. The 5,000-strong initial South African invasion force was divided into three contingents, each of which was insufficient for the offensive. South Africa's "C Force" landed unopposed at Luderitz and began to move inland but was slowed by German railway sabotage and waterhole poisoning. Ignorant of the German redeployment, South Africa's "A Force" marched across the Orange River into German territory and where its vanguard was overwhelmed by a German ambush at Sandfontein on September 26. This debacle transpired because the planned movement of Upington-based "B Force," under Manie Maritz, had not happened as it had mutinied against the South African government. On Christmas Day in 1914, South African trawlers landed troops at Walvis Bay, and in mid-January 1915, this force occupied Swakopmund.

In February 1915, Prime Minister Louis Botha, having recently subdued the Boer rebellion in South Africa, took command of South African forces at Swakopmund and led an advance on the German capital of Windhoek. The Germans redeployed their forces from the south to the center of the territory. In late March, Botha's contingent overwhelmed German forces around Reit, which was then used as a staging area for a renewed advance supported by a dozen Royal Navy armored cars. A German attempt to cut the railway behind the South Africans failed when the former became lost in the dark and was then repelled by South African infantry and armored cars that German aerial reconnaissance had previously mistaken for water trucks. At the beginning of May, Botha's force captured the abandoned Karibib railway junction that brought together the territory's rail systems. On May 12, the South Africans occupied Windhoek, site of an important wireless station, as the Germans continued to withdraw. In the south, a South African motorized column of 3,000 men crossed the Kalahari and penetrated the eastern border of SWA at the end of March 1915. By early April, the South Africans had secured all the Orange River crossings and the German railhead at Kalkfontein. In early May, the remaining German forces in the south withdrew north, given the rapid advance of "C Force" in the south and the success of Botha's Windhoek offensive that threatened to isolate them.

With the loss of southern SWA, German forces moved north along the railway to defend Otavi and Tsumeb. The expansionist Botha rejected a German ceasefire offer that proposed each side occupy half the colony. German commander Francke decided against guerrilla tactics because of overwhelming South African numbers and the potential impact on the small German settler population. Botha took several weeks to build up a strong force of 13,000 troops supported by artillery, 20,000 horses and oxen and 500 wagons carrying three days' provisions. On June 18, 1915, the South Africans resumed the offensive with a four-pronged northward movement to encircle Otavi. The 1,000 German troops at Otavi were meant to delay the South Africans long enough for Francke to organize defenses at Tsumeb. However, the speed of the South African advance caught the Germans unprepared. On July 1, Botha's central column, 3,500 men, attacked Otavi and within a few hours a flanking movement caused the Germans to withdraw from the railway and further north to Gaub. If Botha's column had been delayed for two days, it would have been forced to withdraw for lack of water. The Germans were trapped as South African forces converged from all sides and the Angolan border was blocked by an African rebellion. With Botha refusing conditions, the Germans surrendered on July 9, 1915. Casualties were low given South African encirclements and constant German withdrawals. Among the South Africans, 113 had been killed in action, 153 died through disease or accident and 263 had been wounded. 103 Germans had lost their lives. The South Africans captured 4740 German soldiers and dozens of cannon and machine guns (Strachan, 2004, pp. 61–92; Nasson, 2007, pp. 63–87; Van Der Waag, 2013; Van Der Waag, 2015, pp. 95–106).

East Africa

The most protracted and destructive African campaign of World War I happened in East Africa. While the immediate British objective was to deny German East Africa's Indian Ocean coast to German naval raiders, the territory's occupation would fulfill the British imperial ambition for uninterrupted rule from Cape to Cairo. Although the German governor had wanted the territory to remain neutral, German military commander Colonel Paul Von Lettow-Vorbeck felt a duty to fight so as to distract Allied resources from the European theatre. Bringing troops from India, the British planned to quickly defeat the Germans in East Africa by a simultaneous seaborne assault on the port of Tanga and an overland invasion across the Kenyan border. It proved disastrous. In early November 1914, the 8,000-strong British Indian Expeditionary Force B under Major General A.E. Aitken landed at Tanga but resistance from the reinforced German garrison pushed them back to their ships. Simultaneously, 4,000 men from British Indian Expeditionary Force C under Brigadier J.M. Stewart marching south from Kenya were pushed back at Longido by 600 German troops who caught them in crossfire.

With insufficient forces in the region and the Germans now raiding the Uganda railway, the British turned to South Africa to lead what would become a long campaign to conquer German East Africa. South Africa was Britain's main regional ally, but its involvement in East Africa was delayed by the invasion of SWA and South Africa's October 1915 election during which Afrikaner nationalists objected to participation in the war. Botha's government imagined that once German East Africa was occupied, Britain would cede its southern half to Portugal in exchange for the southern half of Mozambique that would be transferred to Pretoria, giving South Africa the nearby trade outlets of Beira and Lorenzo Marques (now Maputo). In November 1915, South Africa began recruiting for the East Africa campaign but disappointing results among whites prompted the formation of an armed battalion of mixed-race soldiers called the Cape Corps. With time to prepare, Lettow expanded his force from 218 European and 2542 African soldiers to 2712 Europeans, 11,367 Africans and 2591 auxiliaries by January 1916. Although the British sinking of the German cruiser Konigsberg in the Rufigi Delta in July 1916 fulfilled an important objective, Lettow stripped the warship of artillery, small arms and ammunition which bolstered his ground forces.

In early February 1916, South African Defense Minister Jan Smuts took command of British imperial forces in East Africa and launched an invasion of German territory. Envisioning large and fast sweeping maneuvers by mounted units that would compel German surrender, Smuts' approach to the East Africa campaign reflected his military experience during the South African War (1899–1902) and the recent invasion of SWA as well as his political imperative to minimize South African casualties. He did not appear to understand that much of German East Africa, with thick bush and disease-carrying tsetse flies, was unsuitable for horses. At the time Smuts arrived, the British 2nd Division conducted an unsuccessful attack on German positions at Salaita, just east of Mount Kilimanjaro and within British-ruled Kenya. In March, Smuts directed another assault on Salaita by 40,000 mostly Indian and South African troops that compelled the 4,000 German defenders to withdraw south along the railway through Moshi in German East Africa. Thick bush and heavy rain hindered British attempts to block the German retreat. Over the next few months, Smuts' three divisions, two of which were South African, pursued the Germans who conducted fighting withdrawals southward through Morogoro which British forces occupied in August. Although Smuts' forces captured the main port of Dar es Salaam and other coastal centers in September, little was done to ship in supplies and it took almost a year to establish a supply line using the undamaged railway between Dar es Salaam and Morogoro.

Additional to Smuts' invasion from Kenya, other Allied forces entered German East Africa. To the west, the Allies had gained control of Lake Tanganyika by using two small and fast gunboats, transported overland from South Africa, to neutralize several larger German vessels during the first two months of 1916. This facilitated invasion from the Belgian Congo in the west and British-ruled Northern Rhodesia (Zambia) and Nyasaland (Malawi) in the south. In April, several Belgian columns moved into Rwanda and Burundi, and by September, they had taken Tabora in what is now Tanzania, with the German defenders constantly pulling back toward the main force under Lettow. In late May 1916, the 2,500-strong Rhodesia–Nyasaland Field Force began an advance into German East Africa between the southern end of Lake Tanganyika and the northern tip of Lake Nyasa. Operating in a vast area, the force was supported by a fleet of 2,000 canoes bringing food across the swamps of the southern Belgian Congo and by developing a supply route from the Indian Ocean port of Chinde along the Zambezi River to Lake Nyasa. In November, the Rhodesia–Nyasaland Field Force suddenly faced much stiffer resistance when local German forces joined those that had fled Rwanda. Between April and September 1917, a German detachment under Max Wintgens broke off from this southern front and returned north toward Tabora covering 3,200 km and distracting some 6,000 Allied troops sent in pursuit. In March 1916, Portugal joined Britain's war mainly to acquire territory in Africa. Some 2,700 Portuguese troops crossed the southern border of German East Africa in October, but within four weeks, German resistance and tropical disease had obligated their retreat.

By the start of 1917, Smuts' southward advance had stalled along the Rufigi River which was defended by 4,000 German troops under Lettow. Tropical disease had devastated the Allied force. From June to September 1916, 53,000 draught animals died of disease and motor vehicles proved ineffective given few roads. By the end of 1916, around 12,000 South African troops had been invalided home given illness, exhaustion and poor nutrition. For example, in February 1916, the 9th South African Infantry battalion consisted of 1135 men, but by October, its effective strength had been reduced to 116. When Smuts prematurely declared victory and left for a position in the Imperial War Cabinet, British General Reginald Hoskins took command and launched a rapid Africanization of his forces. Indian and South African troops were replaced by African personnel from a dramatically expanded KAR which grew from 3,000 to 30,000 soldiers and he imported West African battalions. Furthermore, many tens of thousands of African civilians were conscripted as supply carriers.

Between July and August 1917, Jaap Van Deventer, the South African general who replaced Hoskins in May, directed a series of British pincer movements against German positions. There were three dozen engagements for control of water supplies and food-producing areas that the Germans gradually relinquished as they moved south. A serious battle that took place in October at Mahiwa, resulting in 600 German and 2,000 Allied casualties, delayed Van Deventer's advance, but it was a massive blow to Lettow who could not replace losses. In November, with some 52,000 Allied troops in German East Africa, Lettow led his last column of 300 European and 1,800 African soldiers into Mozambique where Africans had rebelled against the

Portuguese. After the rainy season, Allied forces pursued Lettow during July and August 1918. However, the elusive Germans crossed back into German East Africa in late September and moved west toward lightly defended Northern Rhodesia. Long out of contact with Germany, Lettow learned about the end of the war from captured British documents. On November 25, the Germans surrendered to Van Deventer at Abercorn, Northern Rhodesia (now Mbala, Zambia) near the southern end of Lake Tanganyika. During the conquest of German East Africa, Britain had deployed 114,000 European, Indian and African soldiers, of whom 10,000 died mostly from disease and conscripted 1 million African supply carriers, of which some 100,000 perished from illness and exhaustion. Their food confiscated by both sides, the inhabitants of the German colony and adjacent territories suffered terribly from famine and disease. It is likely that the East Africa campaign caused the deaths of around 300,000 people (Hodges, 1978; Anderson, 2004; Strachan, 2004, pp. 93–184; Stapleton, 2006; Nasson, 2007, pp. 89–122; Paice, 2007; Van Der Waag, 2015, pp. 111–14).

North Africa

When World War I began, Egypt had been occupied by Britain since 1882 but was technically part of the Ottoman Empire. In late 1914, Britain closed the Egyptian legislature fearing that it would criticize British occupation, and then, after the Ottoman sultan declared jihad against the Allied powers, London imposed a protectorate over Egypt and deposed the pro-Ottoman Egyptian ruler. Some 70,000 Australian, New Zealand and Indian soldiers arrived to defend the strategically vital Suez Canal.

The Ottoman Empire, in 1915, embarked on a plan to attack the Suez Canal with the aim of blocking Allied shipping and igniting an Egyptian nationalist uprising. In mid-January 1915, despite objections from German advisors, a 20,000-strong Ottoman expedition under German Colonel Friedrich Freiherr Kress von Kressenstein set out across the Sinai Desert supported by 5,000 camels carrying water, large water tanks pre-positioned along the route and Bedouin guides who were hostile to the British. The force was easily spotted by British aircraft. At the beginning of February, and under cover of a sandstorm, Ottoman forces tried to cross the canal at three points but were driven off by the well-prepared defenders. Given British counter-attacks, the Ottomans fought their way back across the Sinai, having lost around 1,400 men, of whom half were prisoners. The British lost around 150 men. Egyptian civilians were unaware of the attack and did not revolt. In July 1916, Kressenstein, with 16,000 soldiers supported by arms, artillery and airplanes from Germany, made another attempt on the Canal, intending to block Allied troops passing through to Europe, but his force was defeated in Gaza and lost half its personnel.

In Libya's eastern province of Cyrenaica which borders Egypt, the Sanussi Brotherhood advocated a strict interpretation of Sunni Islam that gained popularity including among Egyptian nationalists. The core of Sanussi military power was a contingent of Ottoman professional soldiers that had been left behind when the Italians seized the area in 1911–12. Since the British closed the western Egyptian border when the war began, the Sanussi were deprived of Egyptian markets and ports and therefore turned to the Ottomans and Germans who landed weapons, supplies and advisors on the eastern Libyan coast. In November 1915, the Sanussi seized the Egyptian border town of Sollum where three quarters of the Egyptian garrison joined them. The Sanussi then attacked British positions along the coast but were repelled by armored cars. While a Sanussi column moved inland and tried to capture the chain of oases in western Egypt that led to the Nile, this was prevented by Anglo-Egyptian reinforcements. Egyptian civilians rejected Sanussi calls for rebellion given the movement's demands for supplies, pack animals and recruits. In late 1916, the British began to expel the dwindling Sanussi forces, and in February 1917, a motorized British column drove the remaining Sanussi fighters back to Libya.

In 1915, Sir Reginald Wingate, British commander of the Egyptian Army, pressured London to approve a British offensive against the Sultanate of Darfur to the west of the Anglo-Egyptian Sudan. Ambitious to conquer Darfur since the late 1890s, Wingate falsely claimed that German/Ottoman agents were encouraging the Sultan of Darfur to attack the British in neighboring Sudan. Wingate also realized that the French wanted to expand east from Chad into Darfur and the end of the Cameroon campaign made this likely. With permission from London, Wingate organized the 2,000-strong Western Frontier Force (WFF) which was British-led but composed entirely of Egyptian army units with many Sudanese soldiers. In late May 1916, the WFF decisively defeated the comparatively poorly armed Fur army and sacked the capital of El Fashir. After Sultan Ali Dinar was killed by a WFF patrol, Darfur was incorporated into the Anglo-Egyptian Sudan (Carver, 2003, pp. 7–9, 187–90; McGregor, 2006, pp. 201–6).

African military service outside Africa

At the beginning of the twentieth century, France made plans to use colonial African troops in the defense of the motherland threatened by a growing German army. France was the only combatant in World War I to make extensive use of African soldiers outside of Africa. In 1914, France imported 10,000 North African troops to throw against the German invaders, and by 1918, some 200,000 black Africans from the French colonial territories, including Madagascar, had fought in Western Europe in every major battle and around 30,000 died. These African troops formed the shock force for French assaults and were central in suppressing a mass mutiny by white French soldiers in 1917. The French also sent African troops to the 1915 Gallipoli campaign and the 1916–17 Allied expedition to the Balkans which supported Serbia against Bulgaria, Germany and Austro-Hungary.

Immediately after the Armistice, French African troops formed the core of the occupation force in the Rhineland, which the racist German press dubbed the "black shame" (Echenberg, 1991, pp. 25–32; Lunn, 1999, pp. 120–56; Fogarty, 2008, pp. 39–44).

Before the war, Britain had decided against using colonial African troops outside their home continent. During World War I, Britain's African soldiers usually remained in Africa, but there were some exceptions. An entirely white South African infantry brigade fought in Western Europe from July 1916 to the end of the war and suffered heavy casualties. In 1918, a Cape Corps infantry battalion, consisting of mixed-race troops who had fought in East Africa, joined the British offensive against the Ottomans in Palestine. As requested by Britain, South Africa dispatched some 25,000 black military laborers from the South African Native Labour Contingent (SANLC) to Western Europe where, between September 1916 and January 1918, they cut timber, loaded and unloaded ships and maintained road and rail systems. In February 1917, more than 600 black SANLC members and a dozen white officers were lost when the Mendi, a troopship taking them across the English Channel, was accidentally hit by another vessel and sank. Mixed-race South Africans also served as unarmed military labor in Europe, as in the two Cape Corps battalions that unloaded ships at French ports, the 2,000-strong Cape Corps Labor Battalion that transported munitions and supplies and the 3,500-strong Cape Auxiliary Horse Transport that also moved goods and worked in logging. Black and mixed-race South African elites hoped that wartime military service represented an opportunity to assert citizenship claims, but they were disappointed as nothing changed. Conversely, the participation of 1,000 men from Bechuanaland (today's Botswana) in the SANLC was significant in enabling the territory's traditional leaders to convince Britain not to incorporate the territory into white supremacist South Africa (Willan, 1978; Clothier, 1987; Grundlingh, 1987; Jackson, 2001; Nasson, 2007, pp. 123–60).

While fears about a possible Egyptian nationalist rebellion made the British hesitant to use Egyptian soldiers outside their home country, most Egyptians remained loyal to Britain. In June 1916, the British sent an Egyptian artillery battery to the Arabian Peninsula to assist the Arab rebellion against the Ottomans. The 170,000 Egyptians of the Camel Transport Corps provided logistical support to British operations in Palestine and Syria. Some 98,000 men were conscripted into the Egyptian Labour Corps which was first used in Gallipoli and eventually sent 23,000 men to work in France, Palestine and Mesopotamia (McGregor, 2006, pp. 207–19).

Rebellions

In Africa, World War I created grievances related to increased colonial demands for manpower, resources and taxation, while at the same time, the departure of soldiers and police for the front weakened the colonial state and created an opportunity for protest. This situation led to rebellions by people who had recently come under colonial rule. In 1915, in Nyasaland, John Chilembwe, a US-educated Baptist minister, objected to British recruitment for the East Africa campaign and allegedly sent a message to the Germans seeking assistance. The rebellion started when Chilembwe's followers killed a white plantation manager with whom they had a long-standing dispute. Though the Nyasaland Uprising involved possibly less than 200 people, the wartime atmosphere prompted swift and overwhelming British reaction in which Chilembwe was killed. While African nationalist historians claim that Chilembwe had been influenced by the history the American abolitionist movement, others argue that his actions had been caused by mental stress or that the dead minister became a convenient scapegoat for colonial maladministration. Fear of another Chilembwe caused paranoid British officials in neighboring Northern Rhodesia to conduct a reign of terror against employees of African Christian missions who were conscripted as supervisors for the Carrier Corps in East Africa (Shepperson and Price, 1958; Mwase, 1967; Rotberg, 1970; Yorke, 1990; Page, 2000).

In 1915 and 1916, riots broke out against abusive and corrupt British-appointed chiefs and local police in the Bongo area of the northern Gold Coast. Resistance to colonial rule in this area had continued until 1911 and was rekindled when colonial agents destroyed local shrines and began military recruitment. Simultaneously, colonial occupation forces were reduced to such an extent that local people believed the British were abandoning the area. The British responded with overpowering force and restored chiefs who had been overthrown. Several rebellions broke out in Nigeria. In the Niger Delta of the east, the Prophet Elijah II mobilized Igbo people against the British. The uprising was connected to a dramatic decrease in price for local palm oil exports, and tensions reduced once this rose again. Several rebellions in western Nigeria reflected discontent with the indirect rule system whereby Europeans governed through appointed African chiefs, which threatened traditional Yoruba power structures. These uprisings were crushed by colonial forces, and in the Egba case, 500 rebels were killed. In Northern Nigeria, where the British cultivated good relations with local Muslims emirs, there were no rebellions during the war (Crowder, 1974; Thomas, 1983).

In French West Africa, resistance was stimulated by mass military recruitment that threatened agricultural production and was often involuntary. Some men tried to avoid military service by hiding in the bush, injuring or starving themselves so they could be judged medically unfit or fleeing into British territory or independent Liberia. There were widespread uprisings in territories like Haut-Senegal-Niger, Dahomey and the Niger Military Territory where rebel Tauregs seized the desert town of Agedes in 1916. Tensions were fueled by the long-standing antagonism between French officials and Muslim leaders, and the 1915 Ottoman declaration of jihad against the Allied powers. To suppress these rebellions, the French used thousands of soldiers who were desperately needed on the Western Front and at times had to turn to the British in northern Nigeria for assistance. By the end of 1917, the Volta-Bani area had been "pacified" in a large military campaign that had engaged in total war and had caused the deaths of 30,000 local people and around 300 French colonial soldiers. In 1919, the French divided the troublesome area into two administrative divisions which later became the independent states of Burkina Faso and Mali (Saul and Royer, 2001).

The entry of South Africa into the war on the side of Britain caused resentment among Afrikaners aggrieved by the memory of the South African War (1899–1902) and who staged a mutiny to recover full independence. A planned September 1914 military coup was undermined when two key leaders were killed driving through a police roadblock. During the initial South African invasion of SWA, the commander of one of the invading columns ignored his instructions and sided with the Germans. By the end of October 1914, 11,500 Boer rebels had been mobilized in the Transvaal and Free State where they briefly seized towns and ambushed trains. Botha's government declared martial law, rejected British military assistance and the prime minister personally led a 32,000-strong force against the rebels. Using encircling tactics and armored cars, Botha's forces quickly suppressed the rebellion in the Orange Free State and Transvaal. Just before Christmas, a combined German and rebel Boer offensive crossed the Orange River into South Africa and threatened Upington, but the Boers withdrew from the operation as they thought it would harm their republican cause. The last rebel force surrendered at the end of January 1915 and some mutineers fled to German territory. Fatalities were low, with 130 loyalists and 190 rebels killed. Botha's government was lenient toward the rebels, only one of whom was executed for treason. By the end of December 1915, there were only fifty rebels still in prison out of the 239 who had been convicted of offenses related to the uprising. While Afrikaner nationalists lauded the rebels as heroes, English-speaking whites considered the light sentences disgraceful and emergent black political leaders noticed a double standard when compared to the harsh treatment of Zulu rebels in 1906 (Davenport, 1963; Swart, 1998; Fedorowich, 2003; Nasson, 2007, pp. 35–59; Van Der Waag, 2015, pp. 99–100).

Loyalism

In January 1918, given massive resistance to its African recruiting, the French government appointed Blaise Diagne as high commissioner for the recruitment of troops in black Africa, with a rank equivalent to governor. Diagne had been the first black Senegalese deputy elected to the French National Assembly where he championed equal rights for the assimilated Africans of Dakar. He accepted the appointment because the French government promised him that after the war it would undertake reforms to ease colonial oppression and facilitate the granting of French citizenship to more Africans. Diagne conducted brilliantly successful recruiting tours using decorated African officers and sergeants. His first recruiting drive was meant to enlist 40,000 men but more than 63,000 came forward in the first two months with the largest continent from the previously rebellious Haut-Senegal-Niger area. However, the French betrayed Diagne as the promised reforms were never implemented (Crowder, 1974, pp. 500–3).

In August 1914, the South African Native National Congress (SANNC – later renamed African National Congress), formed two years earlier as the first South African wide black political organization, did what it considered its patriotic duty by suspending protest against the new Natives Land Act which prevented Africans from buying land outside designated reserves. An SANNC executive member, Walter Rubusana, volunteered to personally raise an armed African contingent for the invasion of German SWA, but the South African government did not take up the offer. Subsequently, westernized African elites in South Africa supported the creation of the unarmed SANLC. The African Political Organization, a group representing mixed-race people, mobilized volunteers for South Africa's Cape Corps. In Southern Rhodesia (now Zimbabwe), the war prompted the formation of the territory's first western-style African organizations. The Loyal Mandebele Patriotic Society adopted the rhetoric of the British Empire but embarked on its own agenda by pursuing a morality crusade to pressurize colonial officials and police to crack down on prostitution. Also formed during the war, the Ndebele National Home Movement comprised members of the Ndebele royal family who engaged legal assistance in an attempt to restore their monarchy and land. Various African chiefs in Southern Rhodesia took collections among their people and made cash donations to the war effort. Unlike settler donations that became part of local patriotic funds, African contributions were sent to the Prince of Wales Fund in Britain so there would be no mistake that they represented an investment in future rights (Ranger, 1970, pp. 55–63; Stapleton, 2002; Nasson, 2007, pp. 160–70).

Impact

World War I resulted in the last major adjustment of the political map of colonial Africa, the legacy of which continues up to the present. Germany was evicted from Africa, with its former territories given to the victorious powers as League of Nations mandates which were supposed to be prepared for self-rule but in practice were treated much the same as other colonies. In West Africa, Togo and Cameroon were split between the French and British, with the former getting the lion's share. A slice of Togo was added to neighboring British-ruled Gold Coast and western Cameroon became part of British Nigeria, though some of it was later returned. This led to

Cameroon's current and contentious bilingual French and English society and post-colonial border disputes between Cameroon and Nigeria. Most of German East Africa became British-administered Tanganyika where an African peasant production economy developed in contrast to the white settler farms of adjacent Kenya. The Belgians took over Rwanda and Burundi, both of which bordered the Belgian Congo, where they would reinvent existing Tutsi, Hutu and Twa identities as hierarchical racial classifications. South Africa gained SWA where it brought in Afrikaner settlers and administered the territory as an unofficial province until it became independent Namibia in 1990.

World War II (1939–45)

Important World War II campaigns were fought in and around the Italian colonies in East Africa which dominated the strategic Red Sea and North Africa where control of the Suez Canal and Middle East was contested. There were also clashes in parts of French colonial Africa which split between pro-Allied Free French and pro-Axis Vichy regimes. Many tens of thousands of African military personnel served outside their continent such as the African colonial soldiers who defended France in 1940, British West and East African units that fought in Burma against the Japanese and the Southern Africans and Free French Africans who advanced up the Italian Peninsula. Allied demands for African manpower and raw materials plus wartime propaganda and urbanization set the stage for important developments in the 1950s.

East Africa

World War II reached Africa in June 1940 when fascist Italy, inspired by the German occupation of France, joined the Axis side. Italian East Africa now represented a threat to Allied shipping through the Red Sea and Suez Canal. Italian forces in East Africa numbered between 250,000 and 280,000 personnel including infantry and cavalry from Eritrea, irregulars from Somalia and various European regular units supported by 3,300 machine guns, twenty-four medium tanks, numerous light tanks and armored cars and 800 artillery pieces. Although mostly outdated, 200–300 fighters and bombers of the Italian Air Force in East Africa were some of the best in the region. While the Italian Red Sea Flotilla consisted of seven destroyers, five torpedo boats and eight submarines, it rarely left the port of Massawa after four of the submarines were lost during attacks on Allied ships in June 1940. With superior Allied naval power, the Italians in East Africa were isolated from Italy, which meant that they suffered supply problems. At the beginning of the East Africa campaign, British forces comprised 30,000 men spread across British Somaliland, Sudan and Kenya, but control of the oceans meant the rapid arrival of reinforcements. In Sudan, two British battalions and the 4,500-strong Sudan Defence Force were supplemented by two Indian divisions. Concentrated in Kenya, the KAR numbered 3,000 men at the start of the war but expanded to 20,000 by March 1940. By the end of 1940, they had been joined by some 27,000 South African troops and two brigades (one from the Gold Coast and one from Nigeria) from the Royal West African Frontier Force (RWAFF). British Somaliland was defended by about 1,400 men including the Somaliland Camel Corps and Northern Rhodesia Regiment (NRR). In terms of air power, the British had three squadrons of obsolete bombers in north Sudan and six biplane fighters at Port Sudan reinforced by a squadron from Egypt and another from South Africa. Four South African Air Force (SAAF) squadrons, two of bombers, one of light dive bombers and one of fighters, and another Southern Rhodesian light bomber squadron were assembled in Kenya.

The East Africa campaign began in mid-June 1940 when Italian aircraft bombed Wajir in northern Kenya and the KAR, supported by Rhodesian aircraft, then raided the El Wak border post in Italian Somaliland. Italian units from Eritrea crossed into Sudan in July and captured the Kassalla railway junction and the British fort at Gallabat, but further advances were hindered by fuel shortage. Furthermore, Italian soldiers advanced 100 km into Kenya seizing the British fort of Moyale and several villages but stopped because of limited supplies. Italian plans to invade French Somaliland (Djibouti) were suspended when the territory's colonial administration sided with the pro-German Vichy regime. In early August, some 25,000 Italian troops invaded British Somaliland where 4,000 British defenders fought a delaying action through Tug Argan to the port of Berbera from where they were evacuated by sea to Aden.

The British in Sudan launched an offensive after the arrival of Indian reinforcements. In early November 1940, an Indian infantry brigade under Brigadier William Slim, later commander of British forces in Burma, re-captured Gallabat but could not continue to Metemma because most of its supporting tanks had been knocked out. During the next few months, Indian troops built dummy airfields and supply depots to deceive Italian intelligence into thinking that the main British thrust from Sudan would be toward Gondar in Ethiopia and not through Kassala into Eritrea. From November 1940 to January 1941, the highly mobile British Gazelle Force, composed of Sudanese and Indian troops, harassed the Italians around the Sudanese border. Simultaneously, the RAF in Sudan received better aircraft to counter the Italians in the sky.

In January 1941, the British initiated a major offensive in East Africa as they knew that the Italians in the region were shifting to the defensive given their defeats in North Africa and the Balkans. Three British forces converged on Addis Ababa in Ethiopia, British troops moved south from Sudan through Eritrea, those in Kenya advanced north and an amphibious force recaptured British Somaliland. Additionally, Ethiopian insurgents expanded their guerrilla campaign. The day before the start of the offensive from Sudan, the Italians withdrew from Kassala and dug in on the foothills of the Eritrean Plateau on the road to Agordat and were quickly pursued by two Indian divisions. In late January, the 5th Indian Division outflanked a strong Italian position at Keru Gorge where 1,200 troops were taken prisoner and the 4th Indian Division outflanked four Italian brigades at Agordat taking 1,000 prisoners. At the start of February, the 5th Indian Division seized the town of Barentu south of Agordat which had been defended by 8,000 Italian troops. Over nine days, British forces from Sudan had advanced 160 km and captured 6,000 prisoners, eighty artillery pieces, twenty-six tanks and 400 trucks. The Italians withdrew and established defenses around Keren, 100 km east of Agordat on the route to the Red Sea port of Massawa. On February 4, the weakened 4th Indian Division attacked Keren but was repelled. After consolidating their forces and with the arrival of Briggs Force (two Indian and two Free French battalions) from Sudan, the British renewed their attack on Keren in early March. By the end of the month, some 13,000 British troops had secured Keren from 23,000 Italian defenders. At the Battle of Keren, 3,000 Italians were killed, several thousand became wounded or ill and most of the remainder captured, while 4,000 British were dead, wounded or missing. Pursuing the demoralized Italians, the 5th Indian Division captured the undefended Eritrean capital of Asmara on April 1. Subsequently, on April 8, elements of the 5th Indian Division and Briggs Force captured Massawa, where the Italians had sabotaged port facilities and 14,000 Italians soldiers and sailors were captured. Several Italian naval vessels left Massawa and broke through the Allied blockade with two cruisers eventually making it to Japan and four submarines rounding the Cape of Good Hope and making the south of France. The Italians' six remaining destroyers were dispatched on a suicide mission to attack British fuel tanks at Port Sudan.

In August 1940, the British launched Mission 101 that sent military advisors, arms and ammunition to Ethiopian guerrillas. In January 1941, the 2,000-strong Gideon Force, commanded by Brigadier Orde Wingate and consisting of Sudanese troops and Ethiopian insurgents, crossed into Ethiopia's Gojjam province from Sudan to bolster rebel forces and attack Italian garrisons. The next month, Emperor Haile Selassie, exiled since the Italian invasion of 1935–36, returned to Ethiopia prompting rebel leaders to declare allegiance to him and inspiring more Ethiopians to join the rebellion including some who deserted the Italian military. With the general retreat of Italian troops, Gideon Force took Bure and Dembecha in early March and Debre Marqos in early April.

In mid-January 1941, British forces in Kenya moved into southern Ethiopia with the aim of motivating an Ethiopian revolt and distracting the Italians from the main push from Sudan. The 1st South African Division captured posts across the border but the uprising did not happen and rains delayed the advance. In mid-February, South African troops captured the Italian fort at Mega after a 3-day battle. In late January, the British 11th and 12th African divisions, mostly African colonial soldiers from the KAR and RWAFF, invaded Italian Somaliland and advanced quickly to the Italian defensive line along the Juba River. During February, these British forces took the Indian Ocean port of Kismayo and surrounded the main Italian position at Jelib where 30,000 Italian troops were killed or wounded or fled. The 11th African Division chased the Italians up the Somali coast with a Nigerian motorized brigade seizing Mogadishu on February 25, and in mid-March, the division reached Jijiga in eastern Ethiopia. After the engagement at Jelib, the 12th African Division moved up the Juba River into Ethiopia. By the end of March, British forces from Kenya had encountered units that had landed by sea in British Somaliland and they all converged on Addis Ababa. Completing a 2,800 km advance in 53 days, they occupied Addis Ababa on April 6 and about a week later a South African brigade along with some Ethiopian scouts was sent further north to meet British forces from Sudan. Dessie, on the road north from Addis to Asmara, was taken by the South Africans on April 20 after a tough fight. However, Amba Alagi, a seemingly impregnable Italian mountain stronghold defended by 7,000 men, prevented the joining of British forces from Kenya and Sudan. During the first half of May, Amba Alagi was surrounded by a brigade from the 5th Indian Division that arrived from the east and northwest, and the South African brigade and Ethiopian forces that arrived from the south. The Italian garrison, including the colonial viceroy, surrendered on May 18 as their water source had been contaminated by a ruptured fuel tank. Haile Selassie had entered Addis on May 5 – a date which came to be celebrated as "Liberation Day" in Ethiopia. A Free Belgian colonial brigade, which had travelled some 2,000 km by road, rail and riverboat from Congo to southern Sudan and then western Ethiopia, blocked an Italian retreat which involved a sharp fight at the Bortai River in May and the seizure of the mountain bastion of Saio in early July where they captured thousands of Italian troops including eight generals. The Italian garrison at Jimma in southwestern Ethiopia surrendered in late June and Italian forces at Gondar in northwest Ethiopia held out until the end of November. Although hampered by lack of fuel, elements of the Italian Air Force in East Africa continued operations until late October 1941. Hoping for an Axis victory in other theatres, some Italian troops fought a guerrilla war against the Allies in East Africa until Italy surrendered in September 1943.

The defeat of the Italians in East Africa represented the first major land victory for the Allies during World War II and facilitated further operations in the Mediterranean Theatre. The British administered Ethiopia until 1944 when the country regained independence under Emperor Haile Selassie. In 1942, Vichy-administered French Somaliland was occupied by the Allies. In 1949, the United Nations returned Italian Somaliland to Italian administration, which lasted until 1960 when both Italian and British Somaliland gained independence and united as the Republic of Somalia. The British administered Eritrea until 1952 when the UN, given the territory's strategic Red Sea location, relinquished it to Ethiopia which was a reliable British and US ally in the developing Cold War (War Office, 1942; Orpen, 1968; Shirreff, 2009; Van Der Waag, 2015, pp. 195–8; Stewart, 2016).

North Africa

When Italy entered World War II, it had 250,000 troops in Libya and quickly organized ten divisions in Cyrenaica near the border with British-occupied Egypt. The fall of France meant that the Italians in Libya did not have to defend the Tunisian border. Despite their numbers, Italian forces in Libya were equipped with outdated light artillery and had just begun replacing old light tanks with newer medium versions. These were augmented by 300 aircraft, mostly designed for ground support. Defending Egypt's border with Libya was Britain's 36,000-strong Western Desert Force including the 7th Armoured Division or "Desert Rats" which had better tanks than the Italians but were supported by obsolete aircraft. Nevertheless, the Royal Navy enjoyed control of the Eastern Mediterranean and could bombard Italian coastal positions and transport British forces and supplies.

In early September 1940, five Italian divisions advanced slowly into Egypt along the coastal road as Italian and British aircraft fought overhead. While the British withdrew to Mersa Matruh about 220 km east of the Libyan border on the coastal road, the Italians followed them for 95 km until they reached the east side of Sidi Barrani where they stopped and dug in because of supply problems. In early December, the British mounted an offensive called Operation Compass supported by RAF strikes on Italian airfields and Royal Navy bombing of Italian positions around Sidi Barrani. An initial raid by British ground forces was so successful that it turned into a general westward advance toward the border. By mid-December, the British had moved through Halfaya Pass into eastern Libya, took Sollum and recaptured Fort Capuzzo which they had briefly seized in June. The British had sustained less than 700 killed and wounded, while the Italians had lost 38,000 men killed or captured, and seventy-three tanks and 237 artillery pieces destroyed or captured. In early January 1941, Australian troops overcame Italian defenses at Bardia and captured 36,000 prisoners. At the end of the month, British and Australian soldiers, continuing the stunning advance along the Libyan coast, seized Tobruk where some 25,000 Italians were captured. The British took Derna at the end of January and Benghazi in early February, and conducted a southward hook manoeuver that isolated Italian forces at Sidi Saleh along the Benghazi-Tripoli road. The ten-week-long Operation Compass saw the British advance 800 km, destroy or capture 400 tanks and 1,300 artillery pieces, capture 130,000 Italian and Libyan prisoners including twenty-two generals which effectively eliminated the entire Italian 10th Army in eastern Libya. The British, who had lost 500 troops in the operation, halted at El Agheila where they established a defensive line and replaced exhausted but experienced units with new ones, some of which were under-strength and partly trained.

Between February and May 1941, the four remaining Italian divisions in Libya were bolstered by the arrival of four more Italian divisions and the German "Afrika Korps" which was led by General Erwin Rommel and consisted of one infantry and one armored division. Although Rommel's orders were to prevent an Italian collapse in North Africa by reinforcing defenses, he realized that the British were weak and quickly launched an offensive. The British were driven east of El Agheila in late March, their defensive position at Mechili was surrounded and 2,700 men captured in early April, and the British and Australians were back at Sollum on the Libyan-Egyptian border by mid-April. Rommel bypassed Tobruk where a garrison of 36,000 men, initially composed of Australians but who were later replaced by British troops including Poles and Czechs, survived a 240-day siege supplied by British and Australian ships. The possession of Tobruk, one of only two ports between Tripoli and Alexandria, by the British meant that the eastward advancing Germans and Italians had to maintain long overland supply lines and they were constantly vulnerable from the rear. Mounted in mid-June, the British Operation Battleaxe failed in its objective of penetrating Axis defenses along the Libya–Egypt border and relieving Tobruk.

In mid-November 1941, the British commenced Operation Crusader that pushed through Axis defenses along the Libyan–Egyptian border as British forces broke out of Tobruk. While an Axis counter-attack defeated British armor and South African infantry at Sidi Rezegh, New Zealand troops took the area and joined forces from Tobruk. With the British 8th Army pushing forward, Rommel realized that success at Tobruk was unlikely and withdrew Axis forces 16 km west to a defensive line around Gazala. In mid-December, given an Allied attack and threatened encirclement of the Gazala line, Rommel ordered another withdrawal back to El Agheila. This left the Axis garrisons of Bardia, Sollum and Halfaya along the Libya–Egypt border cutoff, and during January 1942, they were systematically seized by South African troops who captured almost 14,000 prisoners.

In January 1942, Rommel directed an Axis counteract from El Agheila that recaptured Benghazi at the end of the month and continued east toward Tobruk. The British 8th Army rallied and established a defensive line from Gazala on the coast to Bir Hakeim in the south. In late May, Rommel launched Operation Venezia which involved a diversionary frontal assault on the Gazala line and a mechanized flanking attack to the south which caused the collapse of British defenses. In mid-June, the 8th Army withdrew 160 km east along the coast to Mersa Matruh, leaving the South African 2nd Division to hold Tobruk which was seized by Rommel's advancing units, thus netting some 33,000 Allied prisoners. This represented the second largest British surrender of the war. British forces retreated another 160 km east into Egypt where a new defensive was established at El Alamein with the steep slopes of the Qattara Depression to the south discouraging an Axis flanking attack. Although the weakened Axis forces staged several

Figure 2.1 British soldiers moving forward under cover of smoke screen and
protected by tanks, at the First Battle of El Alamein, July 27, 1942

unsuccessful attacks on the El Alamein line in late June, Italian dictator
Mussolini flew to Libya in anticipation of a glorious entry into Cairo.

At the start of July 1942, in the First Battle of El Alamein, Rommel
directed a major frontal assault by German and Italian divisions on the
Alamein Line, but it was worn down by heavy Allied firepower. Axis forces
then dug in opposite the British positions and attacks, counter-attacks and
raids continued over the next few weeks. Since the British had deciphered
German codes, the British knew that Rommel planned another offensive
against the south of the Alamein Line before Allied reinforcements could
arrive. The new 8th Army commander, Lieutenant General Bernard Montgomery, set a trap by creating a gap in that section of his defenses and
redeployed tanks and artillery along a ridge from where they fired down on
the advancing Axis forces. In early September, heavy losses and supply
problems impelled Rommel to abandon this last Axis offensive in North
Africa. Montgomery did not immediately counter-attack with his tanks as
he favored preparing for an ambitious westward offensive.

At El Alamein, in October 1942, some 220,000 British troops and 1,100
tanks confronted an Axis force of 115,000 men and 560 tanks. On the night

of October 23 and 24, 1942, Montgomery's 8th Army launched Operation Lightfoot that began with a massive artillery bombardment of Axis lines, followed by an attack by four infantry divisions that cut paths through enemy minefields through which tanks would pass. Rommel ordered a withdrawal, given the failure of Axis counter-attacks and limited fuel. On November 2, the British initiated Operation Supercharge which opened with a 7-hour aerial and artillery barrage, followed by an advance of infantry who cleared paths through minefields for tanks. Axis forces withdrew all the way back to El Agheila in Libya. In this Second Battle of El Alamein, the first major Allied land victory against the Germans which British Prime Minister Churchill called "the end of the beginning," the Allies suffered 13 500 casualties which represented a small portion of their total force while the Axis sustained 37,000 casualties or 30% of their manpower.

After a British flanking attack on El Agheila in December, Axis forces retreated west laying minefields to delay Allied advance. To Mussolini's horror, Rommel intended to abandon the open terrain of Libya and withdraw to Tunisia where the mountains would favor defense and he could join other Axis forces opposing Allied landings to the west. As a result, the British 8th Army rolled through western Libya occupying Sirte on Christmas Day and capturing Tripoli on January 23, 1943. The Western Desert campaign was characterized by back and forth movements along the Libyan and Egyptian coastline, with the advancing forces suffering from overextended supply lines and the withdrawing forces benefitting from shortening ones which enabled successful counter-offensives. While the campaign is often portrayed as "a war without hate," Axis forces put thousands of Libyan Jews in concentration camps where hundreds died and a few hundred with British citizenship were shipped to Bergen-Belsen in Germany (Bierman and Smith, 2002; Barr, 2005; Roumani, 2008, pp. 28–37; Van Der Waag, 2015, pp. 198–203).

Launched in early November 1942, Operation Torch involved landings by 35,000 US soldiers at Casablanca on Morocco's Atlantic coast, 18,000 US troops at Oran in Algeria and 20,000 US and British soldiers at Algiers. The invasion of Vichy French territory in North Africa was meant to open the whole Mediterranean to Allied shipping. While there was some resistance to the landings by Vichy forces, Free French leaders took power in these areas. During the rest of November, there was a race to seize Tunisia as British and US troops moved from the west and German forces landed by ship and aircraft. At the Battle of Kasserine Pass, in mid-February 1943, German and Italian forces under Rommel blocked the United States II Corps and the British 6th Armoured Division from moving through the Atlas Mountains into south-central Tunisia. This defeat in their first engagement with the Germans prompted a reorganization of US forces in North Africa and led to the rise of General George S. Patton as corps commander.

Since Rommel was fighting on two fronts and his March offensive against the British 8th Army to the south had failed, he asked Hitler for permission to withdraw from North Africa which was refused and he was then replaced with Colonel General Hans-Jurgen von Arnim. Throughout late March and April, continued pressure from the US II Corps in the west and British 8th Army in the south pushed the Axis forces into an ever-decreasing enclave around Tunis. Allied airfields were moved forward to Tunisia to intercept German reinforcements transported by aircraft and British warships from Malta blocked Axis resupply by sea. British units entered Tunis on May 7 and a week later Axis opposition ended with the submission of 230,000 troops, many of whom had recently arrived from Sicily. Staging out of North Africa, Allied forces invaded Sicily in July and mainland Italy in September 1943 The fighting in North Africa represented one of the great campaigns of World War II and was significant in determining the outcome of the conflict (Watson, 1999; Atkinson, 2002).

Conflict in French Africa

After the 1940 German occupation of France, French colonial administrations in Africa became divided between the exiled Free French and the pro-Axis Vichy regime. French officials in North Africa initially aligned with Vichy. Most of French West Africa sided with Vichy except Cameroon, while most of French Equatorial Africa, influenced by Chad's black Guianese Governor Felix Eboue, supported the Free French with the exception of Gabon. Brazzaville became the Free French capital. In early July 1940, the Royal Navy mounted a surprise attack on the French fleet at Mers-el-Kebir on the coast of Algeria which killed 1,300 French personnel, sunk a battleship and damaged five other French vessels. The British, though not technically at war with Vichy France, were concerned that the French navy in the Mediterranean would assist Germany and Italy. In late September 1940, British vessels carrying 8,000 Free French troops attempted to seize the port of Dakar on the coast of Senegal but were repelled by Vichy warships and coastal batteries. Dakar was attractive to the Allies because it had one of the best harbors in West Africa and it housed the French and Polish governments' gold reserves. In late October and early November, Free French soldiers crossed from Cameroon into Gabon and seized several interior towns. On November 8, British and Free French warships embarked Free French troops at Douala in Cameroon and landed them at Libreville on the coast of Gabon where they overcame Vichy forces. The Vichy governor committed suicide and most of his troops chose captivity in Brazzaville over joining the Free French. Staging in Chad, Free French forces advanced north into southern Libya and attacked the Italian outpost at Kufra in February 1941.

From December 1941, the Allies were concerned that the Japanese would occupy Vichy-ruled Madagascar from where they could dominate the Indian Ocean. Between May and November 1942, during Operation Ironclad, South African and British forces invaded Madagascar by sea, fought some engagements against outnumbered Vichy defenders and occupied the island (Engelbrecht and MacKenzie, 1971; Wessels, 1999; Bimberg, 2002; Smith, 2010; Van Der Waag, 2015, pp. 202–3).

African soldiers outside Africa

Many tens of thousands of African colonial soldiers served outside their continent during World War II. Of the eighty divisions that defended France in 1939, seven were from Africa. In May and June 1940, more than 75,000 West African troops were involved in "the Battle for France," with about 10,000 killed and thousand more missing. The twelve Moroccan regiments in France numbered 90,000 men, of which 83,000 were indigenous Moroccans. Among the many West African troops taken prisoner during the fall of France, between 1,500 and 3,000 were executed by racist German soldiers foreshadowing widespread war crimes later committed in Eastern Europe. Many other black African prisoners-of-war became slave workers for the Nazis. Subsequently, exiled Free French forces operating outside Africa depended heavily on African colonial units. During the July 1943 Allied invasion of Sicily, the presence of fearsome, knife-wielding Free French Moroccan Goumiers (mountain troops) caused a mass Italian surrender. In September 1943, while US and British soldiers were landing in mainland Italy, the French 1st Corps consisting of Moroccan units invaded Corsica. In Italy, the French Expeditionary Corps, 60% of which consisted of indigenous Algerians and Moroccans and rest French settlers from Algeria, fought at Monte Cassino and the Gustav Line during 1944. During Operation Brassard, the 9th French Colonial Infantry Division which included Tirailleurs Senegalais and Moroccan Goumiers was landed on Elba by the Royal Navy in July 1944. In August 1944, as part of Operation Dragoon, Free French Army Group "B" landed in southern France, with two of its four divisions consisting of African troops who then saw considerable combat including in the liberation of Toulon. Fighting in northwest Europe in 1944 and 1945, the Free French 2nd Armoured Division numbered 3,000 Algerian and Moroccan troops out of a total strength of 14,500. The presence of black colonial troops among the Free French forces in France became an embarrassment to white French leaders like Charles de Gaulle. The 2nd Armoured Division was selected to liberate Paris because other Free French units contained many black personnel. During September and October 1944, Free French forces in France undertook a process of "whitening" in which black African veterans were replaced by white Frenchmen. Disarmed and denied a role in the coming victory, thousands of black African soldiers were dispatched to camps in the south of France to await shipment home. Poor living conditions in the camps and lack of back pay for former prisoners led to protest including a serious incident that happened on December 1, 1944, at Thiaroye near Dakar when thirty-five ex-prisoners were shot dead (Echenberg, 1991, pp. 87–104; Scheck, 2006).

From late 1944 to mid-1945, British colonial African troops participated in the Allied offensive against the Japanese in Burma which was characterized by jungle warfare, tropical disease and heavy monsoon rains. Arriving in India in August 1943, the 81st West African Division consisted of a Gold Coast brigade; a Nigerian brigade and a mixed brigade from Gambia, Sierra Leone and Nigeria. While the Nigeria brigade was seconded to the British Special Force or "Chindits" to support behind-the-lines operations, the rest of the division fought in the Second Arakan campaign from January to May 1944 and was the first division in Burma to be supplied entirely by air. With one Gold Coast brigade and two Nigerian brigades, the 82nd West African division arrived in Ceylon in July 1944. Both West African divisions fought in the Third Arakan campaign that began in December 1944 and ultimately expelled the Japanese from Burma. Arriving in Ceylon in June 1943, the 11th East African Division comprised three KAR brigades from Uganda, Nyasaland, Kenya and Tanganyika as well as one NRR battalion. The division also included a field hospital from the Belgian Congo. In August 1944, the East Africa division joined an Allied offensive in Burma's Kabaw Valley, and by mid-December, it had established a bridgehead on the Chindwin River. It was then withdrawn to India and its anticipated return to Burma did not happen because the Japanese surrendered in August 1945. Two independent East African brigades, the 22nd and 28th, were also deployed to Burma and committed to battle at different times and places. The 22nd Brigade fought in the Third Arakan campaign where it experienced the longest continuous contact with the Japanese. In February 1945, the 28th Brigade staged a mock crossing of the Irrawaddy River at Chauk that diverted the Japanese from the real crossings elsewhere. Around 80,000 West Africans and 46,000 East Africans, including soldiers from the Rhodesias and Nyasaland, participated in the Burma campaign (Slim, 1961; Hamilton, 2001; Killingray, 2010; McLynn, 2011, p. 273).

Given the South African policy of not arming black troops, many Southern Africans provided military labor in the Mediterranean Theatre. South Africa's Cape Corps and Native Military Corps had a total strength of 92,000 by 1943 and served in North Africa and Italy. In Italy, the 10,000-strong South African Railway Construction Group repaired hundreds of kilometers of tracks and many bridges. The African Pioneer Corps (APC) was recruited from the Southern African British High Commission territories. Some 10,000 pioneers came from Bechuanaland, 22,000 from Basutoland (today's Lesotho) and 3,600 from Swaziland. APC units supported British operations in the Western Desert and built defenses in Lebanon, Syria, Palestine and the Nile Delta in anticipation of German breakthrough from the Caucasus that looked likely until the Battle of Stalingrad. Although the British War Office wanted to redeploy the APC to Burma like other African units, the Colonial Office refused as it wanted to avoid alienating the traditional leaders of the High Commission territories who had sent their men to fight Hitler before Japan had entered the war.

Following the North Africa campaign, APC units were sent to Malta, Sicily, Italy and Yugoslavia. In mountainous Italy muleteers from Basutoland transported supplies to the front line, Bechuanaland gunners took part in artillery barrages and Swazi pioneers deployed a gigantic smoke screen to conceal the Allied landing at Salerno in September 1943. The SAAF played a vital role in the Allied campaigns in Sicily and Italy, and the 18,000-strong 6th South African Armoured Division arrived in Italy in April 1944 and advanced on Rome and Florence, and through the Apennines Mountains to attack the German Gothic Line (Orpen, 1975; Jackson, 2006, pp. 242–3, 258–68; Bourhill, 2011; Van Der Waag, 2015, pp. 206–10).

Impact

Given the increased demand for African raw materials during World War II, colonial rulers reintroduced forced labor in areas it had not existed for many years, and Africans were often evicted from their land to facilitate commercial agriculture. Since the Japanese had occupied South East Asia, the Belgian Congo became the Allies' chief supplier of rubber and labor practices became nearly as oppressive as under Leopold II. In northern Nigeria, the British forced thousands of men to mine tin. While the international price of agricultural goods rose, African peasant producers were denied the benefit as colonial marketing boards imposed artificially low prices and the extra profits were put toward the war effort. However, some African peasants, particularly those selling higher priced products like cocoa and coffee, prospered during the war and a noticeable socio-economic gap emerged within some rural communities.

The dramatic growth of cities represented one of the most important impacts of World War II on Africa. Urban wage labor became attractive as people left rural areas to escape forced labor and others were lured by wage work in building new harbor and airport facilities. In South Africa, the reduction of imports from Europe bolstered a manufacturing industry which surpassed mining as the main employer. Urban unemployment also became a problem which worsened with the end of the war and the return of former soldiers. Africa's newly enlarged cities would became the venue for elite African nationalist leaders who before the war had humbly requested colonial reform but after it began making radical demands for independence. African nationalists looked to events such as the 1941 Atlantic Charter where the leaders of Britain and the United States declared that all people should have the right to self-determination and the 1944 Brazzaville Conference where Free French leaders promised equal rights to colonial populations. These sentiments were spread by the growth of African newspapers that circulated among an increasingly literate population. Held in Britain in 1945, the Fifth Pan-African Congress was attended by African nationalists like Kwame Nkrumah of the Gold Coast and Jomo Kenyatta of Kenya and called for the independence of Africa. Following the war, the idea that African soldiers had fought for democracy and freedom yet returned home to find none of either gained traction among nationalists and their growing urban support base. This provided the context for the independence struggles of the 1950s and 1960s (Shillington, 1995, pp. 362–72; Killingray, 2007; Byfield, Brown, Parsons and Sikainga, 2015).

Part III

War and conflict in Africa (1945–2000)

3 Decolonization wars (1945–90)

Introduction

Beginning in the late 1950s and continuing into the 1960s, European-ruled African colonies were transformed into independent states. This was a sudden process brought on by the rise of African nationalism that became popular in Africa's expanding cities, the changing international context of a bipolar world dominated by two superpowers (the United States and the Soviet Union) and the growth of an anti-colonial block of newly independent Asian countries such as India. While most African countries became independent through a process of negotiation between colonial rulers and African nationalists, warfare played a prominent role in encouraging European powers to abandon their African empires. At the start of the 1950s the British and French were set to stay in much of Africa for the foreseeable future but the events of the 1956 Suez Crisis, the Kenyan Emergency of 1952 to 1960 and the independence war in Algeria from 1954 to 1962 informed a rapid decolonization. Inspired by the independence of much of the continent, African nationalists used armed force to challenge the stubborn regimes of colonial Portugal and the white minority states of Southern Africa from the 1960s to 1980s. From the 1960s, these anti-colonial wars became proxy conflicts of the global Cold War as African nationalist insurgents were backed by the Eastern Block and the remaining colonial/settler powers were supported by the Western powers.

Insurgency in Kenya (1952–60)

In central Kenya, the Kikuyu people were disproportionally impacted by British colonization as their fertile land had been favored by white settlers and became the "White Highlands." Many Kikuyu became landless squatters and low-paid workers on European commercial farms, and during World War II, many sought employment in the growing city of Nairobi. Simultaneously, there developed a relatively prosperous Kikuyu peasantry loyal to the colonial state. Given the failure of the moderate Kenya African Union (KAU) to eliminate racial discrimination and increase African representation in the legislative council in the 1940s and early 1950s, political momentum shifted to militant African leaders within the trade unions and among squatters in the White Highlands.

In October 1952, a European woman and a Kikuyu chief were killed, which prompted newly arrived Governor Sir Evelyn Baring to declare a state of emergency. Immediately, British security forces mounted Operation Jock Scott that orchestrated the arrest of 180 suspected insurgent leaders in Nairobi along with KAU President Jomo Kenyatta who was later convicted of treason despite lack of evidence. Militants fled to the forest from where they launched more attacks.

When the emergency began, the British had 7,000 soldiers in Kenya. These included the British troops of 39 Brigade flown in from Egypt, the regional KAR of 70 Brigade (East African) and the white settler volunteers from the Kenya Regiment battalion. After a few months, the arrival of 49 Brigade from Britain increased this force to 10,000 soldiers eventually assisted by an expanded 21,000-strong Kenya Police and another 25,000 men from the newly formed Kikuyu "Home Guard."

The Kenya Land and Freedom Army (KLFA) formed small units in the forests of the Aberdare Mountains and around Mount Kenya and organized a passive support wing in African reserves. The British called the movement Mau Mau, though the derivation of the term is uncertain. The KLFA consisted of around 12,000 insurgents, of whom 10% possessed firearms. With a decentralized leadership, insurgent forces were divided into three zones: the Central and Northern Aberdare Mountains led by Dedan Kimathi, the Southern Aberdares under Stanley Mathenge and Mount Kenya directed by Waruhiu Itote called "General China." While Mathenge and Itote were World War II veterans, former colonial soldiers were rare among Mau Mau fighters. Attempts to create a coordinating structure failed as the insurgency consisted of a series of independent and sometime feuding groups. The KLFA lacked a formal revolutionary ideology and strategy, most insurgents were illiterate or semi-literate, there was no foreign sponsor or cross-border sanctuary and weapons ranged from a few captured or home-made firearms to the more common spears and machetes. Insurgent recruits were psychologically bound to the movement by a ritual oath. Rebel groups communicated by "letter boxes" hidden in trees or under rocks and they were skilled at moving quickly and surreptitiously through the bush. British officials in the 1950s saw Mau Mau as a form of psychological disorder caused by rapid westernization, while historians of the late twentieth century debated whether it represented a Kikuyu civil war or a Kenyan nationalist movement.

In June 1953, General George Erskine took over British operations in Kenya, which concentrated on clearing insurgents from specific areas that were then patrolled by the Home Guard and police. Mounted in late April 1954, Operation Anvil sought to deprive the insurgents of resources and recruits from Nairobi. Some 25,000 British troops and police cordoned off the city that was systematically searched. All Africans were detained in barbed wire enclosures, with members of ethnic groups not associated with the insurgency quickly released and Kikuyu, Embu and Meru held. Some 20,000 men were moved to a detention camp and 30,000 women and children were evicted to the rural reserves. From June 1953 to October 1955, the Royal Air Force (RAF) flew reconnaissance, propaganda leaflet dropping and bombing missions over Kenya. The RAF dropped 6 million bombs and killed around 900 insurgents and compelled some groups to disband or flee the forests.

British officials color-coded Kenyan prisoners in a system called the "Pipeline." The "whites" were the most compliant detainees who were sent back to the reserves, the "greys" confessed to having sworn a Mau Mau oath but were cooperative and therefore moved "down" the "Pipeline" to local labor camps before release, and the "blacks" were the most obstinate prisoners who were sent "up" the "Pipeline" to special camps. Torture became common and camp living conditions were terrible, with prisoners suffering malnutrition and typhoid. While most detainees in the "Pipeline" were male including some young boys, a few thousand women and girls were also imprisoned.

Beginning in June 1954, the British forcibly resettled over 1 million Kikuyu into 800 "protected villages" surrounded by barbed wire, trenches with spikes and watch towers, and patrolled by the Kikuyu "Home Guard." As the British had done in Malaya, the protected villages were divided between those suspected of supporting Mau Mau who were denied food and loyalists who were protected and received better treatment. In April 1954, General China surrendered and avoided the death penalty by trying to arrange further capitulations. In May 1955, when General Sir Gerald Lathbury assumed command in Kenya, the number of active Mau Mau had been reduced to 3,000, which led to the withdrawal of the British 39 Brigade. Lathbury phased out large forest sweeps in favor of patrols by smaller tracker combat teams and "counter gangs" of former insurgents who infiltrated real rebel groups to kill or capture them. By early 1956, insurgent numbers had declined to 900, and in October Dedan Kimathi, the last active Mau Mau leader, was captured and eventually hanged.

In 1956, the British enacted a series of reforms in Kenya, providing more land for the Kikuyu, opening profitable coffee growing to the African majority, increasing urban wages for Africans and allowing the direct election of African representatives in the Legislative Assembly. The Mau Mau Emergency showed the British government that it would have to use increasingly expensive and politically embarrassing military force to maintain colonial rule in Africa. In March 1959, one of the most controversial incidents of the war occurred at Hola detention camp where eleven prisoners were beaten to death. Consequently, in 1960, the British ended the emergency, scrapped the rhetoric of African and European "multi-racial" rule in Kenya and pursued a "one-person one vote" majority rule political

Figure 3.1 African leaders listen to the British Governor of Kenya, Sir Evelyn
Baring, unseen, announce the surrender terms that have been offered
to the Mau Mau

system that led to independence in 1963. As the first president of independent
Kenya, Jomo Kenyatta maintained a close relationship with Britain, which
included military cooperation.

There has been debate over the total number of Kenyans who died during
the Mau Mau Emergency. While historian Caroline Elkins claims that the
number could be somewhere between 130,000 and 300,000, demographer
John Blacker puts the figure at around 50,000, half of whom were children.
Most of these deaths related to the detention camps. The British hanged 1090
Kenyans, insurgents killed at least 1819 African, thirty-two European and
twenty-six Asian civilians, while the security forces suffered 600 fatalities
and claimed to have killed 10,500 Mau Mau.

The post-colonial Kenya governments of Kenyatta and Daniel Arap
Moi did not celebrate Mau Mau as a national liberation movement
because of the presence of former loyalists in their administrations and
their alliance with Britain. Since around 2010, given political change in
Kenya, KLFA veterans have been declared national heroes and publically
celebrated on October 20 – the anniversary of the declaration of the emergency, which has become "Heroes Day." This rehabilitation of Mau Mau
in Kenyan historical memory and the publication of new research about

British atrocities during the conflict led to legal action against the British government. In 2013, the British government, after an unfavorable court ruling, agreed to pay compensation to 12,000 elderly Kenyans who had suffered human rights abuses in the 1950s, and this prompted a further legal claim by another 40,000 Kenyans (Page, 1998, pp. 201–20; Anderson, 2005; Elkins, 2005; Blacker, 2007; Branch, 2009; Chapell, 2011; Bennett, 2013).

Rebellions in Madagascar and Cameroon (1947–71)

Now little known, there were several anti-colonial rebellions in France's Sub-Saharan African colonies after World War II. In Madagascar, French authority had been damaged by the British–South African occupation during World War II, subsequent Free French demands for resources and labor that led to famine, and the fact that the island's French settlers opposed post-war colonial reforms. In 1946, a demand by Malagasy delegates in Paris for autonomy within the French Union was rejected. Formed the same year, the nationalist Democratic Movement for Malagasy Renewal (MDRM) was persecuted by French officials and settlers, and its members joined secret societies that advocated violence to achieve independence. In response, the French formed the puppet Party of the Underprivileged of Madagascar that supported the status quo. At the end of March 1947, about 2,000 nationalist insurgents mounted simultaneous attacks on settlers, soldiers and officials around Moremanga and Manakara, and within a few months, the rebellion had spread across the eastern island. Nevertheless, the cities of Tananarive, Fianarantsoa and Diego Suarez were unaffected. Some 15,000–20,000 rebels were poorly armed, lacked coordination and a clear objective, and naively believed that they would gain support from the United States, the British and the United Nations. While MDRM political leaders denied responsibility for the revolt, they were arrested and the party was outlawed.

In April 1947, with the arrival of a French expeditionary force, the number of colonial security personnel in Madagascar increased from 6,000 to 18,000, and by late 1948, there were 30,000 personnel including Foreign Legionnaires and Tirailleurs Senegalais. Reminiscent of methods used to crush resistance on the island in the late 1890s, the pitiless French counter-insurgency campaign of 1947 and 1948 focused on securing a few small areas from where they extended their control. French security forces conducted summary executions, tortured detainees, burned villages, threw prisoners out of flying aircraft and in May 1947 they killed 165 Malagasy hostages in a train. From August 1947, the rebels were forced on the defensive, and in November 1948, the last rebel stronghold was captured. Estimates of the death toll during the conflict ranged from 30,000 to 89,000, out of a total Malagasy population of 3.5million, with most dying from disease and hunger. The rebels killed 550 of the 35,000 Europeans on the island, 350 French troops and almost 2,000 loyalist Malagasy.

The insurgency convinced most Malagasy that freedom and political rights could only come with independence, though within the context of a close relationship with France. The Madagascar revolt, the memory of which is now overshadowed by French defeat in Indochina in 1954 and war in Algeria in the 1950s and early 1960s, contributed to the French colonial reforms of 1956 that introduced universal suffrage and elected local administrations in the colonies (Twaddle, 1993, pp. 201–28; Beigbeder, 2006, pp. 79–92; Randrianja and Ellis, 2009, pp. 173–7).

The September 1945 riots in Douala, Cameroon, motivated by worsening poverty at the end of World War II, impelled the small French settler minority to form armed militias. In April 1948, the Union of the Peoples of Cameroon (UPC), led by Ruben Um Nyobe, was formed by radical nationalists and trade unionists, and demanded independence and accused the French of failing in their obligation to prepare the former German colony and UN mandate for self-rule. The UPC also advocated for the reunification of the British Cameroons, mandated to Britain after World War I, with the rest of the territory. With support from the French communist party, the UPC gained popular support in Cameroon's south and west. In 1954, a new French governor actively sponsored conservative pro-French groups and directed security forces to harass UPC members. Consequently, in May 1955, violence spread across the southwest, including Douala, with UPC activists destroying property of regime supporters. Order was restored by soldiers brought in from nearby French territories. With the banning of their organization in July 1955, UPC leaders fled to British Southern Cameroons and formed an armed wing called the National Organization Committee (CNO). In December 1956, the CNO tried unsuccessfully to use sabotage to derail Cameroon's first Territorial Assembly election that resulted in the rise of pragmatic nationalists allied to the French. At that time, French paratroopers were dropped on the southwestern town of Eseka to restore control. The UPC rebellion continued in the southwest among the Bassa people of Sanaga-Maritime region near Douala and among the Bamileke around the town Bafoussam. From May 1957, with the outlawing of the UPC in British territory, the movement's leaders moved to Sudan, Egypt, Ghana and Guinea and pursued sponsorship from China.

Organized into units of fifty to 200 men, the insurgents sabotaged the railway to cripple the economy and established a liberated zone in the southwest to serve as a base for planned guerrilla operations in the rest of the country. The French initially tried to isolate the UPC militants in the forest by securing roads, railways, towns and industries, but attacks against administration loyalists increased. Starting in November 1957, the French outlawed periodic markets, closed roads to passenger transport and imposed a night curfew in rural areas. In December 1957, Andre-Marie Mbida, prime minister of Cameroon, visited Paris to request military assistance against the rebellion. Almost immediately, the French created the Pacification Zone of Cameroon (ZOPAC) based in Eseka and several battalions from Chad were brought in. ZOPAC launched a concerted counter-insurgency that involved relocating the rural population into fortified villages and mounting patrols to eliminate the rebels. From January to November 1958, some 2,000 rebels surrendered in Sanaga-Maritime, and in September, Nyobe was killed by French forces, which ended the rebellion among the Bassa.

Given Guinea's 1958 rejection of continued association with the French Union and the British announcement that Nigeria would soon become independent, the French co-opted the UPC objectives of independence and reunification of Cameroon. As such, the UPC split, with one faction entering the legal political process and another led by Felix-Roland Moumie creating a new armed wing, the Cameroonian Army of National Liberation (ALNK), which continued the war in the Bamileke region of the west. In January 1960, Cameroon gained independence and its first President Ahmadou Ahidjo requested that French forces crush the insurgency. In mid-February, five French battalions supported by ground support aircraft and armored vehicles began an intensive campaign that ended the rebellion after 8 months. Captive insurgents were publically executed, and in November 1960, French intelligence used poison to assassinate Moumie in Geneva. Although the French claimed to have killed 3,000 guerrillas and lost thirty soldiers, it is probable that thousands of non-combatants perished from disease or hunger. In October 1961, British Southern Cameroons, given the results of a referendum, was merged into independent Cameroon. Ahidjo's Cameroon became an authoritarian one-party state backed a French trained military and intelligence service. Remnants of ALNK continued limited resistance until 1971 when its leader Ernest Ouandie was apprehended and publically executed. Over the next few years, accusations emerged that the French military campaign in Cameroon during the 1960s amounted to genocide against the Bamileke. This view gained some traction with the rise of protest among the Anglophone population of the former British Southern Cameroons who began to resent domination by the Francophone majority. Like Cameroon, many of the French colonies in Africa that received a sudden independence in 1960 remained tied to the former colonial power through a series of agreements relating to military, economic and technical assistance (Joseph, 1974; Atangana, 1997; Atangana, 2010).

The Algerian War of Independence (1954–62)

In Algeria, which was dominated by French settlers, an anti-colonial movement emerged among local Muslims during the 1920s and 1930s. On May 8, 1945, the day World War II ended in Europe, around 4,000 Algerian independence protestors took to the streets of the town of Setif where some were shot by French police. Some 103 French settlers in the countryside were killed in retaliatory attacks by Muslims. French security forces conducted reprisals including summary executions, aerial bombardment of remote villages and naval bombardment of Kerrata. Mobs of French settlers murdered Muslims seized from jails and those who were not wearing white arm bands indicating allegiance to France. These traumatic events radicalized many Muslims, particularly returning soldiers who had fought to liberate France.

In 1954, small independence groups merged to form the National Liberation Front (FLN), which included an armed wing called the National Liberation Army (FLA), which mounted a guerrilla struggle to evict the French and establish an independent state based on Muslim principles. On November 1, 1954, later called "Bloody All Saints Day," FLA insurgents attacked French military and civilian targets across the country. The FLN/ FLA received military support from Egypt's Arab nationalist government. Although the French had recently withdrawn from Indochina, Paris rejected calls for Algerian independence as the North African territory was considered part of France. After an August 1955 FLA massacre of 123 civilians near the town of Philippeville, French security forces and settler gangs sought revenge by killing thousands of Muslims, which drove many formerly moderate Muslims to support the FLN. Abandoning reforms meant to appease the independence movement, the French embarked on an all-out war against the FLN/FLA and granted sweeping police powers to the military.

Commencing in September 1956, the FLA arranged a general strike and a series of bombings in Algiers, which were meant to sway international and French public opinion. Under General Jacques Massu, French paratroopers degraded the FLA structure and recovered control of Algiers by using torture and harshly controlling the population's movement. By 1957, the FLA, which had begun with just a few hundred poorly armed guerrillas, had evolved into a disciplined force with a 30,000-strong conventional army in neighboring Tunisia and Morocco, and from 6,000 to 25,000 insurgents operating within Algeria. During 1956 and 1957, the FLA conducted hit-and-run attacks on security force patrols and camps, economic assets such as settler farms and transportation and communication infrastructure. In Maoist guerrilla style, insurgents dispersed after an attack or ambush and disappeared among the civilian population. The FLN/FLA eventually established liberated zones in mountain areas where they created administrations, collected taxes and enlisted new insurgents.

By 1956, the French maintained 400,000 regular troops in Algeria including 170,000 local Muslim volunteers. In Algeria, the French military pioneered the use of helicopters further developed by the United States in Vietnam during the 1960s. Starting in 1955, the French military recruited around 180,000 Muslim irregular troops called "Harki" (Arabic for war party) who used guerrilla tactics against the insurgents. A few Harki units conducted "pseudo-operations" that sought to foster conflict among the insurgents or discredit them by committing atrocities in their name. The FLA also conducted "false flag operations" by sometimes posing as Algerian volunteers working for the French. In 1957, General Raoul Salan introduced the Quadrillage system that divided the country into sectors, each of which was assigned a security force unit responsible for suppressing insurgents. He also created the Morice Line (named after French defense minister Andre Morice) which was a 320-km-long barrier of electric fences, barbed wire and mine fields meant to prevent infiltration along the Tunisian border. Salan's methods reduced FLA activities, but they tied down large numbers of French troops in static positions. From 1957 to 1960, in a now typical counter-insurgency strategy, some 2 million Algerians were forced into fortified and guarded villages where they experienced poor living conditions. The abandoned villages, orchards and fields were destroyed to deny them to the guerrillas. In late 1958, French commander General Maurice Challe discarded the Quadrillage system and mounted large search-and-destroy operations against FLA strongholds.

In May 1958, French military officers, anxious that French civilian politicians would abandon Algeria, staged a coup in Algiers that established General Salan as head of a ruling junta and they demanded the appointment of Free French hero Charles de Gaulle as leader of a government of national unity, which would prevent decolonization. Furthermore, French paratroopers from Algeria seized the island of Corsica. In the event that their demands were not met or it seemed communists would take over, French forces in Algeria planned Operation Resurrection that involved the seizure of Paris and removal of the government. The French parliament sanctioned de Gaulle's appointment on May 29 just fifteen hours before the launch of Resurrection. While de Gaulle visited Algeria and professed that it would always be French, he doubted the sustainability of French rule and embarked on political, economic and social reforms. Algerian Muslims, including women, were given the vote in a referendum on the draft constitution of France's Fifth Republic which stated that Algeria was not an integral part of France. Seeking to undermine de Gaulle's attempt at a compromise, the FLN tried to spoil the vote by a wave of bombings and raids in France and Algeria, and the formation of a government in exile in Tunis. In September 1959, however, the overwhelming majority of the 80% of Muslims who voted supported the new constitution, and in February 1959, de Gaulle was elected as France's new president. The FLN vehemently rejected de Gaulle's offer to end the war and hold elections that would create an Algeria closely associated with France.

With French and international public opinion turning against France's counter-insurgency war in Algeria, de Gaulle admitted the possibility of independence in September 1959. Enraged French settlers in Algiers staged an uprising in late January 1960 called the "Week of the Barricades" that was crushed by a hesitant French military on the orders of de Gaulle. The leaders of the rebellion fled to Franco's Spain where, in cooperation with retired General Salan, they founded the Secret Army Organization (OAS) in December 1960 and mounted terrorist attacks in France and Algeria aimed at derailing Algerian independence. When 75% of voters in France and Algeria approved Algerian independence in a January 1961 referendum, de Gaulle's government began negotiations with the FLN. In late April, four retired generals, including Challe and Salan, attempted to halt the negotiations by orchestrating an ultimately unsuccessful coup in Algeria and France. In turn, the French government discarded the interests of the French settlers in Algeria and continued talks with the FLN that produced the Evian Accords that imposed a ceasefire in March 1962, granted Europeans religious freedom and property rights for three years after which they would have to choose between French or Algerian citizenship and gave France use of military bases in Algeria and preferential access to Algerian oil. Despite a vicious bombing campaign by the OAS, French and Algerian voters accepted the accords, and on July 3, de Gaulle declared Algeria independent. In June, FLN supporters began attacks on French settlers and Muslim loyalists in which many thousands of former Harkis and their family members were murdered. Within a year, 1.4 million people or 13% of the population including almost the entire Jewish community fled Algeria. After independence, the FLN's Ahmed Ben Bella became the first president of Algeria, though he was overthrown by a military coup in 1965. The external FLA forces in Tunisia and Morocco returned home to become the Algerian military and the FLN imposed an authoritarian one-party state that ruled until the late 1980s.

Algeria's independence war was extremely deadly. Some 25,600 French security force personnel and 3,000 settlers were killed, French forces claimed to have killed 141,000 insurgents, though many of these were probably civilians, some 12,000 FLN members were killed during internal conflicts, around 5,000 people died in France in violence between rival Algerian groups and French authorities claimed that the FLN killed 70,000 Muslim civilians. Debate continues over the overall death toll of the Algerian War, with the French government claiming that 350,000 perished, while the Algerian government puts forth a figure of well over 1 million, which it describes as a genocide against Algerians. Although some historians believe 700,000–800,000 is a fairly accurate number of the total deaths, the war displaced more than 2 million people and the number of them who died of starvation or disease in remote areas will never be known. These figures exclude the victims of post-independence FLN reprisals. While the French public preferred to forget about the war, its latent memory would provide the context for the alienation of France's immigrant Algerian community (Alexander, Evans and Keiger, 2002; Alexander and Keiger, 2002; Aussaresses, 2004; Horne, 2006).

Independence wars in Portuguese Africa (Mozambique, Angola and Guinea-Bissau) (1960–74)

Although most European powers negotiated the independence of their African colonies in the late 1950s and 1960s, the autocratic regime of Antonio Salazar in Lisbon insisted that its African territories of Mozambique, Angola and Guinea-Bissau were integral parts of Portugal. However, Portuguese colonial rule had been particularly oppressive, and frustrated African nationalists in these territories decided to fight for independence. The global Cold War impacted on all three unfolding insurgencies as Portugal, a member of the North Atlantic Treaty Organization, was supported by Western powers and the liberation movements were sponsored by the Eastern Block (Cann, 1997).

The war in Mozambique began in 1960 when Portuguese security forces massacred 500 protestors in the northern town of Mueda. In 1962 African nationalist groups from Mozambique, exiled in newly independent Tanganyika (later Tanzania), formed the Front for the Liberation of Mozambique (FRELIMO) led by the US-educated Eduardo Mondlane. In 1964, FRELIMO launched a guerrilla war in northern Mozambique. With Tanzania as a staging area, FRELIMO received military assistance from the Soviet Union and China, Scandinavian countries provided humanitarian support, and it was also aided by the newly created and anti-colonial Organization of African Unity (OAU). In the late 1960s the insurgents created "liberated zones" in northern Mozambique where medical care and education were provided, and cooperative agriculture dispossessed chiefs and landlords. Starting in 1968, FRELIMO traversed sympathetic Zambia to infiltrate Tete province and challenge the Portuguese in central Mozambique. With about 8,000 fighters in Mozambique, small FRELIMO units harassed and ambushed Portuguese forces, planted landmines and gained supplies and recruits from rural communities. In the late 1960s, the Cabora Bassa dam project on the Zambezi River became a focal point for insurgent operations, though it was not attacked because of its future economic importance. Within FRELIMO, African nationalists with a local agenda clashed with Marxists who saw themselves as part of a global anti-imperialist and anti-capitalist revolution. When Mondlane was assassinated by a Portuguese parcel bomb sent to him in Tanzania in 1969, the Marxist and pro-Soviet Samora Machel assumed leadership of the organization.

In 1970, the Portuguese mounted the six-month-long Operation Gordian Knot which involved an offensive by 35,000 troops under General Kaulza de Arriaga using helicopters and artillery barrages in an effort to block FRELIMO's infiltration routes from Tanzania and eliminate its Mozambican bases. The Portuguese also pursued insurgents into Tanzania. FRELIMO sustained 650 fatalities and had 1,800 insurgents captured, but heavy rains and politically worrisome Portuguese casualties limited the operation's impact. During the early 1970s, the Portuguese in Mozambique Africanized their security forces, constructed "strategic hamlets" to separate civilians from insurgents and concentrated on small search and destroy operations. A FRELIMO offensive in Tete led to Portuguese reprisals including the 1972 massacre of several hundred civilians around Wiriyamu. Simultaneously, FRELIMO launched operations in southern Mozambique from where most of the movement's leaders originated, which caused

Portuguese morale to decline. By 1974, FRELIMO controlled a third of the country, and with newly supplied Soviet ground-to-air missiles, it threatened Portuguese air superiority (Newitt, 1995, pp. 517–40).

In 1961, a number of rebellions against oppressive Portuguese rule broke out in Angola. In January, a dissident Christian group destroyed European crops and property on the central plateau and was brutally suppressed by the Portuguese army. In February, a Portuguese cruise liner was hijacked at sea and several hundred supporters of the Popular Movement for the Liberation of Angola (MPLA) attacked a Luanda police headquarters and a prison. A more serious revolt erupted in the north among the Bakongo who had grievances over land and Portuguese intervention in appointing their traditional king. The Union of Peoples of Angola (UPA) was based in neighboring and newly independent Congo where the group's leader Holden Roberto obtained arms from his brother-in-law Joseph Mobutu, head of the new Congolese army. In turn, the UPA infiltrated small groups of insurgents into northern Angola. In mid-March, 4,000–5,000 insurgents attacked coffee plantations in the north where they killed 200 Portuguese and many more of their African loyalists. UPA insurgents thought they could force the Portuguese to quickly abandon Angola as the Belgians had with Congo. The Portuguese were unprepared, with only 3,000 mostly local troops and a small number of military aircraft in the colony. Since the rainy season delayed the transport of Portuguese soldiers to the north, the Portuguese Air Force supported Portuguese farmers and their African allies who fortified their plantations and formed a militia that burned and massacred villages suspected of rebel sympathies. In May, Portuguese reinforcements began to arrive in Angola and restored colonial control in the north. Although the army halted settler atrocities, it conducted aerial bombing with napalm and forced African civilians into concentrated settlements. The poorly armed and trained insurgents adopted guerrilla tactics against Portuguese forces and fled into Congo when pursued. In August and September, the Portuguese army took the main insurgent strongholds after heavy fighting that fatally weakened the rebellion which fizzled over the next two years. Around 2,000 Europeans and 50,000 Africans had been killed during the fighting and thousands of refugees crossed into Congo.

A divided Angolan nationalist movement emerged during the first half of the 1960s. In 1962, Roberto's UPA merged with another organization to form the National Liberation Front of Angola (FNLA) that set up a government in exile in Leopoldville (today's Kinshasa) in Congo with support from Mobutu and the OAU. The MPLA, under Agostinho Neto, continued to derive most of its support from around Luanda. In 1966, Jonas Savimbi established the National Union for the Total Independence of Angola (UNITA) among the Ovimbundu of the south. Additionally, in 1963, three groups seeking independence for oil-rich Cabinda, physically disconnected from the rest of Angola, amalgamated into the Front for the Liberation of the Cabinda Enclave.

In 1963, MPLA established an armed wing called the "People's Army for the Liberation of Angola" (EPLA) and adopted Maoist guerrilla strategy. Expelled from Congo-Kinshasa and rejected by the people of Cabinda, the MPLA moved to Zambia, acquired Eastern Block Weapons and in 1966 launched armed operations against the Portuguese in southern and eastern Angola. During the late 1960s, the Portuguese considered the 2,000 EPLA fighters their most significant military threat. However, the MPLA tried to expand operations across the whole country rather than liberating specific areas and mobilized 250-man units that were easy for the Portuguese to locate during their six-week march from Zambia to parts of Angola. In the north, the MPLA/EPLA was attacked by the Portuguese army and FNLA and escape into Congo was impossible. The number of EPLA fighters grew to 5,000, but the abovementioned issues meant that only a small portion could operate within Angola. In late 1971, an EPLA offensive involving several thousands of fighters who sought to destroy UNITA and attack the Portuguese failed miserably. Throughout the next year, large Portuguese–South African offensives in Moxico Province pushed EPLA fighters back to Zambia.

In the early 1970s, the Chinese-armed FNLA had around 4,000 insurgents based in Zaire (Congo) who staged small raids across the border into Angola. The FNLA also maintained 200–300 fighters in the Dembos Mountains where they tied down many Portuguese troops and another 300 insurgents along Angola's eastern border countered the MPLA. While UNITA was initially based in Zambia from where it launched incursions into Angola, it was expelled in 1967 given a raid on the Benguela railway that was important for Zambia's copper export. Without a foreign sanctuary, UNITA did not expand much beyond 500 insurgents mostly in the eastern highlands where Savimbi attempted a Maoist guerrilla war with limited Chinese support. UNITA and FNLA formed a loose alliance against the MPLA.

By 1970, Portugal had 60,000 troops, a third of whom were local Africans, in Angola with most military resources assigned to the north and Cabinda. Portuguese intelligence formed special small units called Flechas (arrows) recruited from captured and turned insurgents and minority Khoisan (Bushmen) who tracked insurgent forces. The Portuguese military understood that it needed to gain the "hearts and minds" of local people but lack of training meant that this was not operationalized. Portugal's greatest military advantage in Angola was its unopposed control of the air. By the early 1970s, the Portuguese Air Force in Angola consisted of 3,000 personnel with fifty-one ground strike aircraft, fifty reconnaissance planes, sixteen transports and more than sixty helicopters. The air force supplied ground patrols, evacuated casualties, destroyed insurgent agriculture, sprayed defoliant to reduce bush cover, provided combat support and transported soldiers. Studying French counter-insurgency in Algeria, the Portuguese divided Angola into grids each with a garrison and mounted sweeps with air mobile forces. By 1973, 1 million people had been pushed into protected villages which created food shortages and further alienated rural communities. Portuguese operations in Angola were more successful than in their other two African territories because the country was vast, the insurgents divided and Lisbon devoted more resources to protect its source of oil (Van Der Waals, 1993; Clayton, 2004, pp. 35–47; George, 2005, pp. 14–48).

In 1956, the African Party for the Independence of Guinea and Cape Verde (PAIGC) was founded and engaged in a peaceful political campaign for the autonomy of these small Portuguese West African territories. However, the 1959 Portuguese massacre of fifty striking dockworkers incited PAIGC leader Amilcar Cabral to flee to the adjacent and recently independent Republic of Guinea from where he launched an armed struggle for independence. With a broad socialist ideology that sought to unite mixed-race Cape Verdeans and the Balante of the mainland, PAIGC used political cadres to mobilize rural people within Portuguese territory, and from 1963, it established liberated zones governed by elected councils. Militarily, PAIGC focused on interior rural areas that, after political preparation of locals, were infiltrated by insurgents who sought to restrict Portuguese forces to towns and attack communication lines. While small insurgent units attacked Portuguese posts and economic facilities, there was to be no general violence against Africans loyal to the colonial administration. By 1971, the PAIGC armed wing had 6,000 members. Based in the Republic of Guinea and Senegal, the insurgents were armed and trained by Soviet, Cuban and Czechoslovakian instructors. Wounded fighters were treated in field hospitals across the border, and some were evacuated to Eastern Europe. At times, PAIGC operations were supported by Guinean artillery firing across the border, and from 1971, the insurgents used their own 122 mm rocket launchers.

Guinea was not economically profitable and had few settlers, but Lisbon felt that its loss would weaken control of Angola and Mozambique. The Portuguese military presence in Guinea increased from a few hundred men in 1963 to 30,000, half locally recruited, in 1971. Portuguese forces used the territory's many waterways as an alternative transport system to roads where ambush became common. From 1964, Portuguese strategy focused on defending a network of strong points. Between 1964 and 1968, the Portuguese re-asserted control of major roads and drove rural people into protected villages which created popular resentment. In 1968, General Antonio de Spinola, a student of US counter-insurgency in Vietnam, took command in Guinea and initiated a massive development program called "Better Guinea," which included tarring roads and building hospitals and schools. The fortified village scheme was made voluntary. At the same time, Spinola used newly arrived French-made helicopters to step up operations against the insurgents. Although the Portuguese did not chase insurgents into neighboring countries, they conducted a November 1970 amphibious raid called "Operation Green Sea" on Conakry in the Republic of Guinea where twenty-six Portuguese prisoners were rescued and five PAIGC supply boats destroyed. The raid was ultimately counter-productive as it generated international condemnation and prompted the Soviet Union to send warships to the Guinean coast.

In 1973, Cabral was assassinated by rivals within his own organization, with Portuguese involvement strongly suspected. Around the same time, PAIGC began to use Soviet surface-to-air missiles to destroy Portuguese aircraft and Soviet heavy artillery to bombard Portuguese posts from long range. Portuguese garrisons were besieged, Portuguese pilots refused to fly and Portuguese control was relegated to the capital and some towns. Spinola resigned when Lisbon rejected his advice to join a peace process initiated by Senegalese President Leopold Senghor. In September 1973, PAIGC declared the independence of Guinea-Bissau which was recognized by the UN. While the death toll in the Guinea-Bissau independence war remains unknown, Portugal admitted that 1875 metropolitan troops were killed and it is likely that 6,000–8,000 African colonial soldiers and around 12,000 insurgents lost their lives (Costa Pinto, 2003, pp. 21–2; Clayton, 2004, pp. 51–6; Cann, 2007, pp. 209–29).

In April 1974, the Portuguese military, responding to the great unpopularity of the costly African wars, staged a coup in Lisbon which overthrew the government of Marcello Caetano, the late Salazar's successor, and initiated democratization. This led to the sudden independence of Portugal's colonies. While MPLA took power in Angola and FRELIMO did so in Mozambique, both groups faced challenges from other forces which resulted in post-independence civil wars and military intervention by neighboring states.

Zimbabwe's Liberation War/Rhodesian Bush War (1965–80)

In 1953, Britain created the Central African Federation which brought together white minority-ruled Southern Rhodesia with the mining economy of Northern Rhodesia and the African labor reservoir of Nyasaland. For Britain, the federation represented a new regional ally to replace South Africa which had elected the republican minded Afrikaner Nationalist Party in 1948 and introduced apartheid. At a time of rising African nationalism across the continent, the federation was governed by a tiny white settler population and its government engaged in the meaningless rhetoric of "multi-racialism." African nationalists in all three territories protested against the federation and demanded independence and majority rule. Increasingly violent protest and state repression led to the dissolution of the federation in 1963, and Britain, now eager to withdraw from Africa, granted independence to Northern Rhodesia as Zambia and Nyasaland as Malawi in 1964. In Southern Rhodesia, where the white minority had enjoyed internal self-government since 1923, the reactionary Rhodesian Front party of Ian Smith came to power. The much-harassed African nationalists of Southern Rhodesia split into two groups: Joshua Nkomo led the Zimbabwe African People's Union (ZAPU) that sought to mobilize international sanctions and Ndabaningi Sithole led the new Zimbabwe African National Union (ZANU) that was more committed to popular protest. Most of the top leaders of both organizations were arrested and imprisoned. In November 1965, given British demands that the Rhodesian Front agree to eventual majority rule before the granting of dominion status similar to Canada or Australia, Smith unilaterally declared independence and London did little to stop it.

Both ZAPU and ZANU formed military wings to pursue armed struggle against settler-ruled Rhodesia. Based in neighboring Zambia, ZAPU established the Zimbabwe People's Revolutionary Army (ZIPRA) and ZANU formed the Zimbabwe African National Liberation Army (ZANLA). Smith's Rhodesia gained support from apartheid South Africa, the Portuguese colonial rulers of Mozambique, and some Western powers that saw Rhodesia as an anti-communist stronghold. ZAPU and ZANU gained Eastern Block support and adopted socialist revolutionary ideology. In the late 1960s, ZIPRA and ZANLA sent armed units from Zambia into Rhodesia, but the natural obstacle of the Zambesi River border, the semi-open and sparsely populated terrain of the Zambesi Valley and lack of support from rural people led to the elimination of all these groups by Rhodesian security forces. The conflict began in April 1966 when a group of twenty-one ZANLA insurgents was neutralized by security forces at Sinoia (today's Chinhoyi). In 1967 and 1968, ZAPU embarked on joint operations with the exiled African National Congress (ANC) of South Africa which led to disastrous battles with Rhodesian security forces around Wankie and Sipolilo. These engagements prompted apartheid South Africa to send security forces to assist Rhodesia as a buffer to African nationalist infiltration.

Throughout the 1970s, the two Zimbabwe liberation movements took different paths. ZAPU–ZIPRA remained in Zambia where, given Soviet influence, it adopted a Leninist strategy focused on developing a conventional army that could invade Rhodesia which would be weakened by sanctions and irregular warfare. Staging out of Zambia and eventually Botswana from around 1974, ZIPRA recruited mostly from the ethnic Ndebele, Karanga or Sotho of southwestern Rhodesia where the movement gained popularity. With Chinese assistance, ZANU–ZANLA adopted Maoist revolutionary strategy that emphasized politicizing Rhodesia's rural African communities and fighting a guerrilla war with many small units. ZANLA insurgents held all-night community meetings in which they would lead local people in revolutionary songs and denunciation of traitors who would be killed, and villagers were expected to provide food, information and recruits or face reprisals. Trying to win over rural people, ZANLA emphasized grievances over land and used Shona spirit mediums who were popularly associated with the memory of the 1896–97 rebellion or the First Chimurenga (War of Independence). ZANLA portrayed itself as leading the "Second Chimurenga."

A new phase of the conflict began in 1972 when ZANLA, under Josiah Tongogara, moved to Mozambique's Tete province where it allied with FRELIMO that was fighting the Portuguese. Since the problem with staging areas in Zambia was the natural obstacle of the Zambezi River, ZANLA insurgents in Mozambique more easily entered the forests and hills of northeast Rhodesia. When FRELIMO took over Mozambique in 1975, the conflict in Rhodesia expanded as ZANLA began using the entire eastern border as a staging area. Given its focus on eastern Rhodesia's Mashonaland region during the 1970s, ZANLA developed primarily among the country's Shona ethnic majority. Rhodesian forces responded to the heightened insurgency by launching lightning strikes against ZANLA camps in Mozambique such as at Nyadzonya in 1976 and Chimoio in 1977. Rhodesian forces also conducted cross-border raids against ZIPRA camps in both Zambia and Botswana. In 1978 and 1979, ZIPRA, now commanded by Lookout Masuku, used Soviet ground-to-air missiles to shoot down two Rhodesian civilian airliners which severely damaged white Rhodesian morale. In 1979, ZIPRA infiltrated 3,000 insurgents into Rhodesia to prepare for a conventional invasion that never took place and this was countered by an incursion of ZANLA fighters into the southwest where the two forces clashed with each other and the Rhodesians.

Rhodesian counter-insurgency was largely informed by the 1950s British campaign in Malaya, though it was much less effective. Rural people were herded into "protected villages" and large tracts were declared "free fire zones" where anyone was considered an insurgent and killed. Formed in the early 1970s, the Selous Scouts used "turned terrorists" to infiltrate insurgent cells and call in air mobile "fire forces" to destroy them. A typical "fire force" consisted of a helicopter-borne commander circling a suspected enemy position, several four-man teams landed by helicopter to block escape routes and a larger attack unit of perhaps platoon strength parachuted from an airplane. Insurgents responded to such operations by fleeing in all directions whenever they heard an aircraft which meant that "fire forces" often failed to locate the enemy but sometimes they trapped and killed many. Furthermore, Rhodesian security forces tried to kill insurgents by circulating poisoned clothing and tinned food, and transistor radios containing bombs in rural areas. Rhodesian commanders stressed racking up an insurgent body count, but many rural non-combatants were killed by mistake, and this pushed the increasingly brutalized rural people toward the liberation movements. The Rhodesian Front government hesitated to expand its armed African security personnel until the late 1970s by which time it was too late. Struggling with manpower problems, Rhodesian forces relied on young white conscripts and white reservists who were called up for increasingly long periods which further hindered the sanctions plagued economy.

Both sides came under pressure to negotiate after Portuguese decolonization. Failed talks in late 1974 led to the release of detained nationalist leaders such as Nkomo and it was then that Robert Mugabe, who had also spent a decade in prison, assumed leadership of ZANU as Sithole had allegedly renounced the armed struggle. Smith's regime was entirely dependent on South Africa for imports such as oil but Pretoria, which faced a surge of internal African protest from 1976, began to see the Rhodesian conflict as a threat to its new policy of using economic means to passively dominate black-ruled neighbors. In addition, the OAU and the Zambian government were concerned that the war was crippling the Zambian economy that depended on exporting copper through Rhodesia and South Africa. During the "internal settlement" of 1978, South Africa and Smith arranged for the installation of a pro-Western Rhodesia–Zimbabwe government under moderate black leader Bishop Abel Muzorewa in which whites retained significant power. The war continued as this solution proved unacceptable to the liberation movements. The British-sponsored Lancaster House talks of 1979, which included Nkomo and Mugabe, produced an agreement in which Zimbabwe would formally gain independence in 1980 with universal adult suffrage and some concessions to the white minority including no forced land redistribution for a decade. Under Commonwealth supervision, insurgents gathered at assembly areas for planned absorption, along with former Rhodesian personnel, into a new Zimbabwe security force structure. The newly renamed ZANU-Patriotic Front won the elections and formed independent Zimbabwe's first government with Mugabe as prime minister. During the early and middle 1980s Mugabe's security forces crushed ZAPU and imposed a reign of terror on southwest Zimbabwe in which around 20,000 people were killed (Martin and Johnson, 1981; Lan, 1985; Ranger and Bhebhe, 1995; Nhongo-Simbanegavi, 2000; Sibanda, 2005; Moorcroft and McLaughlin, 2008; Wood, 2009).

South West Africa (1966–89)

Although South Africa gained a League of Nations mandate over the adjacent former German colony of South West Africa (SWA) after World War I, Pretoria ruled the territory as another province, and in 1946, it refused to transfer the mandate to the United Nations. After 1948, South African apartheid policies were extended to SWA which resulted in a 1959 police massacre of eleven protestors during the forced removal of their community from Windhoek. African nationalists from the South West African National Union (SWANU) and South West African People's Organization (SWAPO), led by Sam Nujoma, demanded that the territory come under UN trusteeship with a view to eventual independence. In 1962, exiled SWAPO activists formed the People's Liberation Army of Namibia (PLAN) to fight South African occupation. PLAN was based in Tanzania and Zambia and received support from the Soviet Union. SWANU eventually dissolved, given lack of OAU and UN support and hesitance to engage in armed struggle.

During the 1960s and early 1970s, PLAN experienced problems infiltrating insurgents into SWA as the Portuguese colonial regime in Angola was working with South African security forces and newly independent Botswana was vulnerable to Pretoria's economic and military pressure. At this time, PLAN's staging areas in Zambia were a long distance from its main area of support in northern SWA's Ovamboland region and insurgents had to traverse Portuguese Angola or SWA's narrow and therefore easily guarded Caprivi Strip. The war in SWA began in August 1966 when a detachment of South African paratroopers and police destroyed a PLAN camp at Omgulumbashe in Ovamboland. Given such problems, PLAN operations at that time focused mostly on Caprivi where insurgents planted landmines and attacked local headmen. In 1972, labor unrest in SWA prompted PLAN to accelerate its activities which resulted in increased South African security force deployment.

The 1975 independence of Angola meant that the MPLA state began to host SWAPO camps which resulted in the dramatic expansion of the insurgency across the border in northern SWA. The insurgency in SWA would become closely linked to the events of the Angolan civil war and prompted various South African military incursions into Angola. While PLAN was able to establish liberated zones in parts of Ovamboland and on occasion insurgents advanced south into the white farming areas during the late 1970s, a number of factors once again limited its activities during the 1980s. South African cross-border operations into Angola pushed SWAPO/PLAN bases further away from the border and the presence of South African-backed UNITA rebels in southeastern Angola restricted PLAN access to that area and hence to northeastern SWA. Importantly, the South Africans developed aggressive mechanized reaction units like the police's Koevoet (crowbar) and the military's 101 Battalion, both recruited from the local Ovambo population, which performed well in the environment of northern SWA and inflicted staggering losses on PLAN. Unlike many counter-insurgency forces, the South Africans in SWA did not resort to herding rural people into "protected villages," but as the war unfolded, the "hearts and minds" approach was largely abandoned. Since the insurgency in SWA continued but was mostly confined to Ovamboland, the political fate of the territory would be decided by the large conventional battles fought in southern Angola in the late 1980s. The last SADF combat operation in SWA occurred in April 1989 when around 1,500 PLAN insurgents crossed from Angola to establish a military presence before the upcoming November elections. With SWAPO in violation of a ceasefire and a UN peacekeeping force yet to arrive, the UN authorized the departing SADF and the SWA Police to intercept the insurgents who lost 250 men and were pushed back into Angola. SWAPO eventually won the elections and formed the first government of Namibia that became independent in 1990 under the presidency of Nujoma (Katjavivi, 1988; Leys and Saul, 1995; Namakalu, 2004; Stiff, 2004; Esterhuyse and Jordaan, 2010; Kamongo and Bezuidenhout, 2011; Wallace, 2011; Udogo, 2012; Scholtz, 2013).

South Africa (1961–94)

In March 1960, the South African Police shot into a crowd of anti-apartheid protestors in Sharpeville, an African community near Johannesburg, killing sixty-nine. This event signaled the end of passive resistance to the strict racial segregation of apartheid and the beginning of the armed struggle. The South African government outlawed the long-established ANC and the new Pan-Africanist Congress (PAC) that were the main anti-apartheid groups. In July 1961, joint members of the South African Communist Party and the ANC including Nelson Mandela established a military organization called Umkhonto we Sizwe (Spear of the Nation or MK) that would engage in controlled violence against the apartheid state. MK was technically separate from the ANC as some members of the latter group remained committed to a non-violent approach. In December, MK operatives began a bombing campaign across South African cities and towns which would last for the next year and published a manifesto declaring war on the apartheid government and announcing that they were fighting for democracy. MK members secretly left South Africa for military training in Algeria and Ethiopia. In October 1962, the ANC publically recognized MK at a meeting in British colonial Bechuanaland (Botswana from 1966). In 1963, most MK leaders including Mandela, highly recognizable given their previous career as prominent activists, were arrested, convicted of treason and sentenced to life imprisonment. Those who escaped, such as Joe Slovo, joined the ANC political leadership in exile.

The PAC, an Africanist organization that split from the more inclusive ANC in 1959, engaged in less restrained violence. After the Sharpeville massacre, the PAC planned a nation-wide mass uprising for 1963 and formed armed groups loosely referred to as "Poqo" (alone). During 1962 and 1963, Poqo groups armed with axes and machetes attacked policemen, whites and state-paid African traditional leaders mostly in the western and eastern parts of the Cape. The PAC-armed campaign petered out given a crackdown by South African Police and a police raid on PAC offices in British Basutoland (Lesotho from 1966) in which membership lists were seized. The 1963 uprising never took place, and as with the ANC, PAC leaders were either imprisoned or fled the country.

After 1964, the exiled ANC/MK shifted military training to the Soviet Union and established training camps in Tanzania. At this time, MK lacked a staging area from which to conduct operations within South Africa which was protected by a ring of allies such as the Portuguese colonies and white ruled Rhodesia and small, dependent African states such as Botswana and Swaziland. This inspired MK to join with ZAPU during the ultimately disastrous Wankie and Sipolilo campaigns that some activists called a suicide mission. At the 1969 Morogoro conference in Tanzania, the ANC decided to better integrate political and military issues and to cultivate popular support at home before mounting revolutionary war. The 1976 Soweto

Uprising in South Africa, inspired by the rise of the Black Consciousness movement, revitalized the ANC/MK as many young people joined the exiled movement. Beginning in the late 1970s, MK established camps in Angola where they learned conventional and guerrilla warfare from Soviet instructors, and in the 1980s, MK fighters were deployed against UNITA rebels. Morale problems and the perception of fighting someone else's war led to mutiny in ANC camps in Angola. During the late 1970s and early 1980s, hundreds of MK operatives infiltrated South Africa to build covert networks and conduct limited military missions called "armed propaganda" which targeted police stations, railways and other state institutions to motivate mass action. An MK special operations unit orchestrated high-profile attacks such as the bombing of an oil refinery in 1980 and a nuclear plant in 1982, and a rocket attack on a military base near Pretoria in 1981. With increased popular protest and a state of emergency in South Africa during the mid- to late 1980s, MK expanded its definition of legitimate targets. A program of landmine planting was aimed at killing white farmers as they were active in the part-time security forces, there were bombings and mortar attacks inside South Africa and in some instances white civilians were intentionally killed in shopping centers and restaurants. In 1986, the ANC launched "Operation Vula" (Open) that involved smuggling weapons into South Africa, infiltrating South African security forces and orchestrating a military coup in the Transkei homeland which then became something of a sanctuary.

In the late 1960s, the exiled PAC adopted Maoist guerrilla warfare doctrine and sent some members for training in China. In 1968, the PAC officially renamed its armed wing the Azanian People's Liberation Army (APLA) that was based in Zambia and Tanzania. The PAC/APLA was expelled from Zambia several times, given pressure from South Africa and the group's ill-discipline. Conflicts between PAC factions, including African nationalists, Black Consciousness devotees, Leninists and Maoists, limited the movement's ability to militarily engage South Africa during the 1970s and 1980s. In 1979, the Tanzania military had to restore order in one of the PAC camps in that country, and in 1985, Lesotho expelled a number of PAC activists who had clashed with local security forces. Lacking effective sponsors, APLA members attended training in Gaddafi's Libya, Idi Amin's Uganda and Pol Pot's Cambodia. In 1986, APLA launched its first operations in South Africa; by 1988, it was well established in the western Transvaal, and two years later, it had a strong presence across the country. The insurgents attacked police stations and white farmers, and created a "robbery unit" to garner funds. Although legalized during South Africa's reforms of 1990, the PAC refused to enter negotiations with the South African government and continued its armed struggle with attacks on white civilians at hotels, a golf club and a Cape Town church (Lodge, 1995; Williams, 2000; Maaba, 2004; Magubane et al., 2004; Shubin, 2008; Cherry, 2012; Simpson, 2016).

By 1990, South Africa's apartheid system had become untenable, given crippling international sanctions, internal protest, military defeat in Angola which had led to a withdrawal from Namibia and the end of the Cold War. Notwithstanding continued violence from disenchanted groups like right-wing Afrikaners, Zulu nationalists and the PAC, negotiations between the ANC and the ruling Nationalist Party during the early 1990s produced a non-racial constitution. In April 1994, South Africa's first democratic election ushered in an ANC-led government of national unity under President Mandela. As part of the transition, a new South African National Defence Force (SANDF) was created by amalgamating members of the old SADF and African homeland (Bantustan) armies as well as former insurgents from MK and APLA (Frankel, 2000; Williams, 2002; Van Der Waag, 2015, pp. 283–308).

4 Post-colonial civil wars (1955–2000)

Introduction

The colonial legacy and the nature of the post-colonial African state led to many rebellions and civil wars in the continent after 1960. Since the new African countries inherited colonial borders that had been imposed without consideration of physical or human geography, regional armed separatist movements emerged in, for example, Congo, Nigeria, Sudan and Ethiopia. Colonial favoritism of a particular region or ethnic group within a larger territory led to violent shifts in power relations as in Uganda and Rwanda. These late twentieth-century African conflicts were often also Cold War proxy wars as the superpowers, the United States and Soviet Union, supported rival combatants. A tradition of tit-for-tat support of rebel groups developed in post-colonial Africa in which neighboring states sponsored rebels in each other's territories. The end of the Cold War at the start of the 1990s and the subsequent collapse of superpower-backed authoritarian regimes destabilized parts of Africa and caused more civil wars some of which continued into the twenty-first century. After 1990, armed groups in Africa supported themselves by exporting resources such as diamonds and minerals related to the burgeoning electronics industry, and cut costs by press-ganging child soldiers from among Africa's youthful population. Although African secessionist groups had been unsuccessful during the Cold War era as international organizations and African states sought to maintain existing borders, the dramatic post-Cold War changes facilitated armed separatism as in Eritrea and eventually South Sudan.

The Congo Crisis (1960–7)

In the Congo, where very few local Africans had gained administrative experience or western higher education during the colonial era, the Belgians did little to prepare for independence during the 1950s. In 1959, Brussels, responding to the decolonization ethos of the time, provided the Congo with just six months' notice of independence, intending the new country to remain dependent on its assistance. Since the Belgians had never governed the vast territory as a single entity, Congolese political parties developed along regional and ethnic lines. At the end of June 1960, the first independent government was led by Prime Minister Patrice Lumumba, a Pan-Africanist of the Congolese National Movement centered in the northeast around Stanleyville (now Kisangani), and President Joseph Kasavubu of the ethnic-oriented Bakongo Alliance (ABAKO) that was based in the west around the capital of Leopoldville (now Kinshasa). In early July, African soldiers mutinied against their Belgian officers which prompted wider attacks on Belgian civilians. To quell the rebellion, the military's title was changed from the colonial Force Publique to the Congolese National Army (ANC), Belgian officers were replaced by rapidly promoted Africans including former journalist Colonel Joseph Mobutu and all troops were promoted by one rank.

Supported by Western mining interests, regional separatists took advantage of the army mutiny. In diamond-rich South Kasai, Albert Kalonji proclaimed a self-governing state. With Belgian backing, Moise Tshombe declared the independence of the southern province of Katanga which was home to the Congo's largest mining industry. A Katanga military was formed with mercenaries from Rhodesia, South Africa, France and Belgium. When Belgian troops arrived to protect Belgian civilians, Lumumba demanded their withdrawal and requested UN assistance. However, since UN Operation in the Congo (ONUC) troops protected Western interests and refused to suppress the Katanga secession, Lumumba called for Soviet military support which led to US and Belgian plots to assassinate him. Portraying Lumumba's military campaign against South Kasai as genocidal, President Kasavubu dismissed the prime minister who was placed under arrest by Mobutu's soldiers. Following an unsuccessful escape attempt, Lumumba was flown to Katanga in January 1961 and executed on Tshombe's order.

In February 1961, the UN Security Council authorized ONUC to act against the Katanga secession. ONUC forces in Katanga were bolstered by the arrival of an Indian combat brigade. In August, ONUC conducted Operation Rum Punch which involved the arrest and deportation of some foreign mercenaries working in Katanga. The Katangese siege of 150 Irish peacekeepers at Jadotville, which was bombed by Katanga's French-supplied aircraft, inspired further UN action. In September, the now 20,000-strong ONUC launched Operation Morthor in which they attempted to seize Elisabethville, Katanga's capital, but were repulsed. The next month, the ANC also launched a failed incursion into Katanga. Although Tshombe's state was enjoying military success on the ground, the United States was beginning to shift away from the anti-communist separatist regime to backing a friendly government in the entire Congo. Countering Katanga's dominance of the sky, ONUC created a UN air force in Congo with jet fighters and bombers from Ethiopia, Sweden and India. In December 1962, after a long but failed negotiation, ONUC initiated Operation Grand Slam involving air operations that destroyed Katanga aircraft and a ground offensive by Indian and Swedish troops that crushed the separatist regime.

The 1964 withdrawal of ONUC provided an opportunity for rebellion in other parts of the Congo. After Lumumba's murder, many of his supporters fled to Congo-Brazzaville and Burundi where they organized the National Liberation Council and obtained Eastern-bloc support. In January 1964, fighters under Pierre Mulele launched an insurgency in the western region of Kwilu. In May, "Simba" (lion) rebels, led by Gaston Soumialot and including many exiled Tutsi fighters from Rwanda, began seizing towns in eastern Congo, and in August, they took Stanleyville. The rebels proclaimed the People's Republic of Congo which was recognized by the Soviet Union, China and Cuba. Supported by the United States, the Congolese government of Prime Minister Moise Tshombe formed an air force with Cuban exile pilots and supplemented ANC ground forces by hiring foreign white mercenaries many of whom had recently worked for separatist Katanga as well as recalling Katangese troops who had fled the country. In Kwilu, the ANC re-established control in April but fighting continued until December. In late 1964, mercenary and ANC units began to recapture towns in eastern Congo. During Operation Dragon Rouge, in late November, a mercenary-ANC mechanized ground column and Belgian paratroopers dropped from US aircraft-seized Stanleyville. A few days later, a similar operation, Dragon Noire, captured the town of Paulis (Isiro). While two other planned Dragon operations were cancelled given international outcry, Rouge and Noire rescued almost 2,000 hostages and killed 10,000 rebels, with minimal ANC-Belgian losses. With the withdrawal of Belgian forces, South African mercenary leader Mike Hoare led Operation White Giant which blocked rebel supplies from Uganda and Sudan, and took the northeast town of Bunia in December. In June 1965, Hoare and French mercenary leader Bob Denard directed Operation Violettes Imperiales which secured the northern border with Central African Republic. The arrival of several hundred Cubans under Ernesto "Che" Guevara could not salvage the rebellion which was contained in several isolated and shrinking pockets. In late 1965, rebel links with Tanzania were hindered by the arrival of US-supplied gunboats with Cuban exile crews on Lake Tanganyika and mercenary-ANC amphibious operations along the western lake shore finally crushed the insurgency. In November 1965, the US-sponsored Mobutu, the real power in Congo since 1961, overthrew President Kasavubu and dismissed Prime Minister Tshombe who fled the country. Mobutu established an anti-communist dictatorship that would last for thirty years and become infamous for corruption and oppression. In 1966, a mutiny by Katangese troops in the east was suppressed by mercenaries and other ANC forces. Given that Mobutu would not renew their contracts, white mercenaries in the east also rebelled the next year, though their plot to restore the exiled Tshombe was thwarted by the US CIA. The arrival of overwhelming ANC forces, some transported in US aircraft, compelled many mercenaries to flee into Rwanda from where they were repatriated (De Witte, 2002; Villafana, 2012; Owen, 2015).

Figure 4.1 Joseph Desire Mobutu, later known as Mobutu Sese Seko, rolls up his
sleeves during a speech in December 1965 in Leopoldville, Congo, after
seizing power in November

The Nigerian Civil War (1967–70)

British officials and Nigerian nationalists spent much of the 1950s negoti-
ating a transition to independence, but the process was problematized by
Nigeria's regional, ethnic and religious divisions. The southern portion of
the country was generally more prosperous and populated by Christians who
were divided between a predominantly Yoruba West around the city of
Lagos and a mostly Igbo East around the Niger Delta that had recently
become the site of oil production. In the economically marginalized north,
the Hausa-Fulani were mostly Muslims and governed by conservative emirs
who with the support of the British had limited the development of western
education. The colonial army in Nigeria, which would soon become a
national force, was dominated by northerners, given previous British
recruiting patterns. Politically, the nationalist leaders from the East favored
a future unity government for independent Nigeria, while those from the
north desired a federal system in which their region would have some
autonomy. These goals would eventually be reversed.

In 1960, Nigeria became independent as a federation of three regions but
with an elected federal government dominated by northerners. Easterners
began to feel that their oil wealth was being stolen to develop the north and
that the electoral system was being manipulated against them. In January

1966, a group of mostly Igbo army officers led by Major Kaduna Nzeugwu seized power killing northern Prime Minister Abubakar Balewa and northern premier and traditional leader Ahmadu Bello. This coup resulted in the takeover of General Johnson Aguiyi-Ironsi who was also Igbo. In July, a counter-coup by northern army officers, prompted by Ironsi's abolition of the federal system which confirmed northern fears of southern domination, installed Lieutenant Colonel Yakubu Gowon as head-of-state and resulted in the killing of southern officers including Ironsi. As the new military regime seemed unwilling or unable to stop massacres of Easterners living in the North, Eastern Governor Lieutenant Colonel Chukwuemeka Odumegwu Ojukwu refused to recognize Gowon. Although the January 1967 Aburi Conference in Ghana resulted in a negotiated settlement, this was never implemented, and in May, Ojukwu and a council of Eastern leaders declared the region's independence as the Republic of Biafra.

The ensuing Nigerian Civil War was a highly unequal contest. Internationally, the federal military government was supported and armed by Britain and the Soviet Union as the need for oil trumped Cold War rivalries. The United States, distracted by war in Vietnam, deferred to Britain on Biafra and imposed an arms embargo on the secessionist republic. Several powers provided covert assistance to Biafra such as France which wanted to take over British oil interests there and Portugal, Rhodesia and South Africa which were desperate for a black-ruled African ally and also wanted oil. The Biafran government garnered unofficial international support by hiring a Swiss public relations firm to portray it as defending its Christian people from genocide by Nigerian Muslims. With around 8,000 troops at the start of the war, the federal military expanded quickly to 120,000 in 1968 and 250,000 in 1970. Conversely, Biafran forces began the conflict with 3,000 personnel and ended with 30,000. While the federal air force used up-to-date Soviet-made bombers and fighters sometimes with foreign pilots, the Biafran air force was tiny, with a few World War II era aircraft and eventually five Swedish-made light planes fitted with rockets. Biafra's lack of a navy meant that federal ships could blockade the Biafran coast and were free to land forces in the Niger Delta.

In early July 1967, Nigerian federal forces launched an offensive to suppress the Biafran secession. Located in the north, the First Infantry Division formed two columns and advanced south into Biafra, quickly capturing several centers such as Nsukka. Attempting to distract federal forces, Biafran troops invaded the newly formed mid-western region west of the Niger River where they occupied Benin City and threatened the federal capital of Lagos. The Biafran government hoped that the mixed Yoruba and Igbo population of the mid-west would support them, but this incursion backfired as it discredited Biafra's self-defense claims. By late September, the federal Second Infantry Division had pushed east and expelled the Biafrans from Benin City to the Niger River's east bank. Around the same time, the Third Marine Commando Division was landed on the Biafran coast where it captured the cities of Bonny, Okrika and eventually Calabar. As such, Biafra lost its oil industry and its access to the outside world was limited to the Port Harcourt airport. In early October, the federal First Infantry Division seized the Biafran capital of Enugu which restricted Biafran forces to the Igbo heartland which was becoming packed with refugees. From the start of 1968, the war stalemated with the gradually shrinking and overcrowded Biafra under federal blockade. In early 1968, the Second Infantry Division abandoned its poorly orchestrated attempts to cross the Niger River and took Onitsha by moving overland. A federal offensive from April to June 1968 further reduced Biafra's territory. The Third Marine Commando Division, at the end of April, traversed the Cross River from Calabar to Port Harcourt which was taken a few weeks later and continued its advance to seize Aba and Owerri. To the north, the federal First Division advanced carefully, capturing Abakaliki and Afikpo. At the close of 1968, the Biafrans clung to a small area but were strengthened by international humanitarian airlifts and the arrival of some foreign mercenaries. The federal forces then concentrated on starving secessionist Biafra into submission.

In April and May 1969, the federal First Division embarked on an offensive that secured Biafra's new capital of Umuahia. Biafra responded with a desperate counter-offensive which recaptured Owerri but separatist forces were insufficient. In December 1969, federal commanders initiated operations to end the war. In January 1970, the Third Marine Commando Division, under future President Colonel Olusegun Obasanjo, advanced from the coast to penetrate Biafran lines. On January 9, federal troops again captured Owerri, and on January 13, they took Amichi which was the last Biafran-held town. Ojukwu flew to Cote d'Ivoire, leaving General Phillip Effiong to formally surrender. While the war caused between 90,000 and 120,000 military casualties, approximations of civilian deaths vary from 0.5 million to 3 million, with the overwhelming majority having died of starvation or disease related to the federal blockade of Biafra. After the war, the Gowon regime launched a reconstruction and reconciliation program. However, many easterners resented loss of property, lack of compensation for Biafran currency and the continued federal enjoyment of oil revenue derived in their region. The end of military rule in Nigeria in the late 1990s, together with the environmental disaster caused by the oil industry, informed a resurgence of Biafran separatism which was met with great hostility by the central government (De St. Jorre, 1972; Stremlau, 1977; Obasanjo, 1980; Siollun, 2009).

Sudan (1956–99)

British colonial rule in Sudan had polarized regional identities. By independence in 1956, the Muslim-Arab northerners who dominated the new government had come to see themselves as superior to the Christian-traditionalist and black southerners. A limited insurgency began in the south in 1955 when members of the colonial Sudan Defence Force rejected the impending transition and mutinied. In the early 1960s, given the 1958 military takeover in Khartoum and the subsequent promotion of northern Muslims and repression of southern Christians, educated southerners fled to neighboring countries such as Uganda where they created the Sudan African Nationalist Union as a separatist organization. An insurgency unfolded within southern Sudan with different local groups of fighters, collectively known as Anyanya (snake venom), fighting the northern-dominated state and each other. In January 1964, the Anyanya conducted their first significant operation by attacking Wau, capital of Bahr al-Ghazal province. Lacking external support, a total of around 5,000 Anyanya rebels depended on captured weapons including intercepting arms shipments that Khartoum intended for Simba rebels in eastern Congo. The July 1965 Sudanese army massacre of 1,500 civilians in Juba prompted many southerners to escape to Uganda and Congo, while others joined the Anyanya. The government drove the rural population of Equatoria region into "peace villages" where hundreds died of disease and hunger, and in Bahr al-Ghazal and Upper Nile, ethnic militias were formed to combat the rebels. However, the Anyanya movement alienated southern peasants by stealing their livestock, the fighters resented the exiled and educated political leadership, and Ethiopian and Ugandan support was hesitant as these states had their own problems with separatist movements.

In August 1967, the Southern Sudan Provisional Government (SSPG), the first attempt to unify the insurgents, was formed near Juba, but it quickly collapsed given internal quarrels. However, the SSPG had created the Anyanya National Armed Forces (ANAF) which continued under Colonel Joseph Lagu who had deserted the Sudanese army. During the late 1960s and early 1970s, the ANAF received military support and training from Israel which wanted to open a southern front in its conflict with Arab states. This assistance was facilitated by the pro-Western Ethiopian Emperor Haile Selassie who wanted revenge on Sudan for supporting Eritrean rebels and by Ugandan military commander Idi Amin who originated from his country's northern frontier with southern Sudan. Israeli sponsorship enabled Lagu to extend his authority over all the Anyanya groups and as such he renamed the ANAF the Southern Sudan Liberation Movement. Lagu encouraged the development of Anyanya ethnic units such as the Bari Anyanya in central Equitoria, Dinka Anyanya in Bahr al-Ghazal and Nuer Anyanya in the Upper Nile.

Under Lagu, the hitherto limited insurgency dramatically expanded after 1970, with the Anyanya mining most roads, ambushing trains and river boats and shelling Juba. In September and October 1970, the Anyanya mounted an ambitious attack on Morta, resulting in heavy casualties on both sides. With Soviet military backing including advisors and aircraft, as well as troops from Egypt, Khartoum launched a counter-offensive in 1971 which did not achieve much. After an Anyanya attack on a Sudanese military base at Naupo later that year, the conflict stalemated. Equatoria's forests and mountains favored guerrilla warfare, but in the dry grasslands and seasonal flood plains of Bahr al-Ghazal and Upper Nile, the insurgents moved mostly at night to avoid Sudanese air power and state forces defended population centers. Consequently, Sudanese leader Colonel Ja'afar Muhammad Numayri, who had staged a coup in 1969, negotiated with the southern rebels. The war ended with the 1972 Addis Ababa agreement in which the south gained some autonomy and the rebels abandoned separatism (which had recently failed in Congo and Nigeria) with many integrated into the Sudanese state military. Lagu became a major general and joined the government's politburo. Despite the end of the war, some violence continued in southern Sudan. In 1974 and 1975, problems integrating former rebels into the army led to mutinies. Called Anyanya II, some insurgents who had rejected the Addis Ababa agreement continued limited operations during the 1970s and early 1980s.

Pressured by Islamists in the north, Numayri embarked on a program of Islamization and Arabization in the south in the early 1980s. In January 1983, southern soldiers in Bor and Pibor mutinied given orders transferring them to other parts of the country and after some fighting, many crossed into Ethiopia. In early June, Numayri declared "Republican Order Number One" which imposed direct rule by Khartoum on the south, proclaimed Arabic as the sole official language and cancelled regional integration of the military. This prompted further desertions of southern soldiers who joined Anyanya II fighters in the bush. These dissidents formed the Sudan People's Liberation Movement/Army (SPLM/A) under Colonel John Garang de Mabior. Since the revolutionary military regime in Ethiopia would not back a separatist movement, the SPLA declared its goal of founding a federal Sudan. This alienated Anyanya II fighters and led to violence between the predominantly Dinka SPLA and Nuer militias some of which began to receive arms from Khartoum. In 1984, Garang's SPLA attacked Sudan's most prominent development projects such as a Chevron oil exploration camp and a canal being dug by a French company. By the New Year, the SPLA had 10,000 insurgents in southern Sudan and another 20,000 in Ethiopia where the Mengistu regime compelled them to fight local separatist groups.

A 1985 military coup in Khartoum did nothing to end the war. Most southerners boycotted the 1986 election that brought a moderate Islamist coalition under Sadiq al-Mahdi to power and the new government engaged in negotiations with the SPLA that were suspended in August when a Shilluk SPLA unit shot down a Sudanese civilian airliner. Khartoum then mobilized Anyanya II Nuer militia to attack Shilluk communities. From 1987, the SPLA expanded rapidly as it enticed ethnic militias to its side, prevented the army from seizing food from rural communities and decreased its own food demands, while state forces became increasingly brutal. Sadiq's government, given lack of resources and distrust of its own soldiers many of whom came from the marginalized western region of Darfur, responded by forming local Arab militias that pursued genocidal violence against Dinka people in Bahr al-Ghazal and the inhabitants of the Nuba Mountains during the late 1980s. At the same time, the state military and SPLA conducted offensives and counter-offensives in parts of the south. By the end of 1988, some 3 million people had fled north, 300,000 Sudanese refugees were starving in Ethiopia and more than 250,000 people had died in the south.

In June 1989, another coup in Khartoum installed Brigadier Umar Hasan Ahmad al-Bashir as head of a government strongly influenced by the extremist National Islamic Front (NIF). Islamization and Arabization were renewed and the military expanded with the creation of the paramilitary Popular Defence Force that consisted of 150,000 northern conscripts. With the 1991 fall of Ethiopia's Mengistu regime, the SPLA lost its primary foreign backer. Around the same time, a major conflict developed within the SPLA with the primarily Dinka SPLA forces under Garang fighting several Nuer factions known as SPLA-Nasir and led by Riek Machar. In November 1991, the SPLA-Nasir massacred 2,000 Dinka civilians in Bor. Despite reasserting southern separatism, the SPLA-Nasir (briefly renamed SPLA-United) coordinated with the Khartoum regime from which it also received weapons and ammunition. These contradictions prompted violence within Machar's group which, in 1994, he renamed the South Sudan Independence Movement/ Army (SSIM/A). In 1996, Machar signed a peace agreement with Khartoum which created a federal Sudan and offered a vague promise of a referendum on the south's political future. While peace with the north meant that the SSIM could concentrate on fighting the SPLA, Machar's group lost legitimacy and began to wither. With the decline of the internal Dinka-Nuer conflict, Garang's SPLA recuperated from the mid-1990s and launched a series of successful operations that captured towns across the south. With Khartoum backing rebels in northern Uganda, Kampala now became the main SPLA sponsor. In 1997 Khartoum, continuing its divide-and-rule strategy, created the Council of the South, with Machar as head and national vice president and various pro-government militias were incorporated into state forces. However, rival Nuer militia continued to challenge Machar's fighters in oil-producing western Upper Nile. Machar's remaining credibility was destroyed when he formed the United Democratic Salvation Front in January 1999 to run in an upcoming Sudanese election in which all parties were committed to national unity and Islamic law.

The development of Sudan's oil industry during the 1990s and the 2001 terrorist attacks on the United States prompted Khartoum to improve relations with the West and abandon international Islamist terrorists such as Osama Bin Laden. While Sudan's growing oil revenues allowed it to purchase arms and continue military operations in the south into the early 2000s, the war was hampering oil production and damaging the national economy, and conscription was unpopular in the north. From the SPLA perspective, the long-suffering southern civilians desperately wanted peace. In January 2002, the Bashir regime and the SPLA signed a US-sponsored agreement in Geneva that created a ceasefire in the Nuba Mountains. In June, at talks in Kenya, the Sudanese government agreed to hold a referendum in the south on self-determination and the SPLA accepted Islamic law in the north. Bashir and Garang met in Uganda in July 2003 and launched a peace process. With rebellion in western Sudan's Darfur region, the establishment of the Government of South Sudan was delayed until 2005 when Garang became its president and a national vice president only to be killed shortly thereafter in a helicopter crash. In 2011, the people of South Sudan voted for independence which became official in July with SPLA veteran Salva Kiir Mayardit as president. Machar became a vice president but fled the country in 2013 when civil war broke out between Nuer and Dinka elements of the SPLA (Collins, 2010; Jok, 2015).

Ethiopia (1961–91)

Since the British had restored Haile Selassie's regime in Ethiopia during World War II, the emperor pursued a pro-Western policy during the early Cold War which included sending troops to fight as part of the UN force in the Korean Conflict (1950–3). Given this context, the UN federated the former Italian colony of Eritrea to Ethiopia in 1952 which was annexed a decade later. While Eritreans had been divided on the future of their strategically important Red Sea coastal territory with Christians wanting to join Ethiopia and Muslims favoring independence, they were not consulted on the federation. In 1960, Eritrean nationalists in Egypt formed the Eritrean Liberation Front (ELF) which, a year later, mounted hit-and-run attacks against Ethiopian occupation forces. Supported by Arab states such as Syria and Iraq, the ELF grew from 250 to 2,000 fighters during the first half of the 1960s and established some liberated zones in predominantly Muslim northern Eritrea. A fleet of high-speed boats maintained ELF supply lines with Yemen. During the late 1960s and early 1970s, Ethiopia, backed by the United States and Israel, pursued a brutal counter-insurgency campaign that alienated many Eritreans including Christians. By 1974, Ethiopian forces in Eritrea were restricted to major centers and used convoys to travel by road. However, around this time, the insurgent movement split between the Muslim-led ELF and the new Eritrean People's Liberation Front (EPLF) that had a revolutionary socialist agenda and predominantly Christian intellectual leadership. The two groups fought each other, while the EPLF also launched a conventional military campaign to liberate territory from the Ethiopians. Since Ethiopian forces were distracted by the overthrow of Haile Selassie in 1974 and the Ethiopia–Somalia War of 1977–8, the ELF and EPLF expanded to 30,000 and 40,000 fighters, respectively, and gained control of most of Eritrea, except the cities Asmara and Massawa.

In late 1978, Ethiopia's Mengistu regime, bolstered by massive Soviet military assistance and recent victory against Somalia, launched a major offensive in Eritrea that fatally weakened the ELF and pushed the EPLF back into the mountains. From 1978 to 1983, the Ethiopians mounted seven separate offensives that claimed the lives of 30,000 Eritreans and more than 50,000 Ethiopians. At times, the EPLF counter-attacked capturing weapons, and in the early 1980s, it eliminated the ELF. In January 1982, the Ethiopian government launched the Red Star campaign that was partly planned by Soviet advisors and involved 136,000 troops joining the 30,000–40,000 already in Eritrea. With tanks, artillery and aircraft, Ethiopian forces attacked the EPLF in the north, but the former were repulsed suffering heavy casualties. The EPLF then counter-attacked expanding into the former ELF area of western Eritrea. EPLF success was remarkable, as unlike Ethiopia, it lacked powerful foreign sponsors. The rebels received some support from Sudan, given Ethiopia's sponsorship of the SPLA, some EPLF leaders trained in China, and the Eritrean diaspora in Europe and North America also contributed. Conscripting recruits from liberated areas, the EPLF tried to create an ethnically and religiously mixed force. In 1987, with the help of Arab countries, it formed a fleet of high-speed boats that maintained a staging area at the Sudanese port of Aqiq and raided the Eritrean coast. When the war stalemated during the famine of the mid-1980s, the EPLF used conventional forces to defend its liberated zones and dispatched guerrillas to raid Ethiopian bases. At the same time, the Ethiopians wasted men in useless frontal attacks, conscription became unpopular, commanders were executed for failure, Mengistu interfered in operations and Eritrean civilians were massacred in reprisal for rebel attacks. The decline of Soviet support in the late 1980s weakened Ethiopian forces which enabled the EPLF to switch to the offensive. In March 1988, at the Battle of Afabet, the EPLF achieved its greatest military victory by killing or capturing 18,000 Ethiopian troops and seizing a huge amount of military equipment including fifty tanks and sixty artillery pieces. In turn, the EPLF gained complete control of northern and western Eritrea and began to move into the Ethiopian province of Tigray where it assisted anti-Mengistu rebels. While Ethiopia's peace with Somalia enabled the former to mount an offensive in Eritrea in May 1988, this failed, and into the next year, the EPLF helped expel Ethiopian forces from Tigray and its fighters moved into eastern Eritrea. In February 1990, the now 100,000-strong EPLF mounted Operation Fenkil, its largest action of the war involving ground and naval actions, which captured the port of Massawa. In May 1991, the EPLF captured the rest of Eritrea including Asmara and formed the core of conventional rebel forces that advanced on Addis Ababa and drove Mengistu into exile. Under an EPLF provisional government, Eritreans voted for independence in an April 1993 UN-supervised referendum, and a few days later, this became official. The EPLF changed its name to the Peoples' Front for Democracy and Justice and established an authoritarian state under former rebel leader Isaias Afwerki. Eritrea's almost thirty-year-long independence war claimed the lives of around 80,000 rebels, 150,000 Ethiopian troops and 100,000 Eritrean civilians. It was the first successful separatist military campaign in post-colonial African history.

Emerging in the early 1980s, the Tigray Peoples' Liberation Front (TPLF) had a pragmatic and well-educated leadership and advocated self-determination for Ethiopian peoples. Following the 1977–8 war with Somalia, the Marxist Mengistu regime alienated the inhabitants of the northern region of Tigray by imposing unpopular land reform, forcibly resettling rural communities, terrorizing urban elites and oppressing the Ethiopian Christian church. During the famine of the 1980s, the TPLF gained legitimacy and support by coordinating food deliveries in Tigray and to Ethiopian refugees in neighboring Sudan which allowed the rebel group to use its territory but not establish military bases. The Tigray rebels also used international humanitarian aid money to buy weapons. Facing a common enemy, the TPLF and EPLF allied and four TPLF brigades were sent to Eritrea to counter Mengistu's Red Star campaign. Although this alliance broke down in 1985, it was re-established in the late 1980s as both movements gained success against the weakened Ethiopian state. Unlike the EPLF that favored conventional warfare, the TPLF focused on guerrilla operations and did not try to control territory until the end of the 1980s. Mengistu's brutal counter-insurgency campaign in Tigray, which aggravated famine by disrupting agriculture and then denied international food aide to people in rebel areas, only made the TPLF more popular. In 1988, after the EPLF victory at Afabet, the TPLF launched its own offensive in Tigray which pushed back government forces, but the Ethiopia–Somalia peace agreement allowed Mengistu to mobilize 150,000 troops for a successful counter-offensive in the province. In 1989, with help from the EPLF which moved forces into Tigray, the TPLF transformed into a conventional army that recaptured many of the province's towns. In turn, the TPLF formed a coalition of anti-Mengistu groups known as the Ethiopian Peoples' Revolutionary Democratic Front (EPRDF) which included the Oromo Peoples' Democratic Organization comprising Oromo former government soldiers captured in Tigray. The war now expanded beyond Tigray and Eritrea. In February 1991, the EPRDF and EPLF initiated Operation Tewodros which ousted the regime from Gondar and Gojjam in the west, and was followed by May's Operation Walleligne which moved into eastern Ethiopia. With Mengistu's departure, the EPRDF formed a new government under former TPLF leader Meles Zenawi who gained favor from the West by dropping his socialist agenda. While Ethiopia theoretically became a multi-party democracy with regular elections, Zenawi developed a dictatorial and Tigrayan-dominated state that prompted insurgencies to flare up in other parts of the country such as among the Oromo majority of the center and south. From 2001, Zenawi's regime gained US support by joining the international struggle against Islamist terrorism which included Ethiopian military incursions into Somalia. Although the leaders of Eritrea and Ethiopia had cooperated in the overthrow of Mengistu, they fell out with each other as a border war flared between the two countries at the end of the 1990s (Tareke, 2009; Zewde, 2009, pp. 112–37; Reid, 2011, p. 164).

Somalia (1978–99)

Somalia's military regime, led by Siad Barre, was weakened by the failure of its 1977–8 invasion of Ethiopia. Since US-backed Somalia continued to encourage insurgents in Ethiopia's Ogaden region, the Soviet-sponsored Mengistu regime assisted a number of clan-based rebel movements that emerged in Somalia during the late 1970s and 1980s. At the end of the 1970s, some dissatisfied Somali military officers mostly from the northeastern Majeerteen clan, after failing to overthrow Barre, fled to Ethiopia where they formed the Somali Salvation Democratic Front (SSDF) that launched an insurgency back home. While SSDF and Ethiopian forces seized towns in central Somalia in 1982, US military assistance to the Barre government and internal conflicts among the rebels meant that the campaign was over by 1985. In 1981, members of the Isaaq clan formed the Somali National Movement (SNM) and launched a rebellion in the north by raiding a prison near Berbera. SNM attacks continued during the mid-1980s and state forces responded by executing civilians and attempting to block insurgent escape routes into Djibouti. The war came to the south in 1987 when exiled members of the southern Hawiye clan, who had occupied senior regime positions but were then persecuted by Barre, formed the United Somali Congress (USC) which split between the Abgal subclan from Mogadishu and the Habar Gidir subclan under former regime general Mohamed Farrah Aidid. In 1988, Mengistu and Barre, both facing escalating internal rebellions and diminishing superpower support, stopped backing insurgents in each other's countries and redeployed forces from the border to internal counter-insurgency operations. Expelled from Ethiopia, SNM forces invaded Somalia where they gained control of the north and captured weapons and vehicles from Barre's military. Half a million people from northern Somalia fled into Ethiopia and Djibouti. Barre fled Mogadishu in January 1991 after his order to bombard Hawiye neighborhoods provoked a widespread uprising. The Somalia military disbanded with soldiers joining various armed factions. Pursued by Aidid's USC, Barre fled to the southwest where he tried to rally his Marrehan clansmen as the Somali National Front (SNF), but he fled into Kenya in May and never returned. The Abgal and Habar Gidir USC factions battled over Mogadishu until July when they agreed to form an interim government. Chaos in the south prompted secession in the comparatively stable north which had once been a British colony. In May 1991, the popular SNM declared the independence of the Somaliland Republic in the northwest, and later, in 1998, Puntland was founded in the northeast. These states survived but were not formally recognized by other countries.

Fighting between the USC factions in Mogadishu resumed in September 1991. By August 1992, there were 500,000 Somali refugees in Ethiopia, 300,000 in Kenya, 65,000 in Yemen, 15,000 in Djibouti and 100,000 in Europe. The UN predicted that 1.5 million Somalis would shortly die from famine caused by war and drought. In Mogadishu and other southern

Figure 4.2 Siad Barre (1919–95), president of the Somali Democratic Republic
from 1969–91

Source: Government of Somalia/Wikimedia Commons

ports, faction leaders blocked the delivery of international food relief, and
Aidid demanded the departure of a few hundred peacekeepers from the
UN Operation in Somalia (UNOSOM) that had been established in April
1992 to supervise an ultimately failed ceasefire. In early December, the
United States launched Operation Restore Hope (also known as United Task
Force or UNITAF) as a US-led and UN-authorized international intervention
to facilitate humanitarian assistance through the creation of a safe zone.
UNITAF's 37,000 personnel, 25,000 of whom were Americans, occupied
Mogadishu harbor and airport, and the port of Kismayo and while food
was distributed, the Somali factions were not disarmed. During this operation, Belgian, Italian and Canadian peacekeepers were involved in abuse
and killing of Somali civilians. In May 1993, UNITAF was replaced by
UNOSOM II which aimed to disarm militias and establish a new government. Most US troops withdrew, but the 22,000 UN peacekeepers were
supported by a US quick reaction force and US navy ships off the coast.
After Aidid's fighters were involved in attacks on UN forces, the American
Clinton administration orchestrated a Special Forces raid to capture him
which backfired with two helicopters shot down and eighteen US troops
killed. The US hunt for Aidid was quickly abandoned, and in March 1994,
US ground forces left Somalia. Given the failure of peacekeeping, the UN

Security Council voted in November 1993 to withdraw UNOSOM II, with its final elements departing via US naval vessels in March 1995. This troubled affair contributed to the "Somalia Syndrome" in which Western countries became hesitant to stage military interventions for humanitarian reasons. Somalia became the quintessential "failed state," given lack of an effective government and continued factional violence. Ironically, after 2001, the United States began to militarily support secular Somali warlords against the rising Islamic Courts Union (ICU) that had begun to stabilize parts of the south. Concerned that southern Somalia would become a sanctuary for Islamist terrorists, the United States encouraged Ethiopia to invade in 2006. While the ICU was pushed out of Mogadishu, Kismayo and other towns, it continued a guerrilla war against the African Union Mission in Somalia (AMISOM) that arrived the next year. When some ICU members joined the transitional Somalia government, a radical ICU faction called Al Shabaab renewed the struggle that included fighting in Mogadishu. Around the same time, some Somalis turned to piracy in the Red Sea, given the absence of state control, the proliferation of small arms and the collapse of the local fishery (Lewis, 2008; Rutherford, 2008; Njoku, 2013, pp. 137–60).

Uganda, Rwanda and Burundi (1981–99)

Regionalism plagued post-colonial Uganda. While southerners had been relatively more influential during British colonial rule, after independence in 1962, the northern-dominated regimes of Milton Obote and Idi Amin became increasingly violent. Following the 1979 Tanzanian invasion of Uganda that overthrew the Amin dictatorship, former President Obote returned to power in a disputed December 1980 election. This was resented by former rebels from the south who had been exiled in Tanzania and who had helped oust Amin. As such, Yoweri Museveni formed the National Resistance Movement/Army (NRM/A) and launched an insurgency in the south. Among the rebels were many Rwandan Tutsi refugees such as Fred Rwigyima and Paul Kagame who had fled their home country's Hutu government many years before but then experienced xenophobia in Obote's Uganda. The rebellion began in February 1981 when thirty-five NRA insurgents, personally led by Museveni, raided a military police academy at Kabamba in Uganda. A guerrilla war unfolded in the Luwero Triangle northwest of the capital Kampala. With only a few weapons sent from Libya, the NRA depended on capturing arms and supplies from Ugandan state forces. Since Museveni had been trained in guerrilla warfare in Mozambique, the NRA focused on political education and gaining support from rural communities. The NRA also enforced a strict code of conduct among its fighters who could be executed for abusing civilians. Simultaneously, the mostly northern Ugandan soldiers sent to the Luwero Triangle imposed a reign of terror, forced people into detention camps and were seen as a foreign occupation army, all of which encouraged local people to support the NRA. Human rights abuses eventually lost the Obote regime most of its foreign support, except for North Korea. While the rebels initially avoided large Ugandan military sweeps of the triangle, the NRA grew, and, by the mid-1980s, had transformed into a conventional army with battalions that effectively challenged state forces. Within the NRA, Rwigyima and Salim Saleh, Museveni's brother, emerged as successful commanders. By 1985, some 280,000 people had fled the Luwero Triangle where around 300,000 people had been killed in the war. In July 1985, the beleaguered Obote was overthrown by northern military officers who engaged in ultimately failed negotiations with the NRA. In late 1985, the NRA received its first significant external support in the form of weapons and ammunition from Libya and Tanzania. In January 1986, a 10,000-strong NRA division assaulted Kampala which was seized after heavy fighting. The remnants of the Ugandan army retreated north, were engaged by pursuing NRA forces at Kitgum in March and then crossed into Sudan. Museveni's predominantly southern NRM formed a one-party state and the NRA transformed into the state military and was renamed the Uganda People's Defence Force (UPDF) in 1995 (Ngoga, 1998; Kainerugaba, 2010).

Beginning with the overthrow of Amin in 1979, northern Uganda became the scene of a number of insurgencies. During the early 1980s, former Amin regime members formed rebel groups in Amin's home West Nile District located in the extreme north of Uganda on the Sudan border. The Former Uganda National Army (FUNA), comprising Amin's Kakwa ethnic group, quickly retreated into Sudan and Zaire. The Uganda National Rescue Front (UNRF), led by Brigadier Moses Ali and composed of ethnic Aringa fighters, gained control of West Nile from 1980 to 1982 but were then driven into Sudan by Obote's army that slaughtered civilians. The seizure of power by Museveni's primarily southern NRA expanded insurgency in the north. The Ugandan army that had been driven into Sudan in 1986 formed the Uganda Peoples' Democratic Army (UPDA) and with Khartoum's support launched a guerrilla war among northern Uganda's Acholi people. Frustrated by their group's ineffective campaign, some UPDA fighters eventually joined other religiously inspired northern rebel groups. Around 1986, the Christian millenarian Holy Spirit Movement (HSM) led by spirit medium Alice Auma emerged within Acholi society and formed the Holy Spirit Mobile Force (HSMF) that fought the NRA. Rejecting guerrilla operations, the HSMF used "Holy Spirit Tactics" that combined conventional warfare with beliefs that holy oil would protect soldiers from bullets, hurled rocks would turn into grenades and the most effective battlefield formation was the shape of a cross. The 6,000 to 10,000-strong HSMF mounted a stunningly successful offensive that pushed the NRA back to the south but was defeated at Jinja, just 50 km from Kampala, in October 1987. The defeat of the HSM gave rise to another religious rebel movement in Acholiland. Led by Joseph Kony, who claimed family relation to Alice Auma who had fled to Kenya, it was called the Lord's Resistance Army (LRA). Although the LRA adopted some of the beliefs and practices of the defunct HSM, Kony pursued a guerrilla war against Museveni's state and brutally extorted food and recruits including children from Acholi rural communities.

The war in the north undermined Museveni's positive international image as a new type of ethical and effective African leader. In 1991, motivated by a World Bank loan conditional on security, Museveni launched Operation North in Acholiland, which involved the arrest of all Acholi political leaders and the detention of tens of thousands in an effort to root out LRA insurgents. The NRM state conscripted thousands of Acholi men into "Arrow Groups" and sent these militias to fight the much better-armed LRA who later targeted these people and their families. Museveni's government then tried to negotiate with the LRA which took advantage of the lull in the fighting to regroup and rearm with the help of Khartoum that wanted to punish Kampala for its support of SPLA insurgents in southern Sudan. The cost of Khartoum's support was that the LRA had to fight the SPLA in southern Sudan which prompted the NRA (renamed UPDF) to conduct cross-border operations. In 1996, the UPDF began driving rural Acholi into "protected villages" near towns where farming was impossible, food was supplied by humanitarian organizations and movement was strictly controlled. Within a few years, 1.5 million people were confined to these squalid rural prisons. By 2006, a combination of factors had driven Kony's LRA out of northern Uganda; Khartoum halted its support to the rebels as it wanted better international relations so it could sell oil and Sudan's north-south civil war had ended, the UPDF launched a number of major offensives in both northern Uganda and southern Sudan, the Ugandan government expanded local militias and Acholi people rejected the insurgents' outrageously vicious behavior. Negotiation between the Uganda government and LRA, which included amnesty offers, was undermined by the 2005 International Criminal Court (ICC) indictment of Kony on war crimes charges. After 2006, the LRA moved to the isolated, forested and lawless border region of the Democratic Republic of Congo (DRC: formerly Zaire) and the Central African Republic where it continued to terrorize communities and abduct children to serve as fighters and/or slaves.

In the mid-1990s, insurgencies developed in other parts of Uganda. While Museveni's government had quieted the situation in West Nile by incorporating UNRF rebels into the NRA, this changed given problems with military integration and the continuing marginalization of the area. In 1994, the West Nile Bank Front (WNBF), led by Juma Oris who had been part of the now defunct FUNA, started a guerrilla war against the state, but its alliance with the LRA led to extreme violence toward civilians and the movement failed to gain popularity. With staging areas in Zaire and support from Sudan, the WNBF disrupted SPLA supply lines from Uganda into southern Sudan. In 1996, disgruntled members of the original UNRF split from the WNBF to form UNRF II which, also encouraged by Khartoum, pursued its own war against the Ugandan state. Around the same time, Sudanese agents orchestrated a rebellion in western Uganda that built on long-simmering tensions in the Ruwenzori Mountains and involved marginalized Ugandan Muslims. The presence of these Allied Democratic Forces (ADF) in neighboring Zaire prompted Museveni's government to join Rwanda's invasion of that country during the First Congo War of 1996–7. It was during that conflict, in 1997, that a unit of 4,000 WNBF fighters escaped encirclement by Ugandan and Rwandan forces by entering southern Sudan where they were ambushed and almost annihilated by SPLA fighters. In 1998, the Ugandan military, which had again intervened in eastern DRC together with Rwanda, attacked WNBF and ADF forces. The WNBF dissolved as it was denied cross-border sanctuary and the Ugandan army mounted an effective counter-insurgency campaign in West Nile that gained the support of local people and convinced rebels to surrender. In 2002, with the end of the Second Congo War (1998–2002) and a decline in Sudanese support, UNRF II signed a peace deal and its rebels were demobilized with some integrated into the Ugandan military. As one of many armed groups in eastern DRC that became involved in illegal mining, the ADF survived the Second Congo War and mounted limited attacks into Uganda as well as a 2010 bombing in Kampala (Prunier, 2009, pp. 80–6, 120–1, 132–3, 193, 196–7, 308, 321–2; Allen and Vlassenroot, 2010; Branch, 2011; Cline, 2013).

In Rwanda, the Belgian colonial rulers had favored the Tutsi minority who they considered a superior race, but during the decolonization process of the late 1950s, a Hutu counter-elite took power, establishing a majoritarian republic that became independent in 1962. Since Tutsi-educated elites were turning to African nationalism and socialism in the 1950s, the Belgians consisted the conservative and anti-communist Hutu leaders as better post-colonial partners. In the early 1960s, an armed and exiled Rwandan Tutsi movement had developed in neighboring countries, particularly in Burundi where local Tutsi retained power with the help of communist China. However, armed incursions into Rwanda by exiled Tutsi in 1964 were thwarted by the Belgian-led Rwandan Hutu military and incited revenge massacres of Tutsi inside Rwanda which some called genocide. For the next few decades, the exiled Rwandan Tutsi movement was in disarray. While a new generation of Rwandan Tutsi refugees in Uganda had joined the NRA in the early 1980s and then continued into Museveni's Ugandan state force, they were eventually sidelined, given Ugandan xenophobia. These Rwandan–Ugandan soldiers, who also formed the exiled Rwandan Patriotic Front (RPF), then decided to use their military skills and resources to take over their country of origin.

At the start of October 1990, some 2,500 Rwandan Tutsi soldiers led by Major General Fred Rwigyima deserted Uganda's NRA with their weapons and equipment and invaded neighboring Rwanda. The 5,200-strong Rwanda Armed Forces (FAR), although it had armored vehicles and helicopters, was surprised by the incursion and lacked combat experience.

The RPF force quickly advanced 60 km south of the border but was slowed by stretched supply lines, roads blocked by refugees and the murder of Rwigyima by two of his officers during a dispute over strategy. The entirely Hutu FAR staged a fake rebel attack on Kigali to justify arresting and killing Tutsi civilians. France, which had a defense agreement with the Rwandan regime of President Juvenal Habyarimana, sent weapons to the FAR and enacted Operation Noroit in which 500 French paratroopers were sent to secure Kigali and assist Rwandan state troops. The Mobutu regime in Zaire sent 1,000 soldiers to support Kigali, but they behaved so badly toward Rwandan civilians that they were promptly sent home. With French support, the FAR launched a counter-offensive in early October that pushed the RPF back to Akagera National Park in the northeast. At the end of the month, Paul Kagame, hastily returned from military training in the United States, took command of the RPF and led it into the Virunga Mountains where it regrouped and initiated a hit-and-run war against the Rwandan state that responded by massacring more Tutsi civilians. Recruits from the Rwandan Tutsi diaspora flocked to the RPF which grew from 5,000 in early 1991 to 12,000 at the close of 1992 to 25,000 in April 1994. Ugandan military officers covertly supplied their former colleagues and money raised from the Rwandan Tutsi diaspora bought weapons from bankrupt former Soviet republics. Recruiting from the Hutu peasantry and unemployed urban youth, the FAR expanded from 5,200 in October 1990 to 30,000 by the end of 1991 to 50,000 by mid-1992. The FAR's minimal training meant that French advisors played an active role in combat. Negotiations and ceasefire were attempted, but both sides lacked commitment to them as the FAR was confident in French military assistance and the RPF believed it was safe in the Virungas. While a shaky ceasefire was implemented in July 1993, a massacre of 300 Tutsi prompted the RPF to mount a February 1993 offensive that doubled the size of its occupied territory. RPF units came to within 23 km of Kigali but stopped as the capital was protected by French troops. In April, both sides returned to negotiations in Arusha, Tanzania, where some progress was made. The Rwandan state was militarily spent and was pressured by the UN to end the war, and the RPF worried about its perceived legitimacy as their occupied area was virtually depopulated, given the flight of terrified Hutu civilians. In August, the Habyarimana government, moderate Rwandan opposition parties and the RPF signed the Arusha Accords in which they promised to form a combined transitional government and state security force, and to allow almost 1 million Tutsi exiles to return. The UN Assistance Mission for Rwanda (UNAMIR), a 2,500-strong force but with only two combat battalions, arrived to supervise the settlement. However, within Rwanda, Hutu extremists decried the deal and used newspapers and radio to spread hate against the Tutsi minority. In early April 1994, Habyarimana's aircraft was shot down while approaching Kigali airport, and elements of the FAR and Hutu militias attempted to exterminate the Tutsi minority so as to avoid the power-sharing deal. Over the next 100 days, some 800,000 people were killed in what amounted to the world's deadliest genocide since 1945. UNAMIR proved incapable of stopping the slaughter. Soon after the killings began, Kagame's RPF set off on an aggressive three-pronged offensive that pushed back the FAR and secured the country by the end of July. The French military, during Operation Turquoise, briefly established an occupied zone in southwestern Rwanda which was officially meant to provide safety to civilians but ended up serving as an escape route for retreating elements of the FAR and Hutu militias who slaughtered Tutsi on their way into eastern Zaire. The RPF seized power in Rwanda, with its fighters forming the new national army. The presence of exiled Rwandan Hutu fighters in eastern Zaire would serve as context for two RPF invasions of that country in the late 1990s (Prunier, 1995; Des Forges, 1999; Mamdani, 2001; Melvern, 2006; Wallis, 2006).

Although Burundi's social structure was/is very similar to Rwanda and it also gained independence from Belgium in 1962, the Tutsi-dominated military toppled the monarchy in 1966 and thwarted the rise of a Rwanda-style Hutu republic. In 1972, an incursion by exiled Burundian Hutu rebels from Tanzania served as an excuse for the Burundian military regime to exterminate the country's educated Hutu and Hutu students to prevent the rise of a Hutu political opposition. In this genocide, some 200,000–300,000 people were killed, but no one was ever held accountable as the Tutsi military regime remained in power for many years. In 1980, exiled Burundian Hutu activists in Tanzania formed the Party for the Liberation of the Hutu People (PALIPEHUTU) that sought to overturn minority Tutsi domination, though its military activities were limited. The 1988 killing of 300 Tutsi by Hutu peasants and the revenge massacre of 20,000 Hutu by the Tutsi military, together with the broader context of liberalization in Africa, prompted political reforms in Burundi. A 1993 election resulted in Melchior Ndadaye of the Front for Democracy in Burundi (FRODEBU) becoming the country's first Hutu president, but within a few months, he was assassinated by Tutsi soldiers. The next Hutu President Cyprien Ntaryamira died in the same 1994 plane crash as President Habyarimana of Rwanda. During this period, violence between Burundi's Tutsi and Hutu resulted in 50,000–100,000 deaths and many people fled into Rwanda which inflamed the situation there. Over the next two years, Burundi's Tutsi security force officials and extremists used intimidation and violence to render elected Hutu FRODEBU officials powerless. In June 1994, some FRODEBU leaders established the National Council for the Defence of Democracy (CNDD) with an armed wing called Forces for the Defence of Democracy (FDD) which launched an insurgency with the goal of restructuring the Burundian military and holding internationally monitored elections. In 1995, as the pro-democracy FDD and the radically anti-Tutsi PALIPEHUTU attacked the army and Tutsi civilians, Burundi's military expelled Hutu from Bujumbura and massacred Hutu in rural areas. In July 1996, the military returned to formal power as Tutsi officer Pierre Buyoya overthrew civilian Hutu President Sylvestre

Ntibantunganyu. Some 300,000 rural Hutu were herded into concentration camps to prevent them aiding the rebels who were now active in eleven of Burundi's fifteen provinces. While the Rwandan and Burundian invasion of eastern Zaire in 1996–7 destroyed CNDD-FDD staging areas and undermined their struggle, PALIPEHUTU shifted back to Tanzania and expanded its insurgency within Burundi. In late December 2000, PALIPEHUTU rebels stopped a bus outside Bujumbura and killed twenty Tutsi passengers plus a British humanitarian worker.

In 2000, a peace process was mediated by South Africa's Nelson Mandela, and although this was initially rejected by Burundi's insurgents, the end of the Second Congo War (1998–2002) prompted the FDD to join negotiations at the close of 2002. In 2003, the African Union Mission in Burundi arrived to supervise a transitional power-sharing agreement, and the following year, these peacekeepers were transformed into the United Nations Peace Operation in Burundi. In 2005, Pierre Nkurunziza, a Hutu CNDD-FDD leader, was elected president, and the next year, PALIPEHUTU abandoned the armed struggle though violence continued until 2008. In 2015, Nkurunziza's decision to seek an unconstitutional third presidential term incited a failed coup attempt and a series of political assassinations as fearful people fled to neighboring countries (Lemarchand, 1994; Watt, 2008; Lemarchand, 2009).

Post-Cold War conflicts in West Africa (1989–99)

During the mid-nineteenth century, freed black slaves from the United States founded the West African Republic of Liberia that their descendants, called Americo-Liberians, dominated until the late twentieth century. In 1980, Master Sergeant Samuel Doe overthrew the Americo-Liberian government and became Liberia's first indigenous head-of-state. However, he ruled the country for the benefit of his small Krahn ethnic group that alienated other Liberians and provoked rebellion. In December 1989, fighters from the National Patriotic Front of Liberia (NPFL), led by Charles Taylor, invaded the country from neighboring Cote d'Ivoire and were sponsored by Libya's Gaddafi who saw himself as a champion of African revolutionary struggles. Within Liberia, the NPLF was supported by the Gio and Mano ethnic groups who had been victimized by the Doe regime. The incompetent Liberian military was unable to halt the NPFL advance to the fringe of Monrovia where a faction calling itself the Independent National Patriotic Front of Liberia (INPFL) broke away. The regional Economic Community of West African States (ECOWAS) dispatched a peacekeeping force called the ECOWAS Monitoring Group (ECOMOG) and made up mostly of Nigerian and Ghanaian troops, but it failed to contain the rebellion. Doe was captured and killed by the INPFL. While Taylor's NPFL was not strong enough to seize Monrovia, it provided timber and iron ore to international companies in exchange for weapons. After ECOMOG suffered heavy casualties repelling an October 1992 NPFL offensive against the capital, the number of peacekeepers was increased to 14,500, but they lacked resolve for a counter-offensive into the countryside. On the other hand, ECOMOG's capture of the port of Buchanan in 1994 reduced Taylor's international connections. Although INPFL declined, other rebel groups emerged such as the United Liberian Movement for Democracy (ULIMO) which split along ethnic lines with a Krahn-oriented ULIMO-J headed by Roosevelt Johnson and a mostly Mandingo ULIMO-K under Alhaji Kromah which was backed by mining companies. The Nigerian military government of Sani Abacha, ECOMOG's major contributor and Taylor's NPFL became tired by four years of war. As such, in mid-1995, ECOWAS and NPFL signed the Abuja Accords which imposed a ceasefire, created a transitional government and promised eventual disarmament and elections. In April 1996, with ECO-MOG unable to enforce the ceasefire, NPFL and ULIMO-K mounted a joint attack on ULIMO-J and other allied groups including the Liberian military in which some 1,500 people were killed in Monrovia. Taylor won a July 1997 election mostly because he threatened to continue the war if he lost. During the civil war, combatants dressed in bizarre costumes including shower caps, carnival masks, Rambo T-shirts and women's wigs, and some leaders took dramatic names such as ULIMO-J's Joshua Milton Blahyi who adopted the nom-de-guerre "General Butt Naked" as he believed fighting without clothes would render him invulnerable. Some 40,000 fighters were under the age of fifteen. Undisciplined ECOMOG troops gained a reputation for looting that earned them the moniker "Every Car or Movable Object Gone." The Liberian civil war destroyed much of the country's limited infrastructure, caused the death of around 200,000 people mostly from starvation and disease, prompted 800,000 refugees to flee to neighboring states and internally displaced some 1.25 million. ECOMOG began to withdraw from Liberia in October 1999, but a few months later, in July 2000, fighters from Liberians United for Reconciliation and Democracy (LURD), a rebel group made up primarily of Mandingos who had been oppressed by Taylor, invaded from Guinea where the government of Lansana Conte armed them in return for agricultural products and diamonds. LURD rebels eventually advanced to Monrovia where another regional intervention force, ECOWAS Mission to Liberia, was deployed in 2002. Taylor fled to Nigeria in 2003 and was eventually sent to the ICC where, in 2012, he was convicted for war crimes and crimes against humanity related to his sponsorship of the Revolutionary United Front (RUF) in neighboring Sierra Leone.

The Liberian civil war destabilized Sierra Leone. Some 100,000 Liberian refugees worsened Sierra Leone's existing economic problems and the involvement of Sierra Leone's military in ECOMOG prompted Taylor to support the rebellion of the RUF which began in 1991. At that time, Sierra Leone, like many African countries, was under a waning authoritarian regime that had been in power since the 1970s. Led by former army corporal

Fodah Sankoh and former student radicals, the RUF quickly captured several towns but was then pushed back by the Sierra Leone military with logistical support from Britain and the United States. Given disruption associated with the 1992 military coup that brought Captain Valentine Strasser to power, the RUF gained control of diamond-producing areas and exported diamonds via Taylor's NPFL in Liberia. By January 1995, the RUF was within 100 km of Freetown. Since the RUF's extremely violent methods damaged its once popular support, villages formed Kamajor militias based on traditional hunting societies. They were derisively called "Sobels," meaning that they were both soldiers and rebels. In March 1995, the Sierra Leone government hired the South African-based mercenary company Executive Outcomes (EO) which provided 500 military advisors and 3,000 combat troops who, together with several helicopter gunships, regained control over much of the country. However, the elected government of Ahmad Tejan Kabbah withdrew the EO contract in 1996 which gave the RUF a chance to recover. The May 1997 coup attempt by Major Johnny Paul Koromah and his Armed Forces Revolutionary Council (AFRC), a faction from the Sierra Leone military, resulted in mass violence in Freetown between newly arrived ECOMOG peacekeepers and some 6,000 RUF rebels who entered the city. ECOMOG secured Freetown by March 1998 and the RUF withdrew into the countryside. In January 1999, the AFRC and RUF again attacked Freetown which compelled beleaguered President Kabbah to end the war. In July's Lome Peace Accord, RUF leader Sankoh became Sierra Leone's vice president and minister of mines in exchange for an agreement to demobilize and disarm the RUF under the supervision of a joint ECOMOG-UN peacekeeping force. The UN Mission to Sierra Leone began arriving in the country in December 1999, and by March 2001, it had become the world's largest peacekeeping mission with 17,500 personnel. In May 2000, the British military launched Operation Palliser which initially was aimed at evacuating British, Commonwealth and European citizens and facilitating the delivery of humanitarian aid. However, British commander General David Richards used his expeditionary force to eliminate the RUF that was still engaged in violence and kidnapping. Sankoh, whose bodyguards had fired at civilians, was arrested and died of a stroke in 2003 while awaiting a war crimes trial by a UN-backed court. By March 2002, more than 50,000 rebels had been disarmed and the RUF disappeared as a fighting force (Ellis, 2001; Levitt, 2005; Dorman, 2009).

When France granted independence to its West African territories in 1960, the historically nomadic Tuareg people of the Sahel and Sahara were divided between the new states of Mali, Niger, Burkina Faso and Algeria. As the Tuaregs became increasingly marginalized and impoverished, their isolated home areas eventually became the scene of developing mining industries including the production of uranium which became of strategic and economic importance to France and the post-colonial Sahelian states. In 1962, Tuaregs in Mali stated a rebellion aimed at creating a new Tuareg state called

Azawad that would consist of parts of several countries in the Sahel/Sahara region. While the 1,500 rebels relied on camels for transport and fought with obsolete small arms, the Malian army was supplied with superior Soviet arms. By 1964, the insurgency was crushed, but the brutality of the state campaign alienated many hitherto moderate Tuaregs and forced many out of the country. A 1968 coup by Moussa Traore returned Mali to the France's network of African client states. During the 1970s and 1980s, many Tuaregs from Mali and Niger, given drought, moved to Libya to work in the oil industry or in Gaddafi's "Arab Legion" which sent them to fight in Chad, Afghanistan and Lebanon. Many of these radicalized and militarily experienced Tuaregs returned home in the late 1980s, given a decline in Libyan oil production and the Soviet withdrawal from Afghanistan. In 1990, several Tuareg separatist groups, well-armed by Libya and including both secular and Islamist fighters, mounted insurgencies in Mali and Niger. After the failure of its vicious counter-insurgency program, the Malian government of Moussa Traore negotiated with the rebels and concluded the 1991 "Tamanrasset Accords" which promised to integrate insurgents into the security forces and grant some autonomy and development funds to the north. However, violence continued, and in 1994, non-Tuaregs in the north formed a state-armed militia called the Malian Patriotic Movement or Ganda Koi that attacked Tuaregs. The 1995 "Ouagadougou Accords" ended the insurgency in northern Niger as the government promised to absorb some Tuareg rebels into the military, and help demobilize others. Problems implementing these peace agreements led to further Tuareg rebellions from 2006 to 2009 in Mali and Niger and in 2012 in Mali which prompted a major French military intervention under the banner of the global "war on terror" (Lecocq, 2010; Keenan, 2013; Webb, 2016).

Following its 1962 independence from France, Algeria was governed by the secular and militaristic National Liberation Front (FLN) which had fought the anti-colonial war of the 1950s. At the end of the 1980s, Algeria, given protest brought on by economic problems and the changing international political context, embarked on multi-party democratic reforms in which the National Islamic Front (FIS) rose to popularity among the urban poor. In January 1992, the Algerian military, dominated by FLN officers who feared the rise of Islamists, took power and cancelled recent elections in which the FIS had done well. With the banning of the FIS, its members turned to guerrilla warfare by forming the Islamic Armed Movement (MIA) in the mountains and the Armed Islamic Group (GIA) in the urban areas. The presence of recently returned veterans of the war against the Soviet Union in Afghanistan furthered Islamist radicalism. In 1993, the more extremist GIA declared war on the relatively moderate FIS and MIA and targeted anyone associated with the government or civil society. Although the Algerian military had lost its Soviet support at the start of the 1990s, it used oil money to buy weapons from cash-strapped Russia and dramatically expanded its paramilitary forces to around 180,000 personnel who did most of the fighting in the civil war. The GIA remained small with 2,000–3,000 insurgents. In 1994, the GIA declared Algiers a liberated zone, proclaimed an Islamic caliphate and extended its attacks to France with the hijacking of a French airliner. In the countryside, the FIS and MIA formed the Islamic Salvation Army (AIS) which condemned GIA violence against civilians and advocated democracy. Following the 1995 election of General Liamine Zeroual who defeated several Islamist candidates to become president, the GIA began to massacre entire villages, seeing anyone not fighting the government as apostates and stepped up its war against the AIS. In September 1997, the AIS declared a ceasefire with the government and negotiated amnesty for its members. After Zeroual's sudden death, FLN veteran Abdelaziz Bouteflika was elected as president in 1999 and embarked on a program that reduced violence by granting amnesty to rebels who had not committed murder or rape. By 2002, the GIA had been effectively destroyed by internal conflict and successful army operations facilitated by US military support that began after the September 2001 attacks on the United States. From 2004, Algeria continued the amnesty program and encouraged the demobilization of many more insurgents. The Islamist struggle was continued by the Salafist Group for Preaching and Combat (GSPC), which had split from the GIA in 1998 and moved south into Niger, Mali and Chad where its members eventually became involved in local conflicts such as the Tuareg insurgency. In 2007, GSPC joined a wider international jihadist network by taking the name Al-Qaeda in the Islamic Maghreb (AQIM). (Willis, 1997; Martinez, 2000).

5 Post-colonial inter-state conflicts (c. 1960–2000)

Introduction

Wars between African states were uncommon in the post-colonial late twentieth century as African governments generally accepted the borders inherited from the colonial powers. Some of the inter-state conflicts that developed from the 1960s to 1980s were expanded and intensified by Cold War superpower involvement. The Soviet Union and the United States sponsored different sides in conflicts between Egypt and Israel, Somalia and Ethiopia, Angola and South Africa, and Chad and Libya. These state-versus-state wars also sometimes took place within the context of civil wars. For example, as Angolan state forces clashed with the South African military they also had to contend with Angolan rebels backed by Pretoria and Washington. Africa also experienced some short border conflicts including the 1977–8 Egypt–Libya War, the 1985 Mali–Burkina Faso War and the 1998–2000 Eritrea–Ethiopia War. The 1979 Kagera War started as border clash but resulted in the Tanzanian invasion of Uganda. Post-colonial Africa's largest inter-state war began at the end of the twentieth century when the Democratic Republic of Congo (DRC) was invaded by a half dozen neighboring states who fought each other, backed local armed factions and plundered resources.

Egypt–Israeli wars (1956–73)

In 1948, the inexperienced Egyptian military participated in a failed effort by Arab countries to prevent the formation of the Jewish state of Israel. Israeli aircraft bombed Cairo and Israeli commandos sunk an Egyptian warship sent to Tel Aviv. This defeat inspired the increasingly popular Muslim Brotherhood to attack British occupation forces and businesses in Egypt. In July 1952, the Free Officers Movement, led by Arab nationalist Colonel Gamal Abdel Nassar, overthrew the feckless King Faruk. The withdrawal of British troops from the Suez Canal zone from 1954 to June 1956 meant that the Nassar regime blocked Israeli shipping and supplied Palestinian resistance fighters. The US and British rejection of Egyptian requests for military assistance pushed Nassar closer to the Soviet Union from which he obtained arms including tanks and jet fighters. This prompted the World Bank to withdraw funding for Egypt's planned Aswan Dam and, in turn, Cairo nationalized the Anglo-French Suez Canal in 1956 so as to use the profits toward dam construction. Consequently, Britain and France, resentful over Nassar's support for anti-colonial movements, colluded with Israel to invade Egypt before the arrival of more Soviet weapons. At the end of October and beginning of November 1956, the Israeli army invaded Egypt's Sinai Peninsula, while British and French troops were landed at Port Said and occupied the Suez Canal. The Egyptian army was unable to stop the invasion and many Egyptian aircraft were destroyed on the ground and an Egyptian warship was sunk. However, the international community widely criticized the intervention and the United States refused to support it given the threat of Soviet intervention. As such, the United Nations dispatched its first peacekeeping force to supervise a ceasefire, and by late December, British and French troops had left the Canal Zone and Israeli forces had withdrawn from Sinai. The Suez Crisis demonstrated that the old colonial powers would have to defer to the two post-World War II superpowers – the United States and the Soviet Union.

In early 1967, violence between Israel and Syria prompted the latter to invoke its defense pact with Egypt. Nassar expelled UN peacekeepers from the Sinai and replaced them with two Egyptian army divisions. It is unlikely that the Egyptians were planning to invade Israel as their forces, at this point, were embroiled in a counter-insurgency campaign in support of the government in Yemen. By this time, the 200,000-strong Egyptian military had been equipped and trained by the Soviet Union. On June 5, 1967, the Israeli Air Force (IAF) conducted a preemptive strike that destroyed the air forces of Egypt, Syria and Jordan. The IAF lost twenty-six aircraft but destroyed 400, most of which were on the ground. On the same day, Israeli mechanized forces advanced through the Sinai and reached the Suez Canal as poorly led Egyptian troops fled. Success in the "Six Day War," which Tel Aviv claimed to have launched to protect itself from eradication, gave Israel the buffer zones of Sinai and Golan Heights against its respective enemies Egypt and Syria, and control of water sources on the West Bank.

After the 1967 war, Israel fortified the eastern bank of the Suez Canal. In 1969, Nassar cancelled the ceasefire that had ended the previous war which led to a short air campaign over the Suez Canal in which Israel destroyed Egyptian air defenses. In September 1970, Nassar died and was replaced by Anwar Sadat, the former vice president, who directed preparations for an offensive in the Sinai, though this was undermined by a purge of the Egyptian officer corps. At the start of October 1973, during the Jewish holiday of Yom Kippur, the Egyptians undertook a massive artillery and aerial bombardment of Israeli defenses along the east bank of the Suez Canal which was then crossed by 80,000 Egyptian troops using Soviet-made bridging equipment. Egyptian forces operated under the cover of a massive air defense system that included surface-to-air missiles and radar-guided anti-aircraft guns. Surprised Israeli forces initially withdrew in the Sinai and focused on defeating the simultaneous and much more dangerous Syrian offensive in the Golan Heights. However, when Egyptian ground forces advanced beyond the cover of their air defense system, they were badly mauled by redeployed Israeli armor and air strikes. Indeed, Israeli units crossed west of the Suez Canal and destroyed Egyptian air defenses which made Egypt vulnerable to air attack. In late October, Sadat agreed to a ceasefire which ended the Yom Kippur War or October War.

Figure 5.1 Egyptian troops guard a petrol container company in the Suez Canal region in March 1955

In 1978, Egypt regained the Sinai by dropping its support for Palestinian resistance which prompted the 1981 assassination of Sadat by Islamist radicals. He was replaced by air force commander Hosni Mubarak. From the late 1970s, Egypt made peace with Israel, distanced itself from the Soviet Union and became a major recipient of US military assistance. During the 1991 Gulf War, Egypt provided two divisions and a brigade to the US-led coalition that expelled Iraqi forces from Kuwait and invaded southern Iraq (Pollack, 2002; McGregor, 2006, pp. 259–83).

Libya's conflicts with Egypt and the United States (1977–89)

Libya, an Italian colony administered by the British from World War II, gained independence in 1951 with a king who favored people from his home eastern region of Cyrenaica and who received military support from the United States and Britain. In 1969, a group of Libyan army officers led by Captain Muammar Gaddafi and who had been inspired by Nassar overthrew the monarchy as it had squandered the country's oil wealth and failed to support the Arab cause against Israel. Under Gaddafi, Libya developed its military with Soviet assistance so as to pursue the aims of Arab unification, the destruction of Israel and defeat of western imperialism. Gaddafi also established the Islamic Arab Legion, recruited from foreign migrant workers, to fight for his dream of an Islamic State of the Sahel. After 1973, Gaddafi attempted to compensate for the defection of Egypt from the anti-Israeli effort by massively expanding the Libyan military and buying billions of dollars' worth of advanced Soviet tanks and aircraft, although there were not enough trained Libyan personnel to operate all of them. Several thousand Soviet, Cuban, Syrian, Pakistani and North Korean military personnel were imported to work as pilots and technicians. The paranoid Gaddafi also undercut his military's effectiveness by purging senior officers, constantly moving around officers and creating a network of political commissars.

When Gaddafi accused Sadat of betraying the Arab cause after the 1973 Yom Kippur War, Egypt moved two mechanized army divisions and eighty aircraft to its western border with Libya. In response, Gaddafi dispatched several thousand troops and 150 tanks to the border and opened training camps for Egyptian Islamist militants who raided across the frontier. During 1977, there were border skirmishes and artillery duels between Libyan and Egyptian forces. Outright warfare began on July 21, 1977 when a Libyan tank column violated the border and was ambushed by Egyptian forces which inflicted heavy casualties. As Egyptian aircraft bombed Libyan air fields close to the frontier, an Egyptian mechanized division moved 15 km into Libya where it destroyed Libyan armor and then withdrew. Over the next few days, both sides exchanged artillery fire across the border, both air forces launched sorties and Egyptian commandos raided Libyan radar stations,

Figure 5.2 Arrival of Muammar Gaddafi of Libya in Beirut, Sunday, June 6, 1970

training camps and an airbase. Sadat declared a ceasefire on July 24. This brief border war cost Libya 400 troops, thirty tanks, forty armored vehicles and twenty jets, while the Egyptians lost 100 men and around four aircraft.

During the 1980s, Gaddafi's sponsorship of international terrorist groups led to conflict with the United States. Gaddafi's claim to the entire Gulf of Sirte (also known as the Gulf of Sidra) stretching 500 km from Tripoli to Benghazi was contrary to international law and prompted the United States to dispatch its navy to enforce freedom of navigation. In August 1981, the US 6th Fleet entered the Gulf of Sirte, and although it was shadowed by Libyan aircraft, only two of these engaged in combat and were shot down without any US losses. United States naval forces were again sent to the Gulf of Sirte in March 1986 which led to the sinking of several Libyan patrol boats and the destruction of the Libyan air defense system. Gaddafi responded by organizing terrorist attacks in Europe which prompted the April 1986 US aerial bombing of Libya. In January 1989, given Gaddafi's production of chemical weapons, the United States once again sent a carrier group to the region and two Libyan fighters were shot down.

With the collapse of his Soviet sponsor at the start of the 1990s, Gaddafi successfully improved his relations with the West by admitting responsibility for the bombing of an airliner over Scotland, surrendering two agents who were involved and paying compensation to victims' families. The United States and Britain lifted sanctions so as to access Libyan oil, and after 2001,

Gaddafi renounced weapons of mass destruction and became a Western ally in the global war on terror. However, he was overthrown and killed in 2011 during a popular Libyan uprising related to wider protest across North Africa and the Middle East which was dubbed the "Arab Spring." Western states quickly turned on Gaddafi as the Libyan rebels were supported by North Atlantic Treaty Organization (NATO) airstrikes and military assistance (Pollack, 2002, pp. 362–8, 412–22; Wright, 2012, pp. 231–42).

Conflict in the Maghreb: Algeria, Morocco, Mauritania and Western Sahara (1963–99)

In the early 1950s, colonial France transferred the mineral-rich Tindouf and Bechar border areas from Morocco to Algeria. Morocco gained independence in 1956 as a conservative, French-backed monarchy, while Algeria emerged from its liberation war in 1962 with a revolutionary socialist regime. In October 1963, French-equipped Moroccan troops seized several towns in the disputed border areas but were quickly repelled by Algerian forces supported by Cuba and Egypt. While the short border conflict ended with an Organization of African Unity (OAU)-sponsored ceasefire, Moroccan forces fortified the frontier and the two countries were alienated from each other for many years.

In 1976, the failing fascist regime in Spain withdrew from its colony of Western Sahara. Although the governments of Morocco and Mauritania agreed to divide the territory, the Popular Front for the Liberation of Saguia el Hamra and Rio de Oro (POLISARIO) declared the area's independence as the Saharan Arab Democratic Republic. POLISARIO had been formed in 1973 to fight against Spanish colonial rule and received assistance from Algeria which was concerned about Moroccan claims to Western Sahara. During the late 1970s, the 10,000 insurgents of POLISARIO, based in camps in Algeria, fought Moroccan and Mauritanian occupation. POLISARIO received small arms, armored vehicles and tanks from Algeria, Libya and the Soviet Union, and in Mauritania, it was assisted by marginalized Tuaregs. Within Mauritania, a POLISARIO column attacked the capital of Nouakchott in June 1976 and the insurgents briefly seized the mining center of Zouerate in May 1977. As a result, the Mauritanian government invited Moroccan troops and French military advisors with air support to help combat POLISARIO. In 1978, a military coup in Mauritania, partly inspired by the presence of foreign troops, led to a ceasefire with POLISARIO and recognition of the Saharan Arab Democratic Republic. Morocco then occupied the southern part of Western Sahara that had been abandoned by Mauritania. In January 1979, POLISARIO mounted an offensive against the Moroccans in Western Sahara that involved highly mobile columns each consisting of 400–600 vehicles carrying 2,000–4,000 fighters. Moroccan forces were confined to garrison towns and their air superiority was challenged by POLISARIO's Soviet-made surface-to-air missiles. During the early and middle 1980s, Morocco, with money from Saudi Arabia, constructed a 2,700-km-long fortification southward from the Moroccan border which protected the economically important mining areas of Western Sahara and confined POLISARIO to the arid interior along the Algerian and Mauritanian frontiers. To fight the late 1970s and 1980s war in Western Sahara, Morocco purchased more than US$ 4 billion worth of arms from France and almost one billion from the United States including jet fighters, transport aircraft, helicopters, tanks, armored personnel carriers, artillery and air defense systems. Much of this military hardware was meant to deter direct intervention by Soviet-supplied Algeria. In addition, several hundred French military advisors were sent to Morocco and 1,500 Moroccan troops were trained in the United States.

By 1990, Western Sahara was occupied by 150,000 Moroccan troops, with more than 300 tanks and 250 artillery pieces, and POLISARIO periodically raided the wall. At this time, POLISARIO was weakened and isolated by the end of Soviet support, Algeria's distraction by internal conflict and the founding of the Arab Maghreb Union consisting of Morocco, Mauritania, Algeria, Tunisia and Libya. In September 1991, POLISARIO agreed to a UN-monitored ceasefire, but Morocco constantly delayed a promised referendum on the future of Western Sahara. As the territory became permanently divided between areas occupied by Morocco and POLISARIO, pro-independence protests during 1999 and into the 2000s were violently crushed in the Moroccan zone (Pennell, 2003, pp. 171–88; Clayton, 2004, pp. 70–1, 163–5; Willis, 2012, pp. 82–5, 90–4, 112–15).

The Ogaden War (1977–8)

Colonialism split the Somali people between five different territories: British, Italian and French Somaliland, British-ruled Kenya and independent Ethiopia. In 1960, British and Italian Somaliland were combined as the independent Republic of Somalia, though the inhabitants of the French territory (today's Djibouti) voted to remain separate. During the 1960s, the concept of Pan-Somalism, the desire to unite all Somali people under one state, emerged and prompted insurgency among Somalis living in Ethiopia's Ogaden Desert region and the northern districts of Kenya. In 1964, Ethiopian military forces sent to suppress Somali rebels in the Ogaden crossed the border and briefly clashed with Somalia's army. From 1963 to 1967, Kenyan security forces conducted a brutal but successful counter-insurgency campaign against Somali rebels. Since its sympathy with Pan-Somali insurgents put it at odds with pro-Western Ethiopia and Kenya, Somalia began to look toward the Soviet Union for military support. Taking power in 1969, Siad Barre deepened Somalia's relationship with the Soviet Union which built a naval facility at the strategically located port of Berbera. Under Barre, Somalia developed Africa's fourth largest military and Somalia ranked first among African countries in terms of percentage of gross national product devoted to military spending. Given its relatively small population, Somalia's army of the mid- to late-1970s consisted of 35,000 personnel, but it tried to compensate for this limited manpower by acquiring many armored vehicles and combat aircraft from the Soviets. Ethiopia possessed a much larger army in terms of personnel, but it had far fewer armored vehicles and aircraft that were supplied by the United States and Britain.

Developments within Ethiopia provided Barre with an opportunity to seize the Ogaden region. In 1974, Ethiopian Emperor Haile Selassie was replaced by a military regime led by Haile Mariam Mengistu which, in early 1977, launched an offensive against separatist rebels in Eritrea. Furthermore, Mengistu was a Marxist who expelled Ethiopia's US military advisors. In June 1977, some 5,000 fighters from Somalia infiltrated the Ogaden and attacked towns in support of the insurgent Western Somali Liberation Front (WSLF). The following month, Somalia launched an all-out mechanized invasion of eastern Ethiopia which quickly pushed back Ethiopian ground forces while the Ethiopian Air Force dominated the sky. In September 1977, Somali troops captured Jijiga and began repeated attacks on Harar. In late 1977, the Soviet Union broke ties with Somalia where Barre was proving a difficult partner and fully backed Ethiopia which represented a potentially much stronger regional ally. The Soviets sent more than a billion dollars' worth of military hardware, including helicopters, aircraft, tanks and air defense systems, to Ethiopia as well as 1,000 Soviet military advisors. Furthermore, by February 1978, the Soviets had transported 18,000 Cuban combat troops to Ethiopia. Directed by a Soviet general, an Ethiopian-Cuban offensive was mounted at the start of February and used mechanized forces to outflank Somali units around Marda Pass and recovered Jijiga the next month. Somali forces retreated, and by late March, they had moved back over the border. During the war, Barre had tried to reposition himself in the Cold War alliance structure by asking for US military resources, but the Carter administration was only willing to provide humanitarian assistance. Ethiopia and Somalia each lost around 6,000 troops during the war, but the number of civilian deaths remains unknown. Barre continued sponsorship of WSLF insurgents in Ethiopia's Ogaden and border skirmishes between Ethiopian and Somali forces continued for the next few years. Since Fidel Castro did not want to get bogged down in Ethiopia's counter-insurgency wars in Eritrea and Tigray, most Cuban troops were withdrawn by 1982. The Ogaden War of 1977–8 illustrates the situational nature of Cold War era superpower involvement in African conflicts that were dominated by local issues (Tareke, 2009).

The Kagera War (1978–9)

During the 1970s, Uganda was ruled by Idi Amin who established a notoriously brutal military dictatorship. While Prime Minister Milton Obote had used Uganda's northern-dominated military to impose northern political control in the late 1960s, this showed military commander Amin his potential power. In 1971, Amin, who was from the Kakwa ethnic group in the far north, overthrew Obote while he was out of the country and began victimizing his northern Acholi and Langi ethnic communities. The next year, Amin expelled Uganda's 80,000-strong Asian community, which badly damaged the country's economy. In neighboring Tanzania, exiled anti-Amin groups emerged including the deposed Obote's Kikosi Maalum (special force) and Yoweri Museveni's Front for National Salvation. The activities of these exile groups prompted Amin to conduct a cross-border raid into Tanzania in September 1971 and to have his air force bomb the Tanzanian towns of Bukoba and Mwanza in September 1972. Amin expanded Uganda's military and developed expansionist ambitions against adjacent Kenya, Tanzania and Rwanda. When Amin's Israeli sponsors rejected his request for armaments with which to invade Tanzania, Uganda's allegiance shifted to the Arab cause and Amin rediscovered his Islamic faith. As such, Amin gained millions of dollars from Saudi Arabia and Libyan troops and Palestinian insurgents were sent to Uganda. In 1976, Amin allowed a French airliner that had been hijacked by Palestinian and German terrorists to land at Entebbe airport where Israeli commandos staged a raid that rescued 100 Israeli and non-Israeli Jewish hostages and destroyed Uganda's thirty Soviet-made jet fighters. The humiliated Amin threatened Kenya, which had allowed the Israeli military to use its territory as a staging area, and took out his anger against his own people.

In October 1978, Amin sent 4,000 Ugandan troops across the border to occupy the Kagera area of Tanzania. It is likely that he did this to keep his military busy after some officers staged a failed coup. In November, 8,000–10,000 Tanzanian People's Defence Force (TPDF) troops, along with a battalion from Mozambique, drove the Ugandans out of Kagera. Throughout December 1978 and January 1979, Ugandan artillery continued to harass the TPDF defenses. Tanzanian President Julius Nyerere saw the border war as a chance to remove the volatile Amin. The TPDF used its reserve system to quickly expand from 17,000 to 45,000 troops and Ugandan exiles were formed into the Uganda National Liberation Front/Army (UNLF/A). Amin's military was bolstered by the arrival of a 2,500-strong Libyan expeditionary force that included tanks, multiple rocket launchers and jet fighters/bombers.

The TPDF and its allies invaded Uganda in January 1979 and advanced slowly so as to provide time for Amin to be toppled internally. The invasion force consisted of five TPDF brigades of around 1,000–1,500 men each, around 1,000 Ugandan exiles and some artillery from Mozambique. The operation was carried out by two converging forces, with one advancing along the western shore of Lake Victoria to Kampala and another moving inland, swinging northwest to Fort Portal near the Zaire (Democratic Republic of Congo [DRC]) border and returning east to Kampala. Amin's troops retreated as they were unpaid, untrained and demoralized. In mid-March, the TPDF lakeside force around Lukaya was initially surprised and pushed back by a Libyan attack, but the Tanzanians regrouped, recaptured the town and pressed forward. In early April, Tanzanian soldiers evicted the Libyan defenders of Entebbe airport and a few days later the UNLA and Tanzanians easily took Kampala. Some 8,000 of Amin's troops fled north into Sudan and Zaire, and Amin himself escaped to Libya and then Saudi Arabia. As 8,500 Tanzanian soldiers occupied the country, a provisional government was established under UNLF leader Yusuf Lule with Museveni as defense minister. Though it became the new national military, the UNLA was divided between those returned exiles who were mostly loyal to Obote and the southern youth who Museveni had rallied during the invasion. After several military coups, Obote was returned as president in a December 1980 election that Museveni condemned as fraudulent. These tensions set the stage for the beginning of insurgency in southern Uganda in 1981. The 1978–9 "Kagera War" resulted in the death of 375 Tanzania soldiers, 150 UNLA fighters, 600 Libyans, around 1,000 Ugandan troops and 1,500 Tanzanian and 500 Ugandan civilians (Avirgan and Honey, 1983; Pollack, 2002, pp. 368–73).

Angola (1975–89)

The 1974 military coup in Lisbon resulted in the independence of Portugal's African territories, including Angola, the following year. The Angolan insurgent groups that had been fighting the Portuguese and sometimes each other now fought over control of the state. A civil war developed between the Popular Movement for the Liberation of Angola (MPLA) around Luanda, the National Liberation Front of Angola (FNLA) in the north near the Zaire border and the National Union for the Total Independence of Angola (UNITA) based in the south. Control of the capital and Cuban military support meant that MPLA quickly seized the Angolan state. This concerned South Africa as Angola would then likely offer assistance to South West African People's Organization (SWAPO)/People's Liberation Army of Namibia (PLAN) insurgents in South West Africa (SWA – Namibia) and the United States worried about Soviet access to Angolan oil. Direct South African military intervention began in early August 1975 when SADF units in SWA crossed the Angolan border to occupy an important hydroelectric plant at Calueque. SADF personnel began supplying and training FNLA and UNITA fighters. With armored vehicles from Cuba and the Soviet Union, MPLA mounted a successful offensive taking control of much of the country.

At the start of October 1975, the SADF launched "Operation Savannah" which amounted to an invasion of Angola in support of UNITA and FNLA. At Balombo, a UNITA force supplemented by some South African-manned armored cars and land rovers fitted with missile launchers unsuccessfully attempted to halt an MPLA advance on the town of Nova Lisboa (Huambo). The MPLA then occupied the entire coast down to the SWA border and most southern Angolan towns. In turn, a SADF contingent of 2,500 men and 600 vehicles moved into Angola. In mid-October, Task Force Zulu, a South African-led column of around 1,000 FNLA and former Portuguese colonial soldiers, advanced into southwestern Angola, drove MPLA forces north and captured Perreira de Eca. A column of South African infantry and armored cars followed Zulu, captured Rocadas and then linked up with Zulu to continue the advance. In late October, Zulu captured Sa da Bandiera (Lubango) and the port of Mocamedes (Namibe). At Catengue, 70 km south of Benguela, MPLA forces with Cuban advisors tried but failed to stop Zulu's advance. Zulu seized the major ports of Benguela and Lobito in early November. Zulu benefited from superior firepower, supply by air, effective training and leadership and the late rainy season. In mid-October, South African aircraft lifted some SADF soldiers and armored cars to Silva Porto (Kuito), UNITA headquarters in central Angola, where they formed Taskforce Foxbat which included UNITA fighters.

In late October and early November 1975, FNLA forces in the north were trying to break through MPLA lines at Quifangondo to take the nearby capital of Luanda. The FNLA was supported by troops from Zaire, CIA-funded Portuguese mercenaries and South African heavy artillery. In early November, Fidel Castro, without consulting Moscow, dispatched a 650-strong Cuban Special Forces battalion by air to Luanda followed by an artillery regiment transported by sea. On the day Angola formally became independent, November 10, FNLA leader Holden Roberto discounted warnings from his South African and Portuguese advisors and directed a frontal attack along the road to Quifangondo that was flanked on both sides by swamp. Preliminary bombing by the South African Air Force was ineffective as the bombers flew high to avoid identification. The FNLA soldiers were funneled down a narrow path where they were slaughtered by fire from recently arrived Cuban multiple rocket launchers and heavy mortars. After this disaster, FNLA no longer represented a significant faction in the Angolan conflict.

South of Luanda, South Africa's Task Force Zulu overcame some MPLA delaying actions and captured Novo Redondo in mid-November. After the destruction of FNLA forces at Quifangondo, two Cuban Special Forces companies moved south to supplement MPLA units confronting the South Africans on the Queve River. By this time, Task Force Foxbat had moved north to capture Cela where an airfield allowed South African reinforcements to be airlifted from SWA. However, in late November, Foxbat's SADF armored cars and UNITA infantry were ambushed by Cuban and MPLA forces while trying to cross a bridge near Ebo. It appears that the Cubans and MPLA suffered no casualties, around ninety South African and UNITA troops were killed or wounded, and seven or eight SADF armored cars were lost. This disaster along with the onset of rains delayed the South African advance which gave the Cubans, numbering 3,500–4,000 in Angola by late December, time to bring in more troops and Soviet weapons. In mid-December, South African forces pushed north from Cela and penetrated Cuban/MPLA defenses on the Nhia River at "Bridge 14" but were stopped a few kilometers further by determined Cuban troops. At the end of December, Cuban forces occupied the Morros de Medunda, two prominent hills between Quibala and Cela, and repelled a South African counter-attack by calling artillery on their own position. Far to the east, the UNITA and South African troops of Task Force "X-Ray" tried to control the Benguela railway up to the Zaire border, but after capturing Luso in mid-December, it proved impossible to advance further.

Several factors, in addition to the Cuban intervention, contributed to the South African withdrawal from Angola. Given a shortage of military personnel, the South African government lengthened the duty of some national servicemen and extended citizen force tours of the operational area. Reports of the South African invasion of Angola in the western press, including news of the capture of four South African soldiers by MPLA, impelled the United States to withdraw support. In Angola, the SADF began to move south, leaving Cela on mid-January 1976, and after some skirmishing Cuban forces entered Novo Redondo late that month. By early February, 4,000–5,000 South African troops were holding an 80-km-deep band of Angola territory along the SWA border. Abandoned by Pretoria, UNITA almost collapsed, and in mid-February, Cuban and MPLA troops occupied Huambo, Lobito and Benguela. However, MPLA sought a political solution as its supply lines were becoming extended and it faced South African minefields. In late March, South Africa withdrew its forces from Angola, given promises from the new Angolan MPLA government to respect the SWA border and protect the Calueque-Ruacana hydroelectric project. The Angolan debacle damaged the military prestige of the apartheid state and partly motivated the June 1976 mass uprising by South Africa's black youth that reinvigorated the anti-apartheid struggle.

As Pretoria had feared, MPLA allowed SWAPO/PLAN to establish bases in southern Angola which increased insurgent activity in northern SWA. Consequently, the SADF embarked on a series of cross-border operations to destroy SWAPO/PLAN infrastructure in Angola which also brought the South Africans into conflict with Cuban units and the MPLA state military now called the Armed Forces for the Liberation of Angola (FAPLA). In October 1977, a South African Special Forces raid on Eheke in southern Angola turned disastrous, with seven operators killed. A much more ambitious offensive, Operation Reindeer, was launched in May 1978 and involved a battalion parachute assault on Cassinga which was 250 km north of the border, and an overland and helicopter-borne attack on Chetequera and Dombondola which were 25 km into Angola. The Cassinga raid resulted in a propaganda battle, with the SADF claiming they had killed 600 armed PLAN insurgents, while SWAPO maintained that the victims were mostly unarmed refugees. During the overland component of the operation, the SADF, using its new Ratel infantry fighting vehicles, killed 248 PLAN fighters and captured 200 while suffering only two deaths. As a result, SWAPO began better concealing its facilities in Angola and moved them closer to protective Cuban and FAPLA units.

At the start of the 1980s, UNITA, given renewed support from South Africa and the United States, took control of southeastern Angola and moved into the central region where they used Mavinga as a staging area. This meant that SWAPO was denied access to southeastern Angola and therefore its infiltration of neighboring SWA was restricted to the north-central region of Ovamboland. In addition, the re-emergence of UNITA distracted FAPLA, and Cuban units from the SWA border and SWAPO, at the insistence of its Angolan hosts, had to divert fighters to that front. South African cross-border operations continued. In June 1980, South Africa launched Operation Sceptic (also known as Smoke Shell) which comprised a sudden mechanized assault by three battle groups on a SWAPO complex around Chifufua in southern Angola and marked the first direct combat between the SADF and FAPLA, and the first employment of SWAPO mechanized units. The SADF captured many Soviet-made vehicles, and 380 PLAN and FAPLA troops and seventeen South Africans were killed. SWAPO then withdrew its forward bases from the border which further hindered its infiltration of SWA and it combined its logistical system with FAPLA. In June and July 1981, the SADF mounted Operation Carnation in which its units destroyed SWAPO/PLAN logistical centers between the border and Cuvelai. In late August 1981, the SADF launched Operation Protea which involved 4,000 troops organized into four battle groups, thus representing the largest South African mechanized operation since World War II, and with the use of 138 aircraft, it was also the largest South African air operation of the Angolan conflict. Protea was aimed at destroying SWAPO/PLAN infrastructure some 50 km into south-central Angola which was adjacent to SWA's Ovamboland. In successful attacks on Xangongo and Ongiva, the SADF killed around 1,000 SWAPO and FAPLA personnel, captured or destroyed almost US$ 250 million worth of Soviet-supplied military equipment and took a Soviet officer prisoner. Exploiting the success of Protea, the SADF launched Operation Daisy at the start of November 1981 and its mechanized and airborne units advanced into southern Angola to destroy a SWAPO complex around Chitequeta. South African incursions into Angola continued throughout 1982 and included a helicopter assault on a SWAPO staging area near Iona in which 200 insurgents were killed and air strikes on SWAPO command centers that killed 345. In early 1983, SWAPO/PLAN, given their reoccupation of bases around Xangongo and Ongiva under the protection of a nearby FAPLA brigade, stepped up its infiltration of SWA. This prompted the South Africans, in December 1983, to embark on Operation Askari which involved four mechanized battle groups advancing against SWAPO positions in southern Angola. At the start of January 1984, SADF units assaulting a SWAPO position near Cuvelai clashed with a FAPLA brigade and two Cuban battalions which suffered 324 deaths and withdrew. The South Africans lost twenty-one men in the engagement.

The South African success during Askari led to the 1984 Lusaka Agreement in which Pretoria promised to withdraw its forces from Angola and the MPLA government in Luanda agreed to prevent SWAPO and the Cubans from deploying along its southern border with SWA. While both sides initially lived up to these commitments, SWAPO was not a signatory to the agreement and returned to southern Angola which meant that South African cross-border "hot pursuit" actions resumed in 1985 as insurgency in SWA intensified.

The Lusaka Agreement also provided FAPLA with an opportunity to mount a 1984 offensive against UNITA, but this failed. Consequently, in 1985, FAPLA embarked on a Soviet-planned offensive called Operation Congresso II in the southeast that involved 20,000 troops supported by tanks, fighter bombers and helicopter gunships. Soviet advisors were assigned to FAPLA battalions and the Cubans likely provided artillery, air defense and air support. The 30,000 lightly equipped UNITA infantry could not stop the mechanized onslaught and despite limited SADF support including airlifts, Savimbi's fighters abandoned Cazombo to focus on defending Mavinga. In September, the SADF, through Operation Wallpaper, escalated its support for UNITA including air strikes that inflicted horrific casualties on FAPLA units approaching Mavinga. Ten Soviet officers who had been dispatched to salvage the now failing offensive were killed when their aircraft was destroyed by a South African fighter jet. By the time the Soviets had ordered FAPLA units back to their staging area at Cuito Cuanavale in October, the Angolan military had suffered 2,500 casualties and lost thirty-two armored vehicles, 100 trucks and more than a dozen aircraft. The Cubans suffered around 120 casualties, while 2,000 UNITA fighters were killed or wounded.

In 1986, the Soviets sent more than 1,000 military advisors and more than $1 billion worth of military equipment to Angola. Some 20,000 FAPLA, 7,000 SWAPO and 900 MK (South African ANC) fighters were assembled around Luena and Cuito Cuanavale, and in late May, they embarked on a renewed offensive against UNITA. The advance was slowed by lack of fuel that had been caused by a South African Special Forces raid on oil storage facilities at the port of Namibe, UNITA ambushes on FAPLA supply lines, a UNITA-South African raid on the Cuito Cuanavale airfield and sabotage of a Cuito River bridge by South African commandos. By late August, the Soviets had cancelled the offensive.

Launched in 1987, Operation Saluting October represented the last Soviet-led FAPLA action against UNITA and included another US$ 1.5 billion of Soviet arms brought to Angola. Since Castro desperately needed a victory to bolster flagging support for the war in Cuba, he authorized the use of Cuban frontline soldiers. Soviet planners ignored warnings from South African MK officers, who had agents implanted in the SADF that

South Africa would intervene to save UNITA. While the upcoming South African elections made Pretoria hesitant to act militarily in Angola, the FAPLA military build-up could not be ignored and the SADF was authorized to send in artillery and anti-tank units and help UNITA with airlifts. In early July 1987, four FAPLA brigades left Cuito Cuanavale and advanced southeast toward UNITA-held Mavinga. At the start of August, the SADF initiated Operation Modular in which mechanized forces comprising around 3,000 men crossed into Angola in direct support of UNITA. Throughout September, the SADF force, supported by air strikes, isolated and destroyed the FAPLA mechanized brigades as they were attempting to traverse the Lomba River. In one engagement at the start of October, a South African battle group surprised a FAPLA brigade as it was trying to construct a bridge across the river, killing 600 Angolan soldiers and destroying or capturing 127 vehicles. The battle was one-sided as a single South African was killed and five wounded. Suffering a total of around 4,000 casualties during the failed Operation Saluting October, FAPLA forces withdrew to Cuito Cuanavale in early October. At the same time, the South Africans reinforced their units in Angola with the addition of tanks and self-propelled howitzers.

As the SADF pursued the fleeing FAPLA troops and then besieged Cuito Cuanavale, the Soviets reduced their military presence in Angola and encouraged a negotiated settlement. Given that FAPLA lost 500 men and thirty-three tanks in the fighting with SADF around Cuito Cuanavale during early November 1987, the Angolan government pleaded for more Cuban support. Castro took direct control of Angolan military operations, dispatched 3,000 Cuban troops and many tanks and artillery pieces to Cuito Cuanavale, sent Cuba's top fighter pilots to Angola and sent another 3,500 Cuban troops into southwestern Angola to threaten that side of the SWA border. Castro hoped that military pressure would compel the South Africans to make concessions during negotiations. Although South African President P.W. Botha had ordered the SADF to destroy all FAPLA units east of the Cuito River, this goal was hindered by UN protests which made South Africa hesitant to dispatch reinforcements into Angola and the political sensitivity of potential white South African fatalities.

By December 1987, Cuito Cuanavale was protected by a three-tier Cuban/FAPLA defense which included tanks, artillery, multiple rocket launchers, entrenchments and massive minefields. In mid-January 1988, South African artillery pounded FAPLA units in the outer defense layer in preparation for an attack by SADF mechanized units and UNITA troops that resulted in tank versus tank combat. After killing 250 FAPLA soldiers and destroying nine tanks, the SADF units pulled back to prepare for another assault which was delayed by a month given a hepatitis outbreak. This gave Castro time to send Cuban reinforcements to Cuito Cuanavale and tighten its defensive perimeter. Cuban artillery was positioned on high ground west of the Cuito River which offered a good view of the battlefield and was beyond the range of South African guns. UNITA maintained pressure on FAPLA units until mid-February when a joint SADF-UNITA offensive, including South African tanks, collapsed the outer tier of the Cuito Cuanavale defense system. A near suicidal counter-attack by seven Cuban tanks prevents the South Africans from capturing the Cuito River Bridge. In this engagement, more than 500 FAPLA solders and thirty-two Cubans were killed, and seventeen tanks and eighteen other vehicles destroyed. UNITA casualties were heavy, but only four South Africans were killed and seven wounded. In late February 1988, Castro enacted a new defensive plan in which all units would be withdrawn west of the Cuito River, except one FAPLA brigade and a Cuban tank battalion that would guard the bridge and the adjacent area known as the "Tumpo Triangle." Vast minefields were laid along every approach to Cuito Cuanavale. As a FAPLA brigade was moving west of the river, several attacks on it by SADF mechanized units were turned back by mines and Cuban artillery and air strikes. This boosted the morale of the Cuito Cuanavale garrison. Although only seventeen of the twenty-eight South African tanks were operational, another attack was mounted at the end of February as the national service period of many of the SADF soldiers was about to expire. This offensive action was also abandoned, given mines, Cuban artillery and mechanical problems with the remaining tanks. South African momentum was lost during the time it took to replace the outgoing 20th Brigade with 82nd Brigade that arrived in March. Once again, the Cubans and FAPLA gained time to repair defenses and plant more mines. In late March, in the context of Operation Packer which included preparatory South African aerial attacks on FAPLA and diversionary actions by UNITA, the newly arrived SADF brigade mounted a mechanized assault that fizzled given the same problems of enemy mines, artillery and air strikes. With the South African government realizing that it could not completely drive Cuban/FAPLA units west of the Cuito River, 82nd Brigade was withdrawn and the SADF planted its own minefields to discourage a counter-offensive against UNITA.

With Cuito Cuanavale secure, Castro sent a Cuban tank brigade into Angola's southwestern Cunene province to reinforce existing FAPLA and SWAPO units. Improved airfields enabled Cuban aircraft to fly over SWA and an advanced air defense system ended South African domination of the skies over southern Angola. In mid-April 1988, the first major combat took place between South African and Cuban forces in southwestern Angola when the former crossed the border in pursuit of SWAPO insurgents. A similar event happened in early May. By the end of May, there were two full Cuban divisions totaling 12,000 men and 200 tanks, in southwestern Angola, and three new mixed SWAPO-Cuban battalions were established. During June, the SADF mounted Operation Excite which halted a southwest Cuban advance from Tchipa toward the border town of Calueque. At the end of June, Cuban aircraft bombed the Calueque hydroelectric station, killing eleven South African soldiers which prompted the SADF to destroy a major bridge on the Cunene River and deploy a division along the south side of the border to prevent a possible Cuban/FAPLA invasion of SWA. At this point, there were 65,000 Cuban troops in Angola. South African and Cuban political anxieties over casualties encouraged them to disengage militarily and conclude a settlement during US-sponsored talks. South African forces left southern Angola and all of SWA in 1989, the Cubans withdrew from southern Angola around the same time and departed from the country in 1991 and Namibia attained independence in 1990 under an elected SWAPO government (Gleijeses, 2002; George, 2005; Gleijeses, 2013; Pollack, 2013; Scholtz, 2013; Van Der Waag, 2015, pp. 245–82).

Given the removal of the South African threat, the Angolan MPLA government launched a major military offensive against UNITA's Mavinga stronghold in December 1989. After this stalled, UNITA mounted a counter-offensive in May and June 1990 that resulted in it capturing the oil port of Ambriz and advancing into the center of the country. However, the end of the Cold War meant that the United States and the faltering Soviet Union pressured their respective allies, MPLA and UNITA, to negotiate. The MPLA government abandoned socialism and the one-party state. In May 1991, MPLA and UNITA signed the Bicesse Accords which stipulated that a UN verification mission would supervise a ceasefire, the conduct of multi-party elections within a year, the demobilization of the country's 150,000 fighters and the creation of a new Angolan Armed Forces (FAA). In September 1992, Savimbi rejected the results of elections which he lost and this led to renewed violence between the MPLA government and UNITA rebels. By mid-January 1993, fighting had spread to fifteen of Angola's eighteen provinces and UNITA embarked on a national offensive in which it captured many towns across the country and threatened the oil-rich Cabinda enclave. Deprived of US support, UNITA sustained itself by smuggling diamonds out of Angola and through Mobutu's Zaire. The success of an offensive by the FAA (the Angolan state military) prompted Savimbi to enter the November 1994 Lusaka Agreement in which the MPLA and UNITA promised to stop fighting and form a coalition government. Fighting once again resumed in 1995 with oil-rich Luanda briefly contracting mercenaries from South African-based Executive Outcomes and buying more arms, and in 1997, the FAA invaded Zaire to cutoff UNITA diamond exports. In January 1999, Angolan President Jose Eduardo Dos Santos declared that peace would be achieved through military means and UN observers departed the rebel areas. Further FAA operations reduced UNITA-held territory and the government drove rural people into the towns to prevent them from assisting the insurgents. After Savimbi was killed in a FAA ambush in February 2002, UNITA returned to the Lusaka peace process and around 81,000 UNITA fighters and 350,000 dependents entered demobilization camps. Angolans had experienced five decades of continuous war which had begun with the anti-colonial rebellion of the 1960s, then morphed into a Cold War proxy conflict during the late 1970s and 1980s and ended as a civil war. By 2003, much of the country's infrastructure was destroyed, agriculture was hindered by large minefields, many Angolans had lost limbs from mine explosions, one-third of the population was internally displaced and the majority of Angolans lacked access to medical care and running water. The MPLA retained a firm grip on power in what some called a "negative peace" (Vines, 1999; Weigert, 2011).

Mozambique (1975–93)

Taking power in Mozambique after Portugal's 1974 departure, the Front for the Liberation of Mozambique (FRELIMO) established a socialist one-party state that improved education and health care, but its autocratic methods and emphasis on collective agriculture alienated some rural people. As an African liberation movement, FRELIMO assisted the Zimbabwe African National Liberation Army (ZANLA) and the African National Congress (ANC) that were engaged in armed struggle against the white minority regimes in Rhodesia and South Africa, respectively. Immediately after Mozambique's independence, Rhodesian agents orchestrated the formation of the Mozambique National Resistance (RENAMO) which launched an insurgency against the FRELIMO state. With Zimbabwe independence in 1980, apartheid South Africa assumed sponsorship of RENAMO using it to sabotage infrastructure with a view to furthering Mozambique's economic dependence on South Africa. RENAMO insurgents were trained in South Africa. In Mozambique, RENAMO was assisted by South African Special Forces teams that sometimes carried out their own raids, the South African Navy which landed supplies on the coast and the South African Air Force which conducted strikes on ANC facilities in Maputo. Since RENAMO actions were threatening Zimbabwe's importation of oil from the Mozambican port of Beira, the Zimbabwe military entered Mozambique and assisted FRELIMO counter-insurgency during the 1980s. Tanzanian forces also joined the war against RENAMO. Under pressure because of the war, the FRELIMO government signed the 1984 Nkomati Accord in which Mozambique and South Africa agreed to stop supporting insurgents from each other's country. While FRELIMO expelled the ANC from Mozambique, South Africa continued covert assistance for RENAMO using Malawi as a conduit for supplies. During the late 1980s, FRELIMO, Zimbabwean and Tanzanian forces expanded operations against RENAMO that made revenge incursions into Zimbabwe.

In the early 1990s, the end of apartheid meant that RENAMO lost its South African support and the changing international political climate prompted FRELIMO to adopt multi-party democracy and a free market economy. After negotiations between FRELIMO and RENAMO, Mozambique's first democratic elections were held in 1994 and resulted in a FRELIMO government and RENAMO opposition. In 1993, the Zimbabwean military withdrew from Mozambique and was replaced by the UN Operation in Mozambique that supervised a peace process until the next year (Minter, 1994, pp. 40–1, 198; Newitt, 1995, pp. 541–74; Stiff, 1999, pp. 158–9, 178–80, 369–405).

Angola and Mozambique were not the only African countries which apartheid South Africa, in its quest to undermine regional support for the anti-apartheid movement, attacked and tried to destabilize during the 1970s and 1980s. South African agents encouraged small rebel movements in Zambia, Zimbabwe and Lesotho. Furthermore, the SADF staged direct attacks on neighboring countries such as at port facilities in Dar-es-Salaam, Tanzania, in 1972; an airbase in Gweru, Zimbabwe, in 1982; ANC houses in Maseru, Lesotho, in 1982 and Gaborone, Botswana, in 1985, and simultaneous raids on Harare, Gaborone and Lusaka in 1986. Although impoverished Botswana decided against forming a military on its independence in 1966, incursions by Rhodesian and South African forces prompted the 1977 establishment of the Botswana Defence Force (BDF) which was developed through revenues from the new diamond industry (Stiff, 1999, pp. 38–42, 46–52, 406–26, 470–97, 506–23; Henk, 2007, pp. 31–47).

Chad, Libya and France (1968–90)

In late twentieth-century Chad, a civil war quickly turned into a complex interstate conflict with Cold War dimensions that pitted Soviet-backed Libya against France. Gaining independence in 1960, the former French colony of Chad suffered from regionalism related to a poor and predominantly Muslim north and a relatively more prosperous and mostly Christian south. In 1968, the National Liberation Front of Chad (FROLINAT) launched a rebellion in the north and eventually received weapons from Eastern Block aligned Egypt, Algeria and Libya. The southern-based government of President Francois Tombalbaye was supported by 3,000 French troops as well as military assistance from Zaire, Israel and the United States. In 1973, Gaddafi's Libya annexed the Aouzou Strip, supposedly rich in uranium, just over its border with Chad and established an air base there. Although Tombalbaye tolerated the Libyan action, he was overthrown and killed in a 1975 coup that brought General Felix Malloum to power. Since Malloum was hostile to the Libyans, Gaddafi sent troops into Chad in support of FROLINAT. At that point, the French military presence in Chad amounted to several hundred advisors who sometimes engaged in combat and protected Malloum from internal threats. The Libyan intervention prompted a split in FROLINAT, with the anti-Libyan minority establishing the Armed Forces of the North (FAN) under Hissene Habre and the pro-Libyan majority creating the People's Armed Forces (FAP) under Goukouni Oueddei. In 1977, FAP, with Libyan-supplied weapons, launched an offensive that pushed Chadian state forces out of most northern towns, except Ounianga Kebir which was held by the French. At the start of 1978, after Malloum and FAN's Habre agreed to form a unity government, FAP and the Libyans mounted another offensive that seized northern government strongholds including Ounianga Kebir and Faya-Largeau. The Libyans mostly provided armor, artillery and air support for rebel troops. In February 1978, France embarked on Operation Tacaud in which 2,500 troops, supported by helicopter gunships and ground attack jets, were sent to Chad to protect the capital of N'Djamena. In May and June, Chadian and French forces repelled another FAP offensive and pushed the rebels northward. As Libyan pilots refused to confront the French in the air and Gaddafi backed a failed attempt to overthrow FAP's Oueddei, the rebels evicted all Libyan troops from northern Chad.

In February 1979, Habre's FAN and Oueddei's FAP joined forces and expelled Malloum's state military from N'Djamena where between 2,000 and 5,000, people were killed and 70,000 displaced. French forces did nothing. Subsequently, the Chadian rebel factions formed a Transitional Government of National Unity (GUNT) with Oueddei as president. After an incursion by 2,500 Libyan troops was repelled by Chadian and French troops, GUNT absorbed some pro-Libyan factions. As such, French troops in the country were meant to be replaced by Inter-African peacekeepers. In March 1980, Habre's FAN and Oueddei's FAP clashed in the capital and the former seized Faya-Largeau in the north. This prompted Oueddei, still president of GUNT, to renew his relationship with Libya and sign a treaty that permitted Libyan forces to enter Chad. Using the Aouzou Strip as a staging area, Libyan and FAP forces including tanks and artillery recaptured Faya-Largeau and then advanced 1,000 km south to occupy N'Djamena in December. The remnants of Habre's FAN retreated east to the border of Sudan's Darfur region where they received military support from Egypt, Sudan and the United States. Although Oueddei agreed to merge Chad with Gaddafi's Libya, the leaders fell out when the latter began backing the northern Chadian Arab rebels of the Volcan Army. In late 1981, Oueddei requested that the 14,000 Libyan troops in Chad leave the country and Gaddafi, trying to winfavor in the OAU, surprisingly agreed. The Libyan soldiers were replaced by a 3,300-strong OAU Inter-African Force mostly from Zaire, Nigeria and Senegal which represented the first attempt by an African international grouping to dispatch peacekeepers to a conflict zone.

The departure of the Libyans from Chad opened an opportunity for Habre's FAN which mounted an offensive from Sudan. In June 1982, Habre's fighters defeated GUNT forces in a battle 80 km north of the capital which they subsequently seized without a fight. Habre's FAN then eliminated elements of the old Chadian armed forces in the south and secured most of the country. The Inter-African Force did nothing and Gaddafi rejected Oueddei's pleas for assistance. Oueddei re-established the GUNT in northern Chad and assembled 3,000–4,000 fighters from various militias who, in December 1982 and January 1983, defeated a series of attacks by Habre's FAN. Gaddafi once again decided to back Oueddei whose forces, along with Libyan troops, captured Faya-Largeau and other northern towns in June. This latest Libyan intervention inspired the French to arm Habre's forces and Zaire sent him 250 paratroopers and the United States delivered food. In July, Habre's fighters, now called the Chadian National Armed Forces (FANT), advanced north and inflicted a stunning defeat on the GUNT/Libyan army south of Abeche which led to the retaking of many northern towns including Faya-Largeau. In turn, the Libyan air force bombarded Faya-Largeau and a force of some 11,000 Libyan troops was assembled nearby. In August, some 3,000–4,000 of Oueddei's GUNT troops supported by Libyan armor, artillery and air power drove 5,000 of Habre's troops out of Faya-Largeau. France then launched Operation Manta which involved 2,700 French troops supported by ground attack jets securing N'Djamena. With Paris unwilling to help Habre reoccupy the north and Gaddafi reluctant to take on the French military, Chad became effectively divided with the south ruled by Habre who was backed by French forces and the north under Oueddei who was bolstered by Libyan troops. In November 1984, after an agreement between France and Libya to mutually withdraw their forces, French troops left Chad but Gaddafi reneged and left 3,000 Libyan troops in the north.

During the mid-1980s, the Libyans constructed an air base at Ouadi Doum in northern Chad and increased the force there to 7,000 troops, 300 tanks and sixty aircraft. Consequently, the American Reagan administration bolstered its support for the Habre regime. In February 1986, Gaddafi restarted the war with an offensive by 5,000 Libyan and 5,000 GUNT troops that attacked Habre's FANT along the 16th parallel which divided the country. With new equipment from France, FANT forces counter-attacked and pushed the Libyans and GUNT fighters back. Almost immediately, French President Francois Mitterrand determined to look strong for the upcoming French legislative elections, authorized Operation Epervier (Sparrow Hawk) which transported 1,200 French troops and some ground attack aircraft to N'Djamena. French jets based in Bangui in the CAR bombed the Libyan air base at Ouadi Doum and Gaddafi retaliated by directing a bomber from Aouzou to fly 1,000 km under French radar to attack N'Djamena airport. In August, the shaky alliance between the Libyans and Oueddei's GUNT collapsed, and in the subsequent violence, the latter was supported by Habre's FANT which sent units north and the French who airdropped supplies.

The new alliance of Habre and Oueddei united most Chadians against the Libyan invasion. While the Chadian forces numbered around 10,000 men with heavy weapons mounted on Toyota pick-up trucks and equipped with French supplied anti-tank missiles, the 8,000 Libyan troops and their 300 tanks in northern Chad now lacked local allies and were confined to desert outposts. In the "Toyota War," which started in January 1987, Chadian forces commanded by General Hassan Djamous and supported by French air power executed a series of quick pincer maneuvers which overwhelmed many Libyan positions and compelled them to depart northern Chad. In August, a Chadian attempt to take the Aouzou Strip was defeated by the Libyans as the French refused to supply the former with air support. In early September, a mobile column of 2,000 Chadian troops under Djamous raided Maaten al-Sarra air base some 90 km inside Libya, killing 1,700 of the 2,500 defenders, taking 300 prisoners and destroying seventy tanks, twenty-six aircraft, surface-to-air missiles and radar equipment. The Chadians lost just sixty-five men. Since the raid meant that the Libyans had no air support in the area, the Chadians planned another attempt to take the Aouzou Strip, but this was aborted, given French worries about potentially expanding the conflict. The war ended in September with an OAU-brokered ceasefire. During the 1987 conflict, some 7,500 Libyans were killed, around 1,000 were captured and Gaddafi lost $1.5 billion worth of military equipment including 800 armored vehicles. About 1,000 Chadians lost their lives. Blaming the United States and France for this disaster, Gaddafi sanctioned the terrorist bombing of a US airliner that exploded over Scotland in December 1988 and a French airliner that was destroyed over Niger in September 1989. Chad and Libya normalized relations in 1989 and the Aouzou Strip dispute was submitted to the International Court of Justice. In 1994, the court ruled in favor of Chad and Libyan troops withdrew from Aouzou.

In 1989, after Habre had military leader Djamous killed given suspicion of a coup plot, Chadian military commander Idriss Deby fled to Sudan where he founded the Patriotic Salvation Movement (MPS) with assistance from Khartoum and Tripoli. An MPS invasion of Chad in March 1990 was called off because of French intervention. In November, the MPS again pressed into Chad and this time the French forces in the country did nothing as Habre's poor human rights record had become an embarrassment. Some 2,000 MPS fighters occupied N'Djamena and Habre went to exile. Subsequently, Deby became an elected but authoritarian president. Beginning in 2003, his regime was challenged by numerous rebel groups in eastern Chad armed by Sudan in retaliation for Chad's sponsorship of insurgents in Darfur, and this situation was complicated by the presence of several hundred thousand Sudanese and Chadian refugees along the border. Two rebel incursions into Chad, in April 2006 and February 2008, failed to capture N'Djamena where the Deby regime was assisted by French forces. Between 2008 and 2010, international peacekeepers, initially from the European Union but eventually from the UN Mission in the CAR and Chad (MINURCAT), deployed to eastern Chad and northeastern CAR to protect and provide humanitarian assistance for some 200,000 refugees from Darfur. In 2010, the governments of Chad and Sudan agreed to stop backing rebels in each other's countries and the border was reopened (Nolutshungu, 1995; Azevedo, 1998; Mays, 2002; Pollack, 2002, pp. 375–423; Clayton, 2004, pp. 98–101, 159–63).

The Christmas War (1985)

After independence in 1960, the former French colonies of Mali and Upper Volta claimed the Agacher Strip as it contained natural gas and minerals. In 1974 and 1975, there were border skirmishes that resulted in OAU mediation accepted by both sides. Marxist-inspired Captain Thomas Sankara seized power in Upper Volta in 1983. Renaming the country Burkina Faso (Land of Upright Men) to symbolize a promised national rebirth, he rejected French neo-colonial influence and reconsidered the Agacher Strip question which rekindled tensions with Mali. Claiming that census officials from Burkina Faso had violated its territory, Mali's military government launched attacks on Burkinabe border posts and police stations on Christmas Day in 1985. Burkinabe forces counter-attacked, but the Malian military was better prepared and seized several villages and conducted an aerial bombardment of the Burkinabe town of Ouahigouya. Given Nigerian and Libyan mediation, a ceasefire was declared on December 30 ending what became known as the "Christmas War" in which 60–300 people were killed. Both countries withdrew their forces to pre-war positions and exchanged prisoners. In 1986, Burkina Faso and Mali accepted an International Court of Justice decision that split the Agacher Strip between them (Engelbert, 1996, p. 154).

The Ethiopia–Eritrea War (1998–2000)

Following the 1991 secession of Eritrea from Ethiopia, the two neighbors quarreled over the border area of Badme which resulted in some frontier skirmishes. In May 1998, Eritrean forces including tanks and artillery invaded Badme and evicted Ethiopian police. An Ethiopian military counter-attack led to four weeks of intense combat along the border area. In June, the Ethiopian Air Force bombed the Eritrean capital of Asmara and Eritrean aircraft bombed the Ethiopian town of Mekele. Given military stalemate, both sides dug in along the 1,000 km border, mobilized hundreds of thousands of troops and imported advanced weapons systems from Russia and Eastern Europe. In February 1999, with the collapse of a US-Rwanda sponsored peace plan, Ethiopia launched an offensive that retook Badme and advanced a few kilometers into Eritrea. The next month, given the failure of an OAU brokered ceasefire, Ethiopian forces advanced south of Asmara, but they were held off by Eritrean defenders. When negotiations collapsed in May 2000, Ethiopian forces moved through the mountains enabling them to outflank the Eritreans, cut their supply lines and threaten Asmara and the port of Assab. Defeated, the Eritrean government accepted an OAU proposal that both sides withdraw to pre-war positions which meant that they abandoned Badme. The conflict cost between 70,000 and 100,000 lives and displaced more than 1 million people. From 2000 to 2008, the UN Mission in Ethiopia and Eritrea patrolled the disputed border, and although an international court eventually awarded Badme to Eritrea, the Ethiopians did not surrender it. These tensions informed Eritrea's support for Islamist insurgents fighting Ethiopian forces in Somalia (Negash and Tronvoll, 2000; Lata, 2003).

The Congo wars (1996–2002)

During the first half of the 1990s, Mobutu Seke Seko, the long-time ruler of Zaire, lost his US support, given the end of the Cold War and clung to power through drawing out negotiations over political reforms. As the economy collapsed, violence broke out in eastern Zaire's North and South Kivu provinces between communities who considered themselves indigenous and others who were seen as foreign since they had historically originated from Rwanda. The conflict was gravely worsened by the arrival of almost 1 million Hutu refugees, soldiers and militia from Rwanda at the end of the 1994 genocide. Many people of Rwandan Tutsi origin, some long resident in eastern Zaire such as the Banyamulenge, fled to Rwanda. Unpaid Zairean military units were sent to stabilize the area but ultimately sided with whichever faction offered them more money. In early 1995, exiled Hutu Power fighters based in eastern Zaire refugee camps began to infiltrate Rwanda where they ambushed buses and raided schools. The victimization of the Banyamulenge by the Zairean military and various militias gave the predominantly Tutsi RPF government in Rwanda an excuse to send its military across the border to deal with the Hutu Power groups. In August 1996, the Rwandan Patriotic Army (RPA) began infiltrating eastern Zaire through Burundi, and in October, the Mobutu government accused Rwanda and Burundi of invading its territory. Poorly equipped, demoralized and incompetently led, the Zairean military retreated as the RPA and allied Banyamulenge fighters advanced to capture the South Kivu towns of Uvira and Bukavu at the end of October. In early November, the RPA crossed into North Kivu to take Goma; later in the month, it seized Masisi and Butembo and in early December, it captured the Bukavu-Goma road junction. Around this time, the Tutsi-led military regime in Burundi briefly sent units into South Kivu to destroy camps belonging to exiled Burundian Hutu rebels of the National Council for the Defence of Democracy (CNDD) and Forces for the Defence of Democracy (FDD). Further north, units of the Uganda People's Defence Force (UPDF) pushed into Zaire at the end of November, and on Christmas Day, they helped local rebels capture Bunia in the Ituri region of Orientale Province. The UPDF incursion was justified as pursuit of western Ugandan insurgents from the Alliance of Democratic Forces (ADF). To portray their invasion as a local rebellion, the Rwandan and Ugandan governments orchestrated the formation of the Alliance of Democratic Forces for the Liberation of Congo (AFDL) led by long-exiled insurgent Laurent Kabila and representing a coalition of anti-Mobutu rebel groups at the core of which were the Banyamulenge.

In mid-November 1996, given international talks about sending a UN peacekeeping force to the region, the RPA forcefully dismantled refugee camps in the Kivus including Mugunga which was inhabited by 600,000 people. While hundreds of thousands of refugees returned to Rwanda, others fled west across Zaire and were pursued by the AFDL and RPA. In May 1997, the AFDL, led by Rwandan officers, massacred hundreds of Rwandan Hutu civilians near the Zairean town of Mbandaka as they were waiting to cross the Congo River into the Republic of Congo. Since Mbandaka is about 1,200 km west of Rwanda, Kigali's argument that these operations were important for the security of their country made little sense, and the next year, a UN investigative team warned that such massacres of Rwandan Hutu in Zaire, of whom 230,000 disappeared in 1996 and 1997, could represent genocide.

Angola entered the war against Mobutu to block the Angolan rebels of UNITA from using Zaire as a channel for smuggling out diamonds to sustain their armed struggle. In February 1997, Angola flew 2,000–3,000 exiled Katangan rebels called "Tigres" who had been incorporated into the Angolan army to Rwanda from where they moved into eastern Zaire and played a key role in the AFDL's capture of Kisangani in mid-March. The next month, they participated in the AFDL occupation of Shaba (Katanga) including some who crossed through Zambia. At the end of April, military units from Angola crossed into southern Zaire to capture Tshikapa and Kikwit on their way toward Kinshasa. At the same time, AFDL rebels and Rwandan and Ugandan troops advanced on Kinshasa from the east.

With an injection of funds from Kuwait which Zaire had supported during the First Gulf War and from France, Mobutu tried to bolster his military by paying soldiers for the first time in months, buying new equipment and hiring mostly Serbian foreign mercenaries. However, it was too little and too late. Zairean forces usually did not fight and abandoned towns sometimes after selling their weapons to the enemy. The last battle of the war took place in early May at Kenge when UNITA rebels from Angola failed to halt the advance of the Angolan army toward nearby Kinshasa. As such, an ailing Mobutu fled to Morocco and died shortly thereafter and Kabila, who entered Kinshasa on May 20, declared himself president and changed the name of the country to the DRC. The fighting of 1996 and 1997 is often called the "First Congo War."

The new Kabila regime quickly fell out with its external sponsors: Rwanda and Uganda. The weak Kinshasa government could do little to prevent exiled Rwandan and Ugandan insurgents from using parts of eastern DRC as a staging area for incursions into their home countries. These foreign rebels included the Army for the Liberation of Rwanda (ALIR) which consisted of Hutu Power fighters many of whom had participated in the 1994 genocide and ADF rebels from western Uganda. Local Congolese militias called Mai Mai became embroiled in this complex web of conflicts. Facing domestic criticism about his reliance on foreign troops, Kabila replaced Rwandan officer James Kabarebe as chief-of-staff of the new Congolese Armed Forces (FAC), and in late July 1998, he ordered all foreign troops out of the country including 600 Rwandan soldiers who were flown from Kinshasa to Kigali. As a result, at the beginning of August, FAC troops in the eastern towns of Goma and Bukavu rebelled against the Kabila government with the support of Rwanda and Uganda. The "Tigres" returned to Angola after some of them who had opposed the rebellion were killed by Rwandan forces. The eastern Congolese rebels eventually adopted the name Rally for Congolese Democracy (RCD) with strong backing by Rwanda which was also supported by the United States given the Clinton administration's guilt over failing to intervene in the 1994 genocide in Rwanda. On the other side of the country, at military camps near Kinshasa, FAC troops massacred Banyamulenge and Rwandan soldiers who had not already left. In early August, a force of 1,200 Rwanda troops under Kabarebe was flown by hijacked civil airliners from Goma in eastern DRC to Kitona in western DRC where they rallied former Mobutu troops and distracted FAC forces from dealing with the rebellion in the east.

Kabila requested military support from the Southern African Development Community (SADC) which the DRC had very recently joined. SADC members Botswana, South Africa and Zambia refused to defend a non-elected government. However, Zimbabwe wanted to protect its new investments in DRC, Angola was concerned about UNITA's warming relations with Uganda and Rwanda, and Namibia supported its ally Angola. Assembled in Angola's Cabinda enclave, an Angolan expeditionary force with armored vehicles and helicopters moved into western DRC where it devastated the lightly armed Rwandan contingent and took Kitona in late August. At the same time, 2,800 Zimbabwean troops were flown to Kinshasa where they fought a three-day battle to defend the airport as the Zimbabwe Air Force destroyed a rebel motorized column heading for the capital.

By early September, RCD rebels, along with Rwandan and Ugandan troops, had secured most of eastern Congo including Kisangani. The capture of strategically important Kindu in October meant that Kabila could no longer fly soldiers to the east and it opened a rebel/Rwandan route to the diamond-rich Kasai region and a possible link with UNITA rebels in Angola. In November, in northern DRC's Equateur Province, the Ugandan army orchestrated the formation of a new rebel group called the Movement for the Liberation of Congo (MLC) led by Jean-Pierre Bemba with links to the old Mobutu regime which had enjoyed support in that region. Since Uganda has been backing the SPLA rebellion in southern Sudan, Khartoum organized a Libyan airlift of 1,000 Chadian soldiers to northern DRC to support the Kabila regime. The government of Sudan also recruited exiled Rwandan and Ugandan fighters for Kabila's forces and dispatched bombers to the DRC. Zimbabwe sent additional aircraft to DRC and trained exiled Burundian Hutu rebels, recruited from camps in Tanzania, to fight on behalf of Kabila in southern DRC. The involvement of so many African countries in this "Second Congo War" inspired another name for it: "Africa's World War."

During the first half of 1999, the RCD rebels and Rwandan military advanced into Kasai and north Katanga but determined Zimbabwean defenders, assisted by Hutu fighters from Rwanda, prevented them from taking the diamond center of Mbuji-Mayi. Around the same time, and to the north, the newly formed MLC force, consisting of many child soldiers from CAR, together with Ugandan troops and UNITA rebels from Angola tried but failed to capture Mbandaka which was essential if they were to continue down the Ubangi and Congo rivers to Kinshasa. Namibian and Angolan aircraft brought Congolese soldiers to CAR from where they moved overland into northern DRC and pushed the MLC/Ugandan alliance away from the border. The only combined rebel offensive of the war was launched in February 1999. While the MLC/Ugandans pushed Congolese forces back into the CAR and took Gbadolite in July, and the RCD/Rwandans expanded their occupation of northern Katanga in mid-March, momentum was lost and the ambitious objectives of seizing Kinshasa and Lubumbashi were not achieved. UNITA forces from Angola moved toward Mbuji-Mayi from the other direction but withdrew given problems at home.

The war stalemated with a stagnant "frontline," a series of pockets where enemies faced one another rather than a continuous war zone, ran from Mbandaka in the northwest through Mbuji-Mayi to Pweto in the southeast. Although Bemba's MLC gained popularity in the north as people anticipated the return of a friendly regime, the RCD in the east lacked legitimacy as it was seen as a puppet of Rwanda and locals were victimized in continuing factional violence. The once strong Uganda-Rwanda alliance broke down as their soldiers and associated rebel groups fought each other for control of Kisangani in August 1999 and May and June 2000. Kampala favored installing a friendly but independent government in Kinshasa, while Kigali wanted a puppet regime. The RCD split into pro-Uganda RCD-Kisangani and pro-Rwanda RCD-Goma factions. While the foreign forces present in the DRC had intervened there for security reasons, they all became involved in looting the country's vast natural resources such as minerals demanded by the growing global electronics industry.

Although the July 1999 Lusaka Agreement technically imposed a ceasefire to be monitored by the UN Mission in the Democratic Republic of Congo (MONUC), the war resumed and the deployment of peacekeepers was delayed. The major rebel groups and their allies advanced down different rivers toward Kinshasa: the MLC/Ugandans on the Ubangi and the RCD-G/Rwandans on the Tshuapa. In late November 1999, Zimbabwean and Congolese forces fought their way up the Tshuapa to relieve a garrison trapped at Ikela. During the first half of 2000, Kabila launched two offensives up the Ubangi which both failed given MLC/Ugandan counter-attack and ambush. Around 120,000 Congolese civilians fled to neighboring

Congo-Brazzaville. Kabila's allies became alienated by his continued under-mining of diplomatic efforts to end the increasingly costly war and Rwanda abandoned its goal of installing a puppet regime in Kinshasa in favor of extracting mineral resources from the areas it occupied. By the end of December 2000, the foreign troops in DRC included 12,000 Zimbabweans, 7,000 Angolans and 2,000 Namibians who supported the Kabila regime and 10,000 Ugandans and 17,000–25,000 Rwandans allied with various local rebel groups.

In January 2001, given strains related to failed government offensives, Kabila was assassinated by his bodyguards, and his son, Joseph Kabila, took power and renewed diplomatic measures to end the conflict. Furthermore, the new George W. Bush administration in the United States, less influenced by guilt over the genocide in Rwanda, pressured Rwanda and Uganda to disengage. During 2001 and 2002, talks facilitated by Botswana and South Africa resulted in foreign forces in DRC withdrawing from the frontline. In April 2002, Kabila and the MLC agreed to form a united, multi-party government and eventually hold elections. In the July Pretoria Accord and the September Luanda Accord, Rwanda and Uganda, respectively, pledged to withdraw their forces from DRC. By June 2003, all foreign state forces had returned home. In December 2002, all the major DRC factions including the Kabila regime, MLC, three RCD groups, the Mai Mai militia and civil society organizations signed the Global and Inclusive Accord (AGI) in which they vowed to form a shared government under a Kabila presidency, integrate armed groups into a new security force structure and hold elections in two years. MONUC, which grew from 200 peacekeepers in December 2000 to 4,200 by the end of 2002, monitored the departure of foreign troops and oversaw the disarmament and demobilization process for the various and usually reluctant "negative" factions such as former Hutu militia from Rwanda which had been left out of the AGI.

The death toll arising from the Second Congo War has been debated. The International Rescue Committee (IRC), an established international humanitarian organization that regularly reported on the impact of the war, claimed that between August 1998 and November 2002, some 3.3 million people had died mostly of hunger, disease and displacement related to the collapse of the state. This would make it the world's deadliest conflict since 1945. However, more recently, the Canadian-based Human Security Report Project criticized IRC research methodology and put the figure at several hundred thousand deaths and up to 800,000 for the longer period between 1998 and 2007.

After the withdrawal of foreign state forces in 2002/3, violence continued in eastern and northeastern DRC. In the northeastern Ituri province, fighting broke out between Hema and Lendu militias, with the former supported by Rwanda. In the eastern region's North and South Kivu provinces, Hutu militias and former soldiers from Rwanda constituted themselves as the Democratic Forces for the Liberation of Rwanda (FDLR) which provoked periodic Rwandan military incursions. Additionally, Congolese Tutsi (Banyamulenge), with the covert support of Rwanda, rebelled against the DRC government from 2006 to 2009 under the banner of the National Congress for the Defence of the People (CNDP) and again from 2012 to 2013 as the March 23 (or M23) movement. Throughout this period, the UN force grew to around 20,000 international troops, tried with mixed results to contend with the different factions and in 2010 renamed itself the UN Organization Stabilization Mission in the DRC (MONUSCO) to reflect that it was now supporting an elected government (Prunier, 2009; Reyntjens, 2009; Sterns, 2011).

Part IV

Documents

Document 1
Peace Treaty of Vereeniging, May 31, 1902

The Second Anglo-Boer War (or South African War, 1899–1902) ended with the signing of the Treaty of Vereeniging. Although they had fought a protracted guerrilla war against the British, the Boer leaders voted 54:6 to surrender their independence. This led to the 1910 creation of the self-governing Union of South Africa which was dominated by Boer leaders, but in 1914, some Boers took advantage of the outbreak of World War I to rebel in a bid to regain republican autonomy.

Peace Treaty of Vereeniging, May 31, 1902

THE FOLLOWING NOTICE is hereby published for general information. By order of His Excellency the High Commissioner and Administrator of the Transvaal.

WE Davidson, Acting Secretary to the Transvaal Administration – 3rd June 1902.

ARMY HEADQUARTERS, SOUTH AFRICA

General Lord Kitchener of Khartoum, Command in Chief

AND

His Excellency Lord Milner, High Commissioner, on behalf of the

BRITISH GOVERNMENT, AND

Messrs S.W. Burger, F.W. Reitz, Louis Botha, J.H. de la Rey, L.J. Meyer, and J.C. Krogh, acting as the GOVERNMENT of SOUTH AFRICAN REPUBLIC,

AND

Messrs W.J.C. Brebner, C.R. de Wet, J.B.M. Hertzog, and C.H. Olivier, acting as the GOVERNMENT of the ORANGE FREE STATE, on behalf of their respective BURGHERS

Desirous to terminate the present hostilities, agree on the following Articles.

1. The BURGHER Forces in the Field will forthwith lay down 'their Arms, handing over all Guns, Rifles, and Munitions of War, in their possession or under their control, and desist from any further resistance to the Authority of HIS MAJESTY KING EDWARD VII, whom they recognise as their lawful SOVEREIGN.

   The Manner and details of this surrender will be arranged between Lord Kitchener and Commandant General Botha, Assistant Commandant General de la Rey and Chief Commandant De Wet.
2. Burghers in the field outside the limits of the TRANSVAAL and ORANGE RIVER COLONY, and all Prisoners of War at present outside South Africa, who are burghers, will, on duly declaring their acceptance of the position of subjects of HIS MAJESTY KING EDWARD VII, be gradually brought back to their homes as soon as transport can be provided and their means of subsistence ensured.
3. The BURGHERS so surrendering or so returning will not be deprived of their personal liberty, or their property.
4. No proceedings CIVIL or CRIMINAL will be taken against any of the BURGHERS so surrendering or so returning for any Acts in connection with the prosecution of the War. The benefit of this Clause will not extend to certain Acts contrary to the usage of War which have been notified by the Commander in Chief to the Boer Generals, and which shall be tried by Court Martial immediately after the close of hostilities.
5. The DUTCH language will be taught in Public Schools in the TRANSVAAL and the ORANGE RIVER COLONY where the Parents of the Children desire it, and will be allowed in co U R T S of LA W when necessary for the better and more effectual Administration of Justice.
6. The Possession of Rifles will be allowed in the TRANSVAAL and ORANGE'RIYER COLONY to persons requiring them for their protection on taking out a licence according to Law.
7. MILITARY ADMINISTRATION in the TRANSVAAL and ORANGE RIVER COLONY will at the earliest possible date be succeeded by CIVIL GOVERNMENT, and, as soon as circumstances permit, Representative Institutions, leading up to self-Government, will be introduced.
8. The question of granting the Franchise to Natives will not be decided until after the introduction of Self-Government.

9. No Special Tax will be imposed on Landed Property in the TRANSVAAL and ORANGE RIVER COLONY to defray the Expenses of the War.
10. As soon as conditions permit, a Commission, on which the local inhabitants will be represented, will be appointed in each District of the TRANSVAAL and ORANGE RIVER COLONY, under the Presidency of a Magistrate or other official, for the purpose of assisting the restoration of the people to their homes and supplying those who, owing to war losses, are unable to provide for themselves, with food, shelter, and the necessary amount of seed, stock, implements etc. indispensable to the resumption of their normal occupations.

His Majesty's Government will place at the disposal of these Commissions a sum of three million pounds sterling for the above purposes, and will allow all notes, issued under Law No.1 of 1900 of the Government of the SOUTH AFRICAN REPUBLIC, and all receipts, given by the officers in the field of the late Republics or under their orders, to be presented to a JUDICIAL COMMISSION, which will be appointed by the Government, and if such notes and receipts are found by this Commission to have been duly issued in return for valuable consideration they will be received by the first-named Commissions as evidence of War losses suffered by the persons to whom they were originally given. In addition to the above named free grant of three million pounds, His Majesty's Government will be prepared to make advances as loans for the same purpose, free of interest for two years, and afterwards repayable over a period of years with 3 per cent interest. No foreigner or rebel will be entitled to the benefit of this Clause.

Signed at Pretoria this thirty first day of May in the Year of Our Lord One Thousand Nine Hundred and Two.

[Signed]

KITCHENER OF KHARTOUM, MILNER, S W BURGER, F W REITZ, LOUIS BOTHA, J H DE LA REY, LJ MEYER, J C KROGH, C R DE WET, J B M HERTZOG, W J C BREBNER, C H OLIVIER

Source: Accessed online at https://nelsonmandela.org/omalley/index.php/site/q/03lv01538/04lv01600/05lv01601/06lv01602.htm.

Document 2
The South African concentration camps

During the last phase of the Second Anglo-Boer War (1899–1902) in what is now South Africa, the remaining Boer fighters pursued a guerrilla warfare campaign against the conventional British forces occupying the former Boer republics. To deny resources and intelligence to the Boer fighters, the British destroyed Boer farms and confined Boer non-combatants in concentration camps where around 25,000 Boers and 20,000 of their African servants died of disease and hunger. British activist Emily Hobhouse visited the camps and wrote scathing reports that prompted British domestic criticism of London's conduct of the war.

The Bloemfontein Camp

January 26

The exile camp here is a good two miles from the town, dumped down on the southern slope of a kopje, right on out onto the bare brown veld, not a vestige of a tree in any direction, nor shape of any description. It was about four o'clock of a scorching afternoon when I set foot in the camp, and I can't tell you what I felt like, so I won't try.

I began by finding a woman whose sister I had met in Cape Town. It is such a puzzle to find your way in a village of bell tents, no streets or names or numbers. There are nearly 2,000 people in this one camp, of which some few are men – they call them "hands up" men – and over 900 children.

Imagine the heat outside the tents and the suffocation inside! We sat on their khaki blankets, rolled up, in Mrs. B.'s tent; and the sun blazed through the single canvas, and the flies lay thick and black on everything; no chair, no table, nor any room for such; only a deal box, standing on its end, served as a wee pantry. In this tiny tent live Mrs. B's five children (three quite grown up) and a little Kaffir servant girl. Many tents have more occupants. Mrs. P. came in, and Mrs. R. and others, and they told me their stories, and we cried together, and even laughed together, and chatted bad Dutch and bad English all the afternoon. On wet nights the water streams down the canvas and comes flowing in, as it knows how to do in this country, under the flap of the tent, and wets their blankets as they lie on the ground. While we sat there a snake came in. They said it was a puff adder, very poisonous, so they all ran out, and I attacked the creature with my parasol. I could not bear to think the thing should be at large in a community mostly sleeping on the ground. After a struggle I wounded it, and then a man came with a mallet and finished it off.

Source: Emily Hobhouse, *The Guardian*, June 19, 1901.

Document 3
The Konigsberg in East Africa

During the early part of World War I, the German cruiser Konigsberg was based in German East Africa and represented a serious threat to British shipping in the Indian Ocean. Using naval and air power in a way that had not been seen previously in Africa, initial British operations in German East Africa focused on neutralizing this strategic threat.

At the commencement of the war our light cruiser Konigsberg had left the harbour of Dar-es-Salaam and had, on the 29th September, surprised and destroyed the English cruiser Pegasus at Zanzibar. Then several large enemy cruisers had arrived and industriously looked for the Konigsberg. On the 19th October, at Lindi, a pinnace steamed up to the steamer Praesident, of the East African Line, which was concealed in the Lukuledi river. The local Defence Force raised at Lindi, and the Reinforcement Company, were at the moment away under Captain Augar, to repel a landing expected at Mikindani, so that nothing could be undertaken against the pinnace.

It was not till the 29th July, 1915, that several whalers went up the Lukuledi and blew up the Praesident.

After successful cruises in the Indian Ocean the Konigsberg had concealed herself in the Rufiji river, but her whereabouts had become known to the enemy. The mouth of the river forms an intricate delta, the view being obstructed by the dense bush with which the islands are overgrown. The various river-mouths were defended by the Delta Detachment, under Lieutenant Commander Schoenfeld; this detachment consisted of Naval ratings, European reservists, and Askari, and its strength was about 150 rifles, a few light guns, and a few machine guns. The enemy made many attempts to enter the river-mouths with light craft, but was invariably repulsed with severe loss. The Adjutant, a small steamer which the English had taken as a good prize, and armed, was recaptured on one occasion, and was used thenceforward by us as an auxiliary man-of-war on Lake Tanganyika. Some English aircraft had also come to grief in the Rufiji delta. A blockship, which the English had sunk in the most northerly of the river-mouths, did not close the fairway.

The frequent bombardments by ships' guns, which he had no means of opposing, Lieut.-Commander Schoenfeld defeated by the skillful design of his positions, and by shifting them in time. Early in July, 1915, the English had brought to the Rufiji two shallow-draught gun-boats, armed with heavy guns. On the 6th July they made the first attack with four cruisers and other armed vessels, and two river gun-boats. The enemy bombarded the Konigsberg, which was at anchor in the river with aeroplane observation. The attack was beaten off, but when it was repeated on the nth July, the Konigsberg suffered severely. The gun-detachments were put out of action. The severely wounded captain had the breech-blocks thrown overboard and the ship blown up. The loss of the Konigsberg, though sad in itself, had at least this advantage for the campaign on land, that the whole crew and the valuable stores were now at the disposal of the Protective Force.

Lieutenant-Commander Schoenfeld, who was in command on land at the Rufiji delta, at once set himself with great forethought to raise the parts of the guns that had been thrown overboard. Under his supervision the ten guns of the Konigsberg were completely salved and got ready for action again; five were mounted at Dar-es-Salaam, two each at Tanga and Kigoma, and one at Muansa. For their transport he made use of several vehicles constructed for heavy loads which were found on a neighbouring plantation. In their concealed positions on land these guns rendered excellent service, and as far as I know not one of them was damaged on this service, although they were often bombarded by the enemy's vessels.

Source: General Paul von Lettow-Vorbeck, *My Reminiscences of East Africa*, London: Hurst and Blackett, 1922, pp. 84–6.

Document 4

Haile Selassie, Appeal to the League of Nations

In 1935–36, fascist Italy invaded and conquered Ethiopia which was one of only two independent states in Africa. Ethiopian Emperor Haile Selassie, who had led the unsuccessful defense of his country, addressed the League of Nations, which had been established after World War I in order to prevent conflict but which did little to prevent Italian aggression.

Appeal to the League of Nations

Haile Selassie

June 1936

I, Haile Selassie I, Emperor of Ethiopia, am here today to claim that justice which is due to my people, and the assistance promised to it eight months ago, when fifty nations asserted that aggression had been committed in violation of international treaties.

There is no precedent for a Head of State himself speaking in this assembly. But there is also no precedent for a people being victim of such injustice and being at present threatened by abandonment to its aggressor. Also, there has never before been an example of any Government proceeding to the systematic extermination of a nation by barbarous means, in violation of the most solemn promises made by the nations of the earth that there should not be used against innocent human beings the terrible poison of harmful gases. It is to defend a people struggling for its age-old independence that the head of the Ethiopian Empire has come to Geneva to fulfill this supreme duty, after having himself fought at the head of his armies.

I pray to Almighty God that He may spare nations the terrible sufferings that have just been inflicted on my people, and of which the chiefs who accompany me here have been the horrified witnesses.

It is my duty to inform the Governments assembled in Geneva, responsible as they are for the lives of millions of men, women and children, of the deadly peril which threatens them, by describing to them the fate which has been suffered by Ethiopia. It is not only upon warriors that the Italian Government has made war. It has above all attacked populations far removed from hostilities, in order to terrorize and exterminate them.

At the beginning, towards the end of 1935, Italian aircraft hurled upon my armies bombs of tear-gas. Their effects were but slight. The soldiers learned to scatter, waiting until the wind had rapidly dispersed the poisonous gases. The Italian aircraft then resorted to mustard gas. Barrels of liquid were hurled upon armed groups. But this means also was not effective; the liquid affected only a few soldiers, and barrels upon the ground were themselves a warning to troops and to the population of the danger.

It was at the time when the operations for the encircling of Makalle were taking place that the Italian command, fearing a rout, followed the procedure which it is now my duty to denounce to the world. Special sprayers were installed on board aircraft so that they could vaporize, over vast areas of territory, a fine, death-dealing rain. Groups of nine, fifteen, eighteen aircraft followed one another so that the fog issuing from them formed a continuous sheet. It was thus that, as from the end of January, 1936, soldiers, women, children, cattle, rivers, lakes and pastures were drenched continually with this deadly rain. In order to kill off systematically all living creatures, in order to more surely to poison waters and pastures, the Italian command made its aircraft pass over and over again. That was its chief method of warfare.

RAVAGE AND TERROR

The very refinement of barbarism consisted in carrying ravage and terror into the most densely populated parts of the territory, the points farthest removed from the scene of hostilities. The object was to scatter fear and death over a great part of the Ethiopian territory. These fearful tactics succeeded. Men and animals succumbed. The deadly rain that fell from the aircraft made all those whom it touched fly shrieking with pain. All those who drank the poisoned water or ate the infected food also succumbed in dreadful suffering. In tens of thousands, the victims of the Italian mustard gas fell. It is in order to denounce to the civilized world the tortures inflicted upon the Ethiopian people that I resolved to come to Geneva. None other than myself and my brave companions in arms could bring the League of Nations the undeniable proof. The appeals of my delegates addressed to the League of Nations had remained without any answer; my delegates had not been witnesses. That is why I decided to come myself to bear witness against the crime perpetrated against my people and give Europe a warning of the doom that awaits it, if it should bow before the accomplished fact.

Is it necessary to remind the Assembly of the various stages of the Ethiopian drama? For 20 years past, either as Heir Apparent, Regent of the Empire, or as Emperor, I have never ceased to use all my efforts to bring my country the benefits of civilization, and in particular to establish relations of good neighbourliness with adjacent powers. In particular I succeeded in concluding with Italy the Treaty of Friendship of 1928, which absolutely prohibited the resort, under any pretext whatsoever, to force of arms, substituting for force and pressure the conciliation and arbitration on which civilized nations have based international order.

COUNTRY MORE UNITED

In its report of October 5th 1935, the Committee of Thirteen recognized my effort and the results that I had achieved. The Governments thought that the entry of Ethiopia into the League, whilst giving that country a new guarantee for the maintenance of her territorial integrity and independence, would help her to reach a higher level of civilization. It does not seem that in Ethiopia today there is more disorder and insecurity than in 1923. On the contrary, the country is more united and the central power is better obeyed.

I should have procured still greater results for my people if obstacles of every kind had not been put in the way by the Italian Government, the Government which stirred up revolt and armed the rebels. Indeed the Rome Government, as it has today openly proclaimed, has never ceased to prepare for the conquest of Ethiopia. The Treaties of Friendship it signed with me were not sincere; their only object was to hide its real intention from me. The Italian Government asserts that for 14 years it has been preparing for its present conquest. It therefore recognizes today that when it supported the admission of Ethiopia to the League of Nations in 1923, when it concluded the Treaty of Friendship in 1928, when it signed the Pact of Paris outlawing war, it was deceiving the whole world. The Ethiopian Government was, in these solemn treaties, given additional guarantees of security which would enable it to achieve further progress along the specific path of reform on which it had set its feet, and to which it was devoting all its strength and all its heart.

WAL-WAL PRETEXT

The Wal-Wal incident, in December, 1934, came as a thunderbolt to me. The Italian provocation was obvious and I did not hesitate to appeal to the League of Nations. I invoked the provisions of the treaty of 1928, the principles of the Covenant; I urged the procedure of conciliation and arbitration. Unhappily for Ethiopia this was the time when a certain Government considered that the European situation made it imperative at all costs to obtain the friendship of Italy. The price paid was the abandonment of Ethiopian independence to the greed of the Italian Government. This secret agreement, contrary to the obligations of the Covenant, has exerted a great influence over the course of events. Ethiopia and the whole world have suffered and are still suffering today its disastrous consequences . . .

I ask the fifty-two nations, who have given the Ethiopian people a promise to help them in their resistance to the aggressor, what are they willing to do for Ethiopia? And the great Powers who have promised the guarantee of collective security to small States on whom weighs the threat that they may one day suffer the fate of Ethiopia, I ask what measures do you intend to take?

Representatives of the World I have come to Geneva to discharge in your midst the most painful of the duties of the head of a State. What reply shall I have to take back to my people?

June, 1936. Geneva, Switzerland.

Source: Accessed online at https://astro.temple.edu/~rimmerma/appeal_to_the_league_of_nations_.htm.

Document 5

Manifesto of Umkhonto we Sizwe

After South African Police killed sixty-nine protestors at Sharpeville in March 1960, members of the South African Communist Party (SACP) and African National Congress (ANC) decided to abandon non-violent activism and embark on an armed struggle to liberate their country from white minority rule and apartheid. Called "Umkhonto we Sizwe" or "Spear of the Nation" by founding member Nelson Mandela, the new group conducted bombings across South Africa and circulated a manifesto in December 1961.

Units of Umkhonto we Sizwe today carried out planned attacks against government installations, particularly those connected with the policy of apartheid and race discrimination.

Umkhonto we Sizwe is a new, independent body, formed by Africans, It includes in its ranks South Africans of all races It is not connected in any way with a so-called 'Committee for National Liberation' whose existence has been announced in the press. Umkhonto we Sizwe will carry on the struggle for freedom and democracy by new methods, which are necessary to complement the actions of the established national liberation organisations. Umkhonto we Sizwe fully supports the national liberation movement, and our members jointly and individually, place themselves under the overall political guidance of that movement.

It is, however, well known that the main national liberation organisations in this country have consistently followed a policy of non-violence. They have conducted themselves peaceably at all times, regardless of government attacks and persecutions upon them, and despite all government-inspired attempts to provoke them to violence. They have done so because the people prefer peaceful methods of change to achieve their aspirations without the suffering and bitterness of civil war. But the people's patience is not endless.

The time comes in the life of any nation when there remain only two choices: submit or fight. That time has now come to South Africa. We shall not submit and we have no choice but to hit back by all means within our power in defence of our people, our future and our freedom. The government has interpreted the peacefulness of the movement as weakness; the people's non-violent policies have been taken as a green light for government violence. Refusal to resort to force has been interpreted by the government as an invitation to use armed force against the people without any fear of reprisals. The methods of Umkhonto we Sizwe mark a break with that past.

We are striking out along a new road for the liberation of the people of this country. The government policy of force, repression and violence will no longer be met with non-violent resistance only! The choice is not ours; it has been made by the Nationalist government which has rejected ever peaceable demand by the people for rights and freedom and answered ever such demand with force and yet more force! Twice in the past 18 months, virtual martial law has been imposed in order to beat down peaceful, non-violent strike action of the people in support of their rights. It is now preparing its forces – enlarging and rearming its armed forces and drawing the white civilian population into commandos and pistol clubs – for full-scale military actions against the people. The Nationalist government has chosen the course of force and massacre, now, deliberately, as it did at Sharpeville.

Umkhonto we Sizwe will be at the front line of the people's defence. It will be the fighting arm of the people against the government and its policies of race oppression. It will be the striking force of the people for liberty, for rights and for their final liberation! Let the government, its supporters who put it into power, and those whose passive toleration of reaction keeps it in power, take note of where the Nationalist government is leading the country!

We of Umkhonto we Sizwe have always sought -as the liberation movement has sought – to achieve liberation without bloodshed and civil clash. We do so still. We hope – even at this late hour – that our first actions will awaken everyone to a realisation of the disastrous situation to which the Nationalist policy is leading. We hope that we will bring the government and its supporters to their senses before it is too late, so that both the government and its policies can be changed before matters reach the desperate state of civil war. We believe our actions to be a blow against the Nationalist preparations for civil war and military rule.

In these actions, we are working in the best interests of all the people of this country – black, brown and white – whose future happiness and well-being cannot be attained without the overthrow of the Nationalist government, the abolition of white supremacy and the winning of liberty, democracy and full national rights and equality for all the people of this country.

We appeal for the support and encouragement of all those South Africans who seek the happiness and freedom of the people of this country.
Afrika Mayibuye! (Return Africa!)

Source: Accessed online at https://nelsonmandela.org/omalley/index.php/site/q/03lv02424/04lv02730/05lv02918/06lv02950.htm.

Document 6
British attitudes toward Mau Mau insurgents

During the 1950s Mau Mau Emergency in Kenya, British colonial security forces engaged in what they called "pseudo operations," whereby captured insurgents who had changed sides were used to infiltrate and eliminate active rebel units. A "pseudo team" directly by British police officer Ian Henderson captured Mau Mau leader Dedan Kimathi who was later tried and hanged. The following account by Henderson highlights some of the British attitudes toward the Mau Mau insurgents.

While a select group of the very best of our converted terrorists was searching for Kimathi in the Tree Tops Salient and the Mwathe, the rest of the force was not idle. They too had been formed into gangs and went back into the forest to work for us. By the end of June we had over ninety hardcore Mau Mau operating in the Aberdares on our side, and success bred success. A hostile gang fighting against us yesterday became a tamed gang fighting for us today. We were not exactly converting these desperate men, but we were certainly recruiting them.

No Mau Mau could merge with the Kimathi gang, but our technique of penetrating and living in with other Mau Mau gangs proved immensely successful. Time after time our collaborators contacted gangs and merged with them without difficulty. Every meeting was celebrated in great fashion with much praying and smearing of smelling animal fat on everyone's foreheads to wash away any impure thoughts that might have entered their minds during the time they had been apart from one another. Everyone would then retire to some secluded part of the jungle where all the available food was eaten.

When the gang fell asleep their guests would lie down with them and pretend to fall asleep also. Sometimes friend and foe would lie beneath the same skin cover, their bodies close together for warmth. But as the night wore on, as their hosts snored and signed and turned, our men would be waiting for the signal to strike. Sometimes someone in the gang would be restless, and the time for action had to be postponed. So as to warn the leader not to rise, warning coughs would echo round the hideout, and all would be silent for another hour or so. But when the moment finally came, the job would be done with the utmost efficiency. The Mau Mau would wake to find that they were being tied by the feet or covered by armed men who were no longer friendly. Every week and average of twenty-two terrorists were accounted for in the forests by our teams using this technique.

Normally it was only when a gang had posted armed sentries round its hideout that anyone was killed, and these were invariably the sentries themselves. This suited us well, for in order to make progress we had to have information, and only live terrorists could supply this. When a team was preparing to capture their sleeping hosts, some of them would sneak away to deal with the sentries. Sometimes they found them leaning against trees blissfully unaware of their danger. These we were able to overpower without noise or resistance; sometimes we found them alert. They would challenge our men, and we would have to have a good excuse for not being asleep. The excuse our men usually gave was that they were going to relieve themselves. Normally our men walked quite boldly up to the sentries, whose positions had been carefully noted beforehand, and as they went they would stretch their arms back and yawn as though they had just risen from deep sleep. They would whisper to the sentries about the coldness of the night, about the noise of an animal, or about a pain in their stomachs. They would watch their man until he relaxed, then, with the speed of a wild cat, they would drop him and hold him down. Any resistance meant death. Nothing but immediate submission was good enough, for they knew their advers-aries, they knew it was a matter of life and death. Mau Mau were not people to take chances with! It was like holding down a leopard – give it a chance to free its foot and you could be clawed to death. But not once throughout these operations did anyone escape.

Sometimes the terrorists, asleep in their hideouts, were remarkably slow in coming to their senses. It always amazed me how tense and sensitive a Mau Mau gang would be when no sentries were guarding them, and yet how utterly oblivious to danger they would become when sentries were posted. One night when a terrorist named Kabangi was captured, all the sentries round about, and all his companions in the hideout, had been securely tied up before he awoke. He had been asleep on the ground with six others, all closely packed together and covered with a single dirty piece of hessian, when our team struck. Four men on his left and two on his right had been pulled to their feet and handcuffed before he stirred. But even then he did not wake up. When one of our men grabbed his hair and shook his head, he turned over on to his side and mumbled, "What are you doing? Do you think I am a woman?" With that he went to sleep again . . .

But these were certainly exceptions. In most cases our teams had to act quickly and decisively, sometimes before they were ready. The Mau Mau practice of laying packed together like kernels on a corn cob sometimes made it very difficult for a team leader to extricate himself without waking the gang. There were cases where sentries screamed out and woke everyone. There were even cases were the gang never went to sleep at all.

For months the sole preoccupation of all these terrorists had been mere survival. They lived like animals. They survived because of their animal skills, and when caught they reacted like trapped animals.

I often saw terrorists a few moments after their capture. Some would stand there wide-eyed, completely speechless, and shivering violently from shock and cold. They would think of the moment of death, and that moment seemed very near. Others would be past the stage of thinking at all. Mad with shock, they would shout and struggle or froth at the mouth and bite at the earth.

Under these circumstances it was not easy to remember that they were fanatics who had enjoyed killing children and slitting open the stomachs of pregnant women. They were savage, vicious, unpredictable as a rabid dog, but because they were now cornered, muzzled, powerless, and terrified, one felt like giving them a reassuring pat.

Those who were suspected of committing specific atrocities or major crimes were handed over to the authorities with the least possible delay to stand trial; those against whom no definite charge could be made, but who were, nevertheless, particularly bad characters, were sent off to detention. Some, we felt, would respond to civilization fairly quickly, others might take longer, others would probably never respond. They would remain a menace to society as long as they lived.

But there were some who were not directly linked to serious acts of terrorism. There were terrorists who, though still hardcore Mau Mau, possessed information which would be of great value to us, and who seemed prepared to give it to us. We kept these and recruited them into our force. I talked to them, Gati talked to them, other members of our team talked to them, and soon they were ready to go back into the jungle to hunt for other terrorists. And so the snowball rolled.

Source: Ian Henderson, with Philip Goodhart, *Man Hunt in Kenya: The True Story of the Man Hunt for the Leader of the Mau Maus*, New York: Doubleday, 1958, pp. 146–9.

Document 7
Biafran Declaration of Independence, 1967

The Nigerian Civil War (1967–70) was one of the world's deadliest conflicts after 1945. Although representatives of Nigeria's federal military and eastern regional governments tried to avert conflict through negotiations held at Aburi, Ghana, in January 1967, the easterners declared the independence of Biafra in May of that year which led to the start of civil war.

The Declaration of Independence Tuesday, May 30, 1967

Fellow countrymen and women, YOU, the people of Eastern Nigeria:

CONSCIOUS of the supreme authority of Almighty God over all mankind, of your duty to yourselves and prosperity;

AWARE that you can no longer be protected in your lives and in your property by any Government based outside eastern Nigeria;

BELIEVING that you are born free and have certain inalienable rights which can best be preserved by yourselves;

UNWILLING to be unfree partners in any association of a political or economic nature;

REJECTING the authority of any person or persons other than the Military Government of eastern Nigeria to make any imposition of whatever kind or nature upon you;

DETERMINED to dissolve all political and other ties between you and the former Federal Republic of Nigeria;

PREPARED to enter into such association, treaty or alliance with any sovereign state within the former Federal Republic of Nigeria and elsewhere on such terms and conditions as best to subserve your common good;

AFFIRMING your trust and confidence in ME;

HAVING mandated ME to proclaim on your behalf, and in your name the Eastern Nigeria be a sovereign independent Republic,

NOW THEREFORE I, Lieutenant-Colonel Chukwuemeka Odumegwu-Ojukwu, Military Governor of Eastern Nigeria, by virtue of the authority, and pursuant to the principles recited above, do hereby solemnly proclaim that the territory and region known as and called Eastern Nigeria together with her continental shelf and territorial waters shall henceforth be an independent sovereign state of the name and title of THE REPUBLIC OF BIAFRA.

AND I DO DECLARE THAT:

(i)   All political ties between us and the Federal Republic of Nigeria are hereby totally dissolved.

(ii)   All subsisting contractual obligations entered into by the Government of the federal republic of Nigeria or by any person, authority, organization or government acting on its behalf, with any person, authority or organization operating, or relating to any matter or thing, within the Republic of Biafra, shall henceforth be deemed to be entered into with the Military Governor of the Republic of Biafra for and on behalf of the Government and people of the Republic of Biafra, and the covenants thereof shall, subject to this Declaration, be performed by the parties according to their tenor;

(iii)   All subsisting international treaties and obligations made on behalf of Eastern Nigeria by the Government of the Federal Republic of Nigeria shall be honored and respected;

(iv)   Eastern Nigeria's due share of all subsisting international debts and obligations entered into by the Government of the Federal Republic of Nigeria shall be honored and respected;

(v)   Steps will be taken to open discussions on the question of Eastern Nigeria's due share of the assets of the Federation of Nigeria and personal properties of the citizens of Biafra throughout the Federation of Nigeria.

(vi)   The rights, privileges, pensions, etc., of all personnel of the Public Services, the Armed Forces and the Police now serving in any capacity within the Republic of Biafra are hereby guaranteed;

(vii)   We shall keep the door open for association with, and would welcome, any sovereign unit or units in the former Federation of Nigeria or any other parts of Africa desirous of association with us for the purposes of running a common services organization and for the establishment of economic ties;

(viii) We shall protect the lives and property of all foreigners residing in Biafra, we shall extend the hand of friendship to those nations who respect our sovereignty, and shall repel any interference in our internal affairs;

(ix)   We shall faithfully adhere to the charter of the Organization of African Unity and of the United Nations Organization;

(x)   It is our intention to remain a member of the British Commonwealth of Nations in our right as a sovereign, independent nation.

Long live the Republic of Biafra!

And may God protect all those who live in her.

Source: Accessed online at http:/globaldialoguecenter.com/Recommittal %20to%20Declaration%20of%20Biafra%20May%2030%202007.pdf.

Document 8
Rwanda genocide

With the 1990 invasion of Rwanda by the predominantly Tutsi Rwandan Patriotic Front (RPF), Hutu extremists engaged in hate propaganda through the Kangura newspaper and radio broadcasts that was meant to intensify racist anti-Tutsi anger among the country's Hutu majority. This informed the 1994 genocide against the Tutsi which took place because elements of the established Hutu Power regime did not want to share power with the rebels. Hutu Power hate propaganda was particularly vicious toward Tutsi women who experienced terrible sexual violence during the genocide.

Kangura No. 6, December 6, 1990

Appeal to the Bahutu conscience (with the Hutu Ten Commandments)

The Batutsi are bloodthirsty and power-hungry and want to impose their hegemony on the people of Rwanda using armed force.
The Ten Commandments [of the Bahutu]

1. Every Hutu male should know that Tutsi women, wherever they may be, are working in the pay of their Tutsi ethnic group. Consequently, shall be deemed a traitor:

   - Any Hutu male who marries a Tutsi woman;
   - Any Hutu male who keeps a Tutsi concubine;
   - Any Hutu male who makes a Tutsi woman his secretary or protégée.

2. Every Hutu male must know that our Hutu daughters are more dignified and conscientious in their role of woman, wife or mother. Are they not pretty, good secretaries and more honest!

3. Hutu women, be vigilant and bring your husbands, brothers and sons back to their senses.

4. Every Hutu male must know that all Tutsi are dishonest in their business dealings. They are only seeking their ethnic supremacy. "Time will tell." Shall be considered a traitor, any Hutu male:

- who enters into a business partnership with Tutsis;
- who invests his money or State money in a Tutsi company;
- who lends to, or borrows from, a Tutsi;
- who grants business favors to Tutsis (granting of important licenses, bank loans, building plots, public tenders . . .) is a traitor.

5. Strategic positions in the political, administrative, economic, military and security domain should, to a large extent, be entrusted to Hutus.
6. In the education sector (pupils, students, teachers) must be in the majority Hutu.
7. The Rwandan Armed Forces should be exclusively Hutu. That is the lesson we learned from the October 1990 war. No soldier must marry a Tutsi woman.
8. Hutus must cease having pity for the Tutsi.
9. The Hutu male, wherever he may be, must be united, in solidarity and be concerned about the fate of their Hutu brothers;

- The Hutu at home and abroad must constantly seek friends and allies for the Hutu Cause, beginning with our Bantu brothers;
- They must constantly counteract Tutsi propaganda;
- The Hutu must be firm and vigilant towards their common Tutsi enemy.

10. The 1959 social revolution, the 1961 referendum and the Hutu ideology must be taught to Hutus at all levels. Every Hutu must propagate the present ideology widely. Any Hutu who persecutes his Hutu brother for having read, disseminated and taught this ideology shall be deemed a traitor.

Source: Accessed online at http://rwandafile.com/Kangura/k06a.html.

This is the testimony of Adeline, a survivor of the Rwandan genocide

I am the only survivor of my family. I was only 19 years old when the genocide took place. My parents, three sisters and two brothers were killed in Gitarama on the 14th of April. When the killing began, my family escaped in many different directions. My two brothers and younger sister, then aged 14, escaped to Butare. Along the way my other sister and I separated from my brothers, managing to hide in a trench.

On 16th April we were discovered by some local villagers, who had joined with the interahamwe. We pleaded with them to leave us alone. We were extremely lucky, because they did just that. At around 2.00 pm, still on the 16th, we naively believed that the situation must have improved. We came out of the trenches.

The killers mocked us saying: "Aha, it is the girls. Let's go and 'liberate' them. We must give them something to celebrate." They took us and another girl who was carrying a baby, to a nearby hill. We passed a roadblock where we saw that people were being killed. Right in front of us people were forced to squat on the floor and were then macheted or killed with a masu. A big truck was on standby where the bodies were piled on and taken away.

When they were tired of killing, the men came to us and ordered us to take off our clothes. They each in turn raped us. One man pleaded with the others to leave my 14 years old sister alone, saying she was only a kid. The other men laughed and said, that we were all going to be killed anyway. That we would have to chose between rape or a cruel death. They raped my 14 year old sister. I stopped feeling my pain. I wanted to protect her, but I couldn't. After raping us they gave us food to eat by the roadside.

Many people were being captured by villagers and brought to the roadblock. Soon there were so many women kept aside for rape. This went on two weeks. My sister and I met many women, some were raped and killed, others were macheted and lay in agony for days before eventually dying. Others were piled on lorries with the dead, even though they were still breathing.

A man called Marcel, who was our neighbour and had a reputation as a killer, came to the roadblock and recognized me. I begged him to save my sister and I. He told the interahamwe who were keeping us that I was his spoil and they let him take me. But I had to leave my sister behind. I was distraught. Marcel accused me of forcing myself on him. Saying that I was a whore that deserved what I got. He took me to his home and raped me every day. His mother was left to guard me whenever he went out so that I would not escape. She was a nice woman. I asked whether she had any daughters of her own. She felt sorry for me. She would clean me up, and treat my injuries. She said that if I become a good wife to her son, she would make sure he never hurts me again. I told her I was sad because I had left my younger sister at a roadblock, and feared I had betrayed her.

When my captor finally returned home after two weeks away, he told that he had a surprise for me. I thought he was going to kill me. Instead he had brought my sister with him. His mother had pleaded with him to save my sister. I couldn't believe he could be that kind. I was eternally grateful to him for saving my sister. But Marcel had a plan. He got one of his relatives to take my sister as his wife.

By mid-June, there were few Tutsis left to massacre, and the killers got more and more agitated. They went from village to village to hunt any surviving snakes. Word got around that Marcel was keeping Tutsi spoils. The local leader ordered a search. I managed to sneak out of the house in time with the help of my mother-in-law, but my sister wasn't so lucky. She was killed. I was so distraught by the news of my sister's death, that I handed myself over to interahamwe to be killed. Instead of killing me, another interahamwe took me to a disused house and raped me. He showed me his grenades and bullets and asked me to choose which death I would prefer. I picked up a grenade and threw it on the ground hoping it would blow me up, but it didn't explode. He then called in his friends to punish me. They gang raped me.

This went on for five days. I was left torn and bleeding. I don't know how I sustained the abuse. After a time I finally passed out. When I awoke, the place was silent. I ventured out of the house, hoping someone would kill me, or even rape me until I would die. I was filth, covered in blood, smelling. I looked like a walking dead. I kept walking calling for the killers to come and get me. By that time, I didn't realise the Rwandan Patriotic Army had liberated the area. Soldiers dressed in uniform came towards me. I was throwing insults at them, demanding that they kill me. Instead they calmed me down and took me to a make shift clinic for treatment.

I have since found out that I am HIV positive. But I don't want to talk about it.

Source: Accessed online at http://un.org/en/preventgenocide/rwanda/education/ survivortestimonies.shtml.

Document 9
The Kagera War

In January 1979, during the Kagera War, the Tanzanian People's Defense Force (TPDF) and allied Ugandan exiles invaded Uganda and overthrew the military dictatorship of Idi Amin. In the following account, one of Amin's officers describes the key engagement that took place around Lukaya in March of that year.

Colonel Abdu Kisuule

In early January 1979 my unit was relieved and went back to Masindi. A week after my return to Masindi, I was called to go to Europe on a special mission to shop for weapons. I went with Yekoko and Major Ndibowa. Our destination was Spain; we went down to Bilbao to test the equipment we wanted.

The list included mortars, the Napalm bomb to counter the Saba-saba,[1] and the 112 planes which were to drop the bombs. The Napalm bomb is a fire bomb and when dropped burns a place like fire.

Unfortunately everywhere we went the Tanzanians were tracking, blocking our orders. This was a blessing in disguise because had the Napalm bomb been brought, it would have been the talking subject and not the Saba-saba.

While we were in Spain looking for arms, the Tanzanians entered Uganda.

When I came back from Spain, I went back to Masindi. One night towards the end of February, I got a call that I was needed at State House. At State House, I was told Masaka was captured and I was to lead the battle to recapture it. I went with Amin up to Buganzi Hill to see what was happening. Amin came back to Kampala, leaving the operation to retake Masaka in my hands. By then, Lukaya was still inn our control but our soldiers had looted everything they could lay their hands on, and the locals had fled. This made us a target anytime and for that reason I decided to put my tactical headquarters in Buwama at the county office, and I order all soldiers to stay 500 meters away from the centre.

Unfortunately, they didn't follow orders and at around 2 pm as I was setting up my tactical base in Buwama, the Tanzanians shot at us and eight of my soldiers were killed. I was not sorry for the loss since I had ordered them out of the centre. That night I decided to move closer and monitor the situation; I slept in Kayabwe just on the way to Nkozi University.

The Libyans had now joined us and we mounted heavy guns which they brought on the hills across Katonga; all of them facing Lukaya and we also deployed tanks. We planned to advance to Masaka on March 9 after briefling the more than 1,000 Libyans at Mitala Maria who had come to boost our ranks. They came with many big guns that we did not have like the 122 mm mortars.

After giving orders to both Libyans and Ugandan troops at around 3 pm, I took valium and gave a tablet to Sule so that we have enough sleep ahead of the long operation to retake Masaka. I was used to taking valium a day before any operation.

A few hours into our sleep we were woken up by the stampede of the fleeing Libyans, their jeeps which had been facing Lukaya were now retreating to Kampala. I told Major Aloysius Ndibowa to block the road so that they don't retreat.

At about 6 pm when the war had started, Sule insisted he was going to move with the tanks. I was coming from the rear from Kayabwe. The fighting was so fierce and many of my men were killed and tens of jeeps were ferrying dead bodies from the frontline to Kampala. The Saba-Saba rocket launcher was giving us a real hard time.

Immediately after Katonga Bridge towards Lukaya, there was a eucalyptus forest on the right hand side. The Tanzanians had laid a death trap for us. Many of our infantrymen, including Libyans, were killed there. Sule, who had been waking behind the tanks, was crushed by one of the tanks as he tried to reverse in retreat. It took me long to know he was dead and the president was asking me of his whereabouts but nobody knew.

At around 10 am, I told the president to send people to look among the bodies that were brought back to Kampala because I was not seeing him on the battle front. That day we lost many soldiers. Amin later sent me word that the body had been found and that the head had been crushed.

We had managed to force the Tanzanians back and moved my headquarters to Kabale Bugonzi. Unfortunately, there was laxity on our side. Had we kept the momentum, we would have taken back Masaka. I am sure that was the last serious battle and that's where we lost the war.

Many of the commanders who had survived up to Nyendo instead retreated back to Kampala. When I got back to Buwama, I found Major General Gowan had also left, all the commanders had deserted the front. I told the remaining forces to withdraw back to Buwama. While at Nuwama information got to me that the withdrawing troops were wreaking havoc in Masindi, looting everything they could.

Note

1   A Soviet-made multiple rocket launcher used by the Tanzanian People's Defense Force.

Source: Henry Lubega, "The Untold Story of the Kagera War by TZ, Uganda Top Soldiers," *The Citizen*, June 2, 2014. Accessed online at http://the citizen.co.tz/News/national/The-untold-story-of-Kagera-War-by-TZ–Uganda-top-soldiers/1840392-2334498-ef678t/index.html.

Document 10
First Congo War

During 1996 and 1997, in what became called the "First Congo War," Rwandan forces invaded eastern Zaire (now Democratic Republic of Congo or DRC) in support of local rebels called the Alliance of Democratic Forces for Liberation (AFDL). Rwanda's justification for this intervention was that exiled Rwandan Hutu fighters who had been involved in the 1994 genocide against the Tutsi in Rwanda were using eastern Zaire as a staging area to threaten Rwanda. However, in 1998, a United Nations investigative team visited DRC and concluded that Rwandan soldiers and AFDL rebels had massacred unarmed Rwandan Hutu refugees and that this might constitute genocide. The UN team could not complete its investigation as it was hindered by the DRC's new AFDL government which, at the time, was dependent on Rwandan forces.

5. Equateur Province

110. By early May (1997), several thousand displaced Rwandans had reached the village of Wendji, 25 kilometres south of Mbandaka, the capital of Equateur province, and more had reached Mbandaka itself. Most of the refugees were young males, but there were also many women and children. Local authorities have told the Investigative Team that that the Rwandans were armed when they arrived in the region, but other sources indicated that local authorities set up a checkpoint to disarm those carrying arms as they arrived. The Investigative Team received 14 statements from women of the village who were raped by the Rwandans. Credible sources corroborated the statements.

111. On 13 May 1997, AFDL troops reached the area, and a massacre ensued. According to the statements of witnesses, the massacre began at the village of Wendji, and later continued along the road to Mbandaka and in the city itself.

112. In Wendji, the troops announced to the local population in Lingala that they "were not there for the Congolese," but rather for the

refugees. Using Lingala, the local language, they ordered the local population to place white headbands around their heads, to allow the soldiers to distinguish them from the Rwandans.

Soon after this, the soldiers began to shoot the latter. The number of victims killed in Wendji is unknown.

Many corpses were thrown in the river. Reliable information was received concerning the location of a mass gravesite containing over a hundred corpses, including women and children.

113. The Team's forensic experts managed to locate this site, and made a preliminary exploration of one grave before being forced to discontinue their work (see Cap. I). The site was located exactly where the testimony indicated it would be found, and the size of the site and number of apparent graves located within it were consistent with the testimony given to the Team concerning the number of corpses buried there in May 1997. The condition of the vegetation within the site was consistent with reports that efforts had been made to remove bodies from mass graves in this area during the weeks preceding the Teams first deployment there, in December 1997. The preliminary exploration of the site produced evidence that it had contained bodies which had decomposed, and subsequently been removed. Two small bones were found, belonging to two different adults (see Annex II).

114. Many Rwandans managed to flee Wendji in the direction of Mbandaka, while others fled into the swamps north of Wendji. Credible statements described how soldiers or local citizens captured some of those who fled into the swamps and brought them out, where they were stabbed, shot or beaten to death.

Testimonies also were received indicating that many persons fleeing Wendji were killed along the road to Mbandaka.

115. At approximately 10H00 during the morning of 13 May 1997, the Rwandans fleeing Wendji by foot began to arrive in Mbandaka. Most fled in the direction of the port, hoping to be able to escape by boat to the Republic of Congo. AFDL soldiers arrived shortly thereafter, first by foot and later in vehicles. When they arrived at the ONATRA (Office Nationale de Transport) port area, they commenced shooting indiscriminately at the Rwandans, including some sitting on a barge. As the port area is surrounded by building or walls on three sides, the Rwandans were trapped, and many jumped into the river. Estimates by witnesses of the number of persons killed at the port vary wildly, from 40 to 500. The most credible sources appear to be those which estimate that at least two hundred persons were killed, excluding deaths by drowning. Photographic evidence provided to the Investigative Team shows that some of the victims, including a child, were dismembered and one victim was beheaded. One witness provided a list of the names of some of the victims.

116. An unknown number of Rwandans were killed elsewhere in the town. Many corpses were left untouched for two days, particularly those not killed in the port area. A clean up was then conducted, and the bodies buried in mass graves. Some of those killed at the port were thrown into the river.

117. The testimonial, forensic and photographic evidence obtained by the Team concerning the events in Wendji and Mbandaka clearly Indicates that several hundred unarmed Rwandans were massacred there on 13 May 1996. The Investigative Team received testimony indicating the names of officers in charge of the massacre at Mbandaka. According to this information, the officer nominally in charge was AFDL, but those in effective control were Rwandan Army officers. These killings violate international humanitarian law and, to the extent that Rwandan officers were involved, Rwanda's obligations under international human rights law.

118. The Team also received testimony from a number of witnesses concerning the killing of unarmed Rwandan Hutus by soldiers in the area of Boende, eastern Equateur Province during April and May 1997. In some cases, the witnesses stated that Rwandan Army (RPA) soldiers were present or participated in these killings.

Source: United Nations, "Report of the Secretary General's Investigative Team Charged With Investigating Serious Violations of Human Rights and International Humanitarian Law in the Democratic Republic of Congo," S1998/581, pp. 50–2.

Glossary

African National Congress (ANC) Formed in 1912 as the South African Native National Congress (SANNC), this was the first South African-wide black political organization. From 1948 to the early 1990s it led the campaign against apartheid.

African Party for the Independence of Guinea and Cape Verde (PAIGC) A nationalist group that fought against Portuguese colonial rule in what is now Guinea-Bissau during the 1960s and early 1970s. It was supported by the neighbouring Republic of Guinea as well as Cuba and the Soviet Union.

Agacher Strip A small area claimed by both Mali and Burkina Faso during the 1970s and early 1980s, and split between them in 1986.

Alliance of Democratic Forces for the Liberation of Congo (AFDL) A Congolese rebel group formed by the governments of Uganda and Rwanda during the First Congo War (1996–7), and led by Laurent Kabila who overthrew Mobutu Sese Seko as dictator of Zaire/Democratic Republic of Congo (DRC).

Allied Democratic Forces (ADF) A rebel group originating from western Uganda that emerged in the 1990s and based itself in eastern Democratic Republic of Congo.

Americo-Liberians Descendants of freed African-American slaves from the United States who settled in Liberia in the nineteenth century and established Africa's first republic. They controlled the government of Liberia until 1980.

Armed Forces for the Liberation of Angola (FAPLA) The title of the Angolan military from 1974 to the early 1990s.

Angolan Armed Forces (FAA) The title of the Angolan military from the early 1990s.

Anyanya Meaning "snake venon," the term refers to groups of rebels fighting government forces in southern Sudan during the First Sudanese Civil War (1955–72).

Aouzou Strip A piece of Chadian territory along the Libyan border that was annexed by Libya during the 1970s.

Armed Forces of the North (FAN)   Beginning as a rebel group in northern Chad in the 1970s, this group was led by Hissene Habre and eventually seized power in the country in the early 1980s.

Armed Islamic Group (GIA)   A rebel group that fought the Algerian Civil War (1991–2002).

Army for the Liberation of Rwanda (ALIR)   During the late 1990s this group of exiled Hutu from Rwanda was based in eastern Zaire (Democratic Republic of Congo) and sought to retake power at home.

Arusha Accords   A power sharing agreement concluded between the Rwandan government, the Rwandan Patriotic Front (RPF) and a few other Rwandan political groups in Arusha, Tanzania in August 1993.

Azanian People's Liberation Army (APLA)   The armed wing of South Africa's Pan-African Congress (PAC) from the late 1960s to the early 1990s.

Azawad   The name for an imagined independent state for the Tuareg people of the Sahara. It would consist of parts of Mali and Niger.

Banyamulenge   People of Tutsi identity with historic ties to Rwanda but long resident in eastern Democratic Republic of Congo (DRC).

Biafra   A region in southeastern Nigeria where a separatist movement tried to create an independent state which led to the Nigerian Civil War (1967–70).

Bittereinders   An Afrikaans word for those Boers who, despite no hope of success, refused to surrender during the last phase of the Second Anglo-Boer War or South African War (1899–1902).

Black Week   A series of three serious battlefield defeats suffered by the British during one week in December 1899 during the early phase of the Second Anglo-Boer War (1899–1902).

Caprivi Strip   A narrow portion of Namibia that protrudes between Botswana, Angola and Zambia. It was the scene of intense military operations during Namibia's war of independence during the 1960s to 1980s.

Carrier Corps   A formation of almost one million Africans who were employed, often coercively, by the British to carry supplies in support of military operations in East Africa during the First World War. Around 100,000 died from exhaustion and disease.

Chadian National Armed Forces (FANT)   The title of Hissene Habre's fighting force, formerly known as the Armed Forces of the North (FAN), once he had taken power in Chad during the 1980s.

Chimurenga   A Shona word meaning "struggle." In Zimbabwe, the First Chimurenga refers to the Ndebele and Shona Uprisings against British colonial rule in 1896–7 and the Second Chimurenga to the war of independence against the white minority state from 1965 to 1980.

Christmas War   A 1985 conflict between Mali and Burkina Faso over the Agacher Strip.

Commando   The basic military organization of the late nineteenth century Boer republics in what became South Africa. Commandos were organized locally, leadership was elected, service was unpaid but compulsory and every member was expected to provide his own rifle and horse.

Congo War, First (1996–7)   Rwanda, Uganda and Angola invaded neighbouring Zaire, formed a local rebel alliance and overthrew the regime of Mobutu Sese Seko. Rebel leader Laurent Kabila was installed as president and the country's name was changed to Democratic Republic of Congo (DRC).

Congo War, Second (1998–2002)   Often called "Africa's World War." In 1998 Rwanda and Uganda again invaded neighbouring DRC where they orchestrated several local rebel movements. The Kabila regime in DRC survived by calling on military intervention by Angola, Zimbabwe and Namibia. All these foreign forces eventually looted natural resources from the Congo. After the assassination of Laurent Kabila, a series of negotiated agreements led to the withdrawal of foreign forces in 2002/03.

Congolese Armed Forces (FAC)   The title of the military of the Democratic Republic of Congo from 1997 until 2004.

Congolese National Army (ANC)   The new name of the Force Publique after the independence of the Congo in 1960.

Congolese National Movement (MNC)   A political party active in the Belgian Congo during the decolonization era of the late 1950s and early 1960s. It was led by Pan-Africanist Patrice Lumumba.

Darfur   The western region of modern Sudan. During the First World War Darfur was an independent Muslim state that was conquered by the British and added to colonial Sudan.

Democratic Forces for the Liberation of Rwanda (FDLR)   Formed in 2000 during the Second Congo War, this exiled Rwandan Hutu Power group is based in eastern DRC and engages in illegal mining and smuggling.

Democratic Movement for Malagasy Rejuvenation (MDRM)   An anti-colonial movement that developed in Madagascar during the late 1940s.

Economic Community of West African States (ECOWAS)   An intergovernmental organization of West African states created in 1975.

Economic Community of West African States Monitoring Group (ECOMOG)   A multi-national military force created by ECOWAS during the 1990s that intervened in the civil wars in Liberia and Sierra Leone.

Eritrean Liberation Front (ELF)   Formed in 1960, it launched an armed struggle to regain Eritrea's independence from Ethiopia. Nationalist in ideology, it was recruited mostly from Eritrea's Muslim community and supported by Arab states.

Eritrean People's Liberation Front (EPLF)   Formed in the 1970s, this socialist revolutionary group fought for the independence of Eritrea from Ethiopia.

Front for Democracy in Burundi (FRODEBU)   A moderate and predominantly Hutu political party that came to power in Burundi in 1993 but that was overthrown by the Tutsi military in 1996.

Front for National Salvation (FRONASA)   A group of exiled Ugandan rebels who fought to overthrow the Idi Amin regime during the 1970s. It was led by Yoweri Museveni.

Front for the Liberation of Mozambique (FRELIMO)   Having fought an insurgency against the colonial Portuguese during the 1960s and 1970s, it became the government of Mozambique with independence in 1975.

Harkis   Muslim Algerian troops who fought for the French during the Algerian War of Independence (1954–62). Many were massacred after independence.

Herero   A society in what is now Namibia that rebelled against German colonial rule in 1904 and as a result was subjected to extermination (now called genocide) by German colonial forces.

Holy Spirit Movement   A Christian prophetic movement in northern Uganda that rebelled against the new southern dominated government in 1986–7.

Interahamwe   Meaning "those who work together," this Hutu militia group conducted killings of Tutsi during Rwanda's 1994 genocide.

International Criminal Court (ICC)   Launched in 2002, this international court is based in The Hague in the Netherlands and is backed by the United Nations.

Islamic Armed Movement (MIA)   A rebel group that fought Algeria's Civil War (1991–2002).

Islamic Courts Union (ICU)   An Islamist movement that emerged from the chaos of 1990s Somalia and established order in parts of the south.

Kagera War   A conflict between Tanzania and Uganda fought in 1978–9. It resulted in the Tanzanian invasion of Uganda and the overthrow of Ugandan dictator Idi Amin.

Katanga   The southern mineral rich province of the Democratic Republic of Congo. Between 1960 and 1963, during the Congo Crisis, a separatist movement led by Moise Tshombe tried to create an independent Katanga. Between 1971 and 1997, during the Mobutu regime, Katanga was called Shaba.

Kenya Land and Freedom Army   Predominantly from the Kikuyu ethnic group, this decentralized movement staged a rebellion against British colonial rule in Kenya during the 1950s.

King's African Rifles (KAR)   The British colonial military in East Africa. It was recruited among local people but led by British officers.

Koevoet   Afrikaans for "crowbar," this South African police counter-insurgency unit specialized in pursuing and eliminating insurgents in the late 1970s and 1980s during Namibia's war of independence.

Lord's Resistance Army (LRA)   A rebel movement that operated in northern Uganda from 1987 to 2006 that sought to impose a Christian theocracy on the country.

Mai Mai Militia groups formed in eastern Democratic Republic of Congo during the late 1990s.

Maji Maji A major rebellion against colonial rule in German East Africa (now Tanzania) in 1905.

Mau Mau A British term for the Kenya Land and Freedom Army that rebelled against colonial rule during the 1950s.

Movement for the Liberation of Congo (MLC) A rebel group in eastern Democratic Republic of Congo (DRC) formed in 1998 and supported by Uganda.

Mozambique National Resistance (RENAMO) Formed in 1975 by Rhodesian agents, this insurgent group fought against the FRELIMO government of Mozambique until the early 1990s. In 1980, with the independence of Zimbabwe, apartheid South Africa took over the sponsorship of this group.

Nama A society in what is now Namibia that rebelled against German colonial rule in 1904 and as a result was subjected to extermination (now called genocide) by German colonial forces.

National Council for the Defence of Democracy (CNDD) Formed in 1994, this Hutu rebel group sought to democratize Burundi and fought the country's civil war of 1993 to 2006. In 2005 CNDD leader Pierre Nkurunziza was elected president of Burundi.

National Liberation Front of Angola (FNLA) A nationalist group that fought Portuguese rule in northern Angola during the 1960s and early 1970s. Although supported by South Africa, Zaire and the United States, it was defeated in the civil war that followed independence in 1975.

National Liberation Front (FLN) An Algerian nationalist group that fought the colonial French during the 1950s and early 1960s. It created an authoritarian state after independence.

National Liberation Front of Chad (FROLINAT) A rebel group that operated in northern Chad during the late 1960s and 1970s.

National Patriotic Front of Liberia (NPFL) Led by Charles Taylor, this rebel group invaded Liberia in 1989 initiating the country's first civil war which lasted until 1997.

National Resistance Movement/Army (NRM/A) A rebel group led by Yoweri Museveni that fought the northern dominated Ugandan government in southern Uganda's Luwero Triangle from 1981 to 1986 when it seized the capital.

National Union for the Total Independence of Angola (UNITA) This group fought against Portuguese rule in southern Angola during the late 1960s and early 1970s. Following independence in 1975, it fought a civil war against the ruling MPLA and received support from apartheid South Africa.

Nkomati Accord A 1984 agreement in which Mozambique promised to stop supporting exiled South African anti-apartheid activists and apartheid South Africa pledged to halt its sponsorship of RENAMO insurgents. South Africa did not respect the agreement.

Ogaden War A conflict between Ethiopia and Somalia fought in 1977–8.

Operation Askari A South African military offensive into Angola during 1983 that led to the Lusaka Agreement of 1984.

Operation Congresso II A 1985 Soviet-planned Angolan military offensive against UNITA rebels.

Operation Dragon Noire A November 1964 military operation in eastern Congo involving the United States Air Force, Belgian paratroopers and mercenary ground forces that seized Paulus (Isiro) from the Simba rebels.

Operation Dragon Rouge A November 1964 military operation in eastern Congo involving the United States Air Force, Belgian paratroopers and mercenary ground forces that took Stanleyville (Kisangani) from the Simba rebels.

Operation Epervier (Sparrow Hawk) A French military intervention in Chad in 1986.

Operation Gordian Knot A major Portuguese counter-insurgency operation mounted in Mozambique during 1970.

Operation Grand Slam The 1962 United Nations military action in the Congo that finally suppressed separatist Katanga.

Operation Green Sea A Portuguese amphibious raid on Conakry, capital of the Republic of Guinea, in November 1970.

Operation Lightfoot A successful British offensive against German and Italian positions at El Alamein in Egypt during October 1942.

Operation Modular A 1987 South African military intervention in Angola to prevent the defeat of UNITA rebels by an Angolan state offensive.

Operation Noroit The French military intervention in Rwanda from 1990 to 1993.

Operation Palliser A British military intervention in Sierra Leone in 2000.

Operation Protea A South African military incursion into Angola in 1981. It was South Africa's largest mechanized operation since the Second World War.

Operation Reindeer A 1978 South African airborne assault on Cassinga, Angola.

Operation Resurrection A 1958 plan by French military officers to stage a coup in Paris unless Charles de Gaulle was appointed president.

Operation Saluting October A 1987 Soviet-planned Angolan military offensive against UNITA rebels.

Operation Savannah The 1975 South African intervention in Angola.

Operation Sceptic A 1980 South African military incursion into Angola during which South African troops experienced their first direct combat with Angolan state forces.

Operation Tacaud A 1978 French military intervention in Chad.

Operation Vula A 1986 program by the African National Congress (ANC) to smuggle weapons and agents into apartheid South Africa.

Organization of African Unity (OAU) Formed in 1963 and based in Ethiopia, this international organization of African states was committed to the complete end of colonialism on the continent.

Pan-Africanism Originating among the African Diaspora in the early twentieth century, this ideology advocated the return of people of African descent to their home continent as well as the independence and political unification of Africa.

Pan-Africanist Congress (PAC) Splitting from the African National Congress (ANC) in 1959, this organization continued its own campaign against South Africa's apartheid state until the early 1990s.

Party for the Liberation of the Hutu People (PALIPEHUTU) Formed by Burundian Hutu exiles in Tanzania in 1980, this group sought to overthrow the Tutsi military regime in Burundi. Although its initial military operations were limited, it fought in the Burundian civil war of 1993 to 2006.

Patriotic Salvation Movement (MPS) A Chadian rebel group led by Idriss Deby that seized power from Hissene Habre in 1990.

People's Armed Forces (FAP) Led by Goukouni Oueddei, this rebel group was initially based in northern Chad and received support from Libya. In 1979, it seized power in Chad but was ousted by Hissene Habre's FAN in 1982.

People's Army for the Liberation of Angola (EPLA) The armed wing of the Popular Movement for the Liberation of Angola (MPLA) during the war of independence of the 1960s and early 1970s.

People's Liberation Army of Namibia (PLAN) The armed wing of the South West African People's Organization (SWAPO).

Popular Front for the Liberation of Saguia el Hamra and Rio de Oro (POLISARIO) Formed in 1973, this insurgent group initially fought Spanish colonial rule in Western Sahara. Between 1976 and 1978, it fought Mauritanian occupation of southern Western Sahara, and from 1976 to 1991 it fought Moroccan occupation. It was supported by Algeria, Libya and the Soviet Union.

Popular Movement for the Liberation of Angola (MPLA) An African nationalist group that fought Portuguese colonial rule in Angola during the 1960s and early 1970s. Following the Portuguese withdrawal of 1974, it defeated rival groups and took power with the assistance of Cuba and the Soviet Union.

Poqo Xhosa for "alone," this was the first armed wing of the Pan-Africanist Congress (PAC) that staged an uprising in parts of South Africa during the early 1960s.

Pseudo-Operations A method used by counter-insurgency forces in Kenya during the 1950s and Rhodesia in the 1970s in which security force members discussed themselves as insurgents and attempted to infiltrate insurgent groups. The use of captured and "turned" insurgents became central to such operations.

Quadrillage System   A counter-insurgency method used by the French in Algeria during the 1950s. The country was divided into portions each of which was assigned a specific military unit responsible for hunting down insurgents.

Rally for Congolese Democracy (RCD)   A rebel group formed in eastern Democratic Republic of Congo (DRC) in 1998 and supported by Rwanda. Over the next few years it split into several factions such as RCD-Kisangani (RCD-K) backed by Uganda and RCD-Goma (RCD-G) sponsored by Rwanda.

Red Star Campaign   A massive Ethiopian military offensive against Eritrean separatist rebels that was launched in 1982.

Revolutionary United Front (RUF)   A rebel group that fought in the Sierra Leone Civil War of 1991–2002.

Rif   A mountainous area of northern Morocco that was the scene of intense resistance to Spanish colonial rule during the 1920s.

Rwanda Armed Forces (FAR)   The name of the Rwandan military under the Hutu republics from the 1960s to 1994.

Rwandan Patriotic Army (RPA)   The name of the Rwandan military from 1994, when the Rwandan Patriotic Front (RPF) took power, until the early 2000s when it became the Rwanda Defence Force.

Rwandan Patriotic Front (RPF)   A group of Rwandan exiles, mostly of Tutsi identity, who invaded Rwanda from Uganda in 1990 and seized power during the 1994 genocide.

Salafist Group for Preaching and Combat (GSPC)   Emerging out of the Algerian Civil War (1991–2002) at the end of the 1990s, this Islamist group moved to other Sahelian countries. In 2007 it renamed itself Al-Qaeda in the Islamic Maghreb (AQIM).

Sanussi (Senussi)   A Muslim religious and political group based in Libya.

Secret Army Organization (OAS)   A terrorist organization formed by dissident members of the French military who tried to undermine Algerian independence in the early 1960s.

Simba   Meaning "lion" in Kiswahili, the term was used to refer to leftist rebels fighting in eastern Congo during 1964 and 1965.

Six Day War   The Arab-Israeli conflict of June 1967.

Somali National Movement (SNM)   A rebel group that fought the Siad Barre regime in northern Somalia during the 1980s. With support from Ethiopia, it declared a separate Somaliland Republic in 1991.

Somali Salvation Democratic Front (SSDF)   A Somali rebel group, backed by Ethiopia, which fought the Siad Barre regime in central Somalia during the early to middle 1980s.

Somalia Syndrome   Inspired by the failed United States actions in Somalia, this term referred to the unwillingness of Western states to use military power in pursuit of humanitarian concerns during the 1990s.

South African Defence Force (SADF)   The title of the South African military from 1957 to 1994 which represented most of the apartheid period.

South West African People's Organization (SWAPO)   A nationalist group that fought the South African occupation of Namibia from the 1960s to the end of the 1980s. It became the elected government of Nambia in 1990.

Southern African Development Community (SADC)   An international organization of southern African states formed in 1980 to confront apartheid South Africa. In 1994, with the end of apartheid, South Africa joined SADC.

Southern Sudan Liberation Movement (SSLM)   Originally called Anyanya National Armed Forces (ANAF), this was a separatist rebel group fighting in southern Sudan during the First Sudanese Civil War of the 1960s and early 1970s.

Sudan African Nationalist Union (SANU)   Founded in the early 1960s, this was the first separatist organization created by southern Sudanese.

Sudan People's Liberation Army (SPLA)   The main rebel group in southern Sudan that fought against the government during the Second Sudanese Civil War (1983–2005).

Sudan People's Liberation Army-Nasir (SPLA-Nasir)   The group, led by Riek Machar and made up of ethnic Nuer, split from the original SPLA and engaged in a violent campaign against it during the early 1990s. It was responsible for atrocities against ethnic Dinka civilians.

Suez Crisis   A 1956 international crisis caused by an Anglo-French and Israeli attempt to intervene in Egypt.

Tanzanian People's Defence Force (TPDF)   The military of post-colonial Tanzania.

Tigray Peoples' Liberation Front (TPLF)   A rebel group in northern Ethiopia that fought the Mengistu regime during the 1980s. Its leaders came to dominate the new government that took power in Ethiopia in 1991.

Tirailleurs Senegalais   The French colonial military recruited from west and central Africa.

Toyota War   A 1987 conflict between Chad and Libya.

Transitional Government of National Unity (GUNT)   The late 1970s government of Chad under Goukouni Oueddei that, after it was toppled by Hissene Habre in 1982, became a rebel group based in the north and received support from Libya until 1986.

Uganda National Rescue Front (UNRF)   A rebel group in northern Uganda's West Nile district during the early 1980s.

Uganda People's Defence Force (UPDF)   The new name for Uganda's National Resistance Army (NRA) that was adopted in 1995. It is Uganda's state military.

Uganda Peoples' Democratic Army (UPDA)   Former Ugandan state forces based in Sudan that launched an insurgency in northern Uganda in the late 1980s.

Uganda National Liberation Front/Army (UNLF/A) A coalition of Ugandan exile groups that participated in the 1979 Tanzanian invasion of Uganda.

Umkhonto we Sizwe (Spear of the Nation or MK) The armed wing of the South African African National Congress (ANC) during the struggle against apartheid from the 1960s to early 1990s.

Union Defence Forces (UDF) The title of the military of the Union of South Africa from 1912 to 1957.

Union of Peoples of Angola (UPA) An Angolan nationalist group based in Congo that staged an uprising in northern Angola in the early 1960s.

Union of the Peoples of Cameroon (UPC) An anti-colonial movement that developed in the French territory of Cameroon in the late 1940s and 1950s.

United Nations Assistance Mission for Rwanda (UNAMIR) A multi-national force dispatched to Rwanda in 1993 to oversee the implementation of the Arusha Accords. It was woefully unprepared for the 1994 genocide.

United Nations Mission in the Democratic Republic of Congo (MONUC) A multi-national peacekeeping force deployed to the DRC from 1999 to 2010 when it was renamed UN Organization Stabilization Mission on the DRC (MONUSCO).

United Nations Mission to Sierra Leone (UNAMSIL) A multi-national force that operated in Sierra Leone from 1999 to 2006. In 2001, it was the world's largest UN peacekeeping force.

United Nations Peace Operation in Burundi (ONUB) Originally the African Union Mission in Burundi (AMIB) which was launched in 2003, this multi-national and mostly African peacekeeping force was deployed from 2004 to 2007.

United Nations Operation in Somalia (UNOSOM) A multi-national force dispatched to Somalia in 1992.

United Nations Operation in Somalia II (UNOSOM II) A multi-national force active in Somalia from 1993 to 1995.

United Nations Operation in the Congo (ONUC) A multi-national force dispatched to the newly independent Congo from 1960 to 1964.

United Somali Congress (USC) A rebel group that fought the Siad Barre regime in southern Somalia during the 1980s. At the start of the 1990s, after Barre's overthrow, fighting between USC factions hindered the delivery of international humanitarian assistance and prompted international military intervention by the United Nations and United States.

United Task Force (UNITAF) The United States military intervention (authorized by the United Nations) in Somalia that was launched in December 1992 and replaced by UN Operation in Somalia II (UNOSOM II) in May 1993.

Volcan Army   An Arab rebel group formed in northern Chad in the 1970s.

West African Frontier Force (WAFF)   The umbrella organization for British colonial forces in West Africa (Nigeria, Gold Coast, Sierra Leone and Gambia) from around 1900 to 1956. In 1927, it became the Royal West African Frontier Force (RWAFF).

West Nile Bank Front (WNBF)   Staging out of eastern Zaire/Democratic Republic of Congo, this group mounted an insurgency in northern Uganda's West Nile district from 1994 to 1998.

Western Somali Liberation Front (WSLF)   Active during the late 1970s and 1980s, this rebel group sought to separate the Ogaden region from Ethiopia.

Yom Kippur War   The Arab-Israeli Conflict of October 1973.

Zimbabwe African National Liberation Army (ZANLA)   The armed wing of ZANU during Zimbabwe's War of Independence (1965–80).

Zimbabwe African National Union (ZANU)   Splitting from ZAPU in 1963, this group opposed white minority rule in Southern Rhodesia (now Zimbabwe) during the 1960s and 1970s. Called ZANU-Patriotic Front (ZANU-PF) and led by Robert Mugabe, it came to power in Zimbabwe upon that country's independence in 1980.

Zimbabwe African People's Union (ZAPU)   A nationalist group that opposed white minority rule in Southern Rhodesia (now Zimbabwe) during the 1960s and 1970s. During the early to middle 1980s, after Zimbabwe's independence, ZAPU was crushed by the ZANU-PF government.

Zimbabwe People's Revolutionary Army (ZIPRA)   The armed wing of ZAPU during Zimbabwe's War of Independence (1965–80).

Bibliography

Books

Abdi Abdulqadir Sheik-Abdi, *Divine Madness: Mohammed Abdulle Hassan (1856–1920)*, London: Zed Books, 1983.

Afigbo, A.E. *The Abolition of the Slave Trade in Southeastern Nigeria, 1885–1950*, Rochester, NY: University of Rochester Press, 2006.

Alexander, Martin S., Evans, Martin. and Keiger, J.F.V. (Eds.), *The Algerian War and the French Army, 1954–62: Experiences, Images and Testimony*, Basingstoke, UK: Palgrave MacMillan, 2002.

Alexander, MartinS. and Keiger, J.F.V. (Eds.), *France and the Algerian War, 1954–62: Strategy, Operations and Diplomacy*, London: Frank Cass, 2002.

Allen, Tim and Vlassenroot, Koen (Eds.), *The Lord's Resistance Army: Myth and Reality*, London: Zed Books, 2010.

Alvarez, Jose E. *The Betrothed of Death: The Spanish Foreign Legion During the Rif Rebellion, 1920–27*, Westport, CT: Greenwood Press, 2001.

Anderson, David, *Histories of the Hanged: The Dirty War in Kenya and the End of Empire*, London: Weidenfeld and Nicolson, 2005.

Anderson, Ross, *The Forgotten Front: The East African Campaign, 1914–1918*, Stroud, UK: Tempus, 2004.

Atangana, Martin, *The End of French Rule in Cameroon*, Lanham, MD: University Press of America, 2010.

Atkinson, Rick, *An Army at Dawn: The War in North Africa, 1942–43*, New York: Owl Books, 2002.

Aussaresses, Paul, *The Battle of the Casbah: Terrorism and Counter-Terrorism in Algeria, 1955–57*, New York: Enigma Books, 2004.

Avirgan, Tony and Honey, Martha, *War in Uganda: The Legacy of Idi Amin*, Dar es Salam: Tanzania Publishing House, 1983.

Azevedo, Mario J. *Roots of Violence: A History of War in Chad*, New York: Routledge, 1998.

Barr, Niall, *Pendulum of War: The Three Battle of El Alamein*, Woodstock, NY: Overlook Press, 2005.

Beigbeder, Yves, *Judging War Crimes and Torture: French Justice and International Criminal Tribunals, 1940–2005*, Leiden: Brill, 2006.

Bennett, Huw, *Fighting the Mau Mau: The British Army and Counter-Insurgency in the Kenya Emergency*. Cambridge: Cambridge University Press, 2013.

Bierman, John and Smith, Colin, *War Without Hate: The Desert Campaign of 1940–43*, New York: Penguin Books, 2002.

Bimberg, Edward L. *Tricolor Over the Sahara: The Desert Battles of the Free French, 1940–42*, Westport, CT: Greenwood, 2002.

Bley, Helmut, *South West Africa under German Rule, 1894–1914*, Evanston, IL: Northwestern University Press, 1971.

Bourhill, James, *Come Back to Portofino: Through Italy With the Sixth South African Armoured Division*, Johannesburg: 30 Degrees South, 2011.

Bowen, Wayne H. and Alvarez, Jose E. *A Military History of Modern Spain*, Westport, CT: Praeger Security International, 2007.

Branch, Adam, *Displacing Human Rights: War and Intervention in Northern Uganda*, Oxford: Oxford University Press, 2011.

Branch, Daniel, *Defeating Mau Mau, Creating Kenya: Counterinsurgency, Civil War and Decolonization*, Cambridge: Cambridge University Press, 2009.

Byfield, Judith A., Brown, Carolyn A., Parsons, Timothy and Sikainga, Ahmad Alawad (Eds.), *Africa and World War II*, Cambridge: Cambridge University Press, 2015.

Cann, John P. *Brown Waters of Africa: Portuguese Riverine Warfare, 1961–1974*, St. Petersburg, FL: Hailer Publishing, 2007.

Cann, John P. *Counter-insurgency in Africa: The Portuguese Way of War, 1961–1974*, Westport, CT: Greenwood, 1997.

Carol, Steven, *From Jerusalem to the Lion of Judah and Beyond: Israel's Foreign Policy in East Africa*, Bloomington, IN: iUniverse, 2012.

Carver, Lord, *The Turkish Front 1914–1918*, London: Sidgwick and Jackson, 2003.

Cherry, Janet, *Spear of the Nation; Umkhonto we Sizwe, South Africa's Liberation Army, 1960s–90s*, Athens, OH: Ohio University Press, 2012.

Childs, Timothy W. *Italo-Turkish Diplomacy and the War over Libya. 1911–12*, Leiden: Bill, 1990.

Clapham, Christopher (Ed.), *African Guerrillas*, Bloomington, IN: Indiana University Press, 1998.

Clayton, Anthony, *Frontiersmen: Warfare in Africa since 1950*, London: Routledge, 2004.

Cline, Lawrence, *The Lord's Resistance Army*, Santa Barbara, CA: Praeger Security International, 2013.

Clothier, Norman, *Black Valour: The South African Native Labour Contingent, 1916–1918 and the Sinking of the Mendi*, Pietermaritzburg: University of Natal Press, 1987.

Collins, Robert O. *A History of Modern Sudan*, Cambridge: Cambridge University Press, 2010.

De St. Jorre, John, *The Nigerian Civil War*, London: Hodder and Stoughton, 1972.

De Witte, Ludo, *The Assassination of Patrice Lumumba*, London: Verso, 2002.

Des Forges, Alison, *Leave None to Tell the Story: Genocide in Rwanda*, Human Rights Watch, 1999.

Dorman, Andrew, *Blair's Successful War: British Military Intervention in Sierra Leone*, Farnham, UK: Ashgate Publishing, 2009.

Drechler, Horst, *"Let Us Die Fighting:" The Struggle of the Herero and Nama against German Imperialism, 1884–1915*, London: Zed Press, 1980.

Echenberg, Myron, *Colonial Conscripts: The "Tirailleurs Senegalais" in French West Africa, 1857–1960*, Portsmouth, NH: Heinemann, 1991.

Elkins, Caroline, *Imperial Reckoning: The Untold Story of Britain's Gulag in Kenya*, New York: Henry Holt, 2005.

Ellis, Stephen, *The Mask of Anarchy: The Destruction of Liberia and the Religious Dimension of an African Civil War*, New York: New York University Press, 2001.

Emerson, Stephen A. *The Battle for Mozambique*, Pinetown, South Africa: 30 Degrees South, 2014.

Englebert, Pierre, *Burkina Faso: Unsteady Statehood in West Africa*, Boulder, CO: Westview Press, 1996.

Falola, Toyin and Heaton, Matthew M. *A History of Nigeria*, Cambridge: Cambridge University Press, 2008.

Fogarty, Richard, *Race and War in France: Colonial Subjects in the French Army, 1914–1918*, Baltimore, MD: Johns Hopkins University Press, 2008.

Forsyth, Frederick, *The Biafra Story*, London: Penguin, 1969.

George, Edward, *The Cuban Intervention in Angola, 1965–1991: From Che Guevara to Cuito Cuanavale*, London: Frank Cass, 2005.

Gershovich, Moshe, *French Military Rule in Morocco: Colonialism and its Consequences*, London: Frank Cass, 2000.

Gewald, Jan-Bart, *Herero Heroes: A Socio-Political History of the Herero of Namibia, 1890–1923*, Oxford: James Currey, 1999.

Giblin, James and Monson, Jamie (Eds.), *Maji Maji; Lifting the Fog of War*, Leiden: Brill Publishers, 2010.

Gleijeses, Piero, *Conflicting Missions: Havana, Washington and Africa, 1959–1976*, Chapel Hill, NC: University of North Carolina Press, 2002.

Gleijeses, Piero, *Visions of Freedom: Havana, Washington, Pretoria and the Struggle for Southern Africa, 1976–91*, Chapel Hill, NC: University of North Carolina Press, 2013.

Grundlingh, Albert, *Fighting Their Own War: South African Blacks and the First World War*, Johannesburg: Ravan Press, 1987.

Grundlingh, Albert, *War and Society, Participation and Remembrance: South African Black and Coloured Troops in the First World War*, Stellenbosch: SUN Media, 2014.

Guy, Jeff, *The Maphumulo Uprising; War, Law and Ritual in the Zulu Rebellion*, Scottsville University of Kwa-Zulu/Natal Press, 2005.

Hamilton, John A.L. *War Bush: 81 (West African) Division in Burma 1943–45*, Norwich, UK: Michael Russell Publishing, 2001.

Henk, Dan, *The Botswana Defence Force in the Struggle for an African Environment*, New York: Palgrave Macmillan, 2007.

Honwana, Alcinda, *Child Soldiers in Africa*, Philadelphia, PA: University of Pennsylvania Press, 2006.

Horne, Alistair, *A Savage War of Peace: Algeria 1954–62*, New York: Review Book, 2006.

Hull, Isabell V. *Absolute Destruction: Military Culture and the Practises of War in Imperial Germany*, Ithaca, NY: Cornell University Press, 2005.

Jackson, Ashley, *Botswana 1939–1945: An African Country at War*, Oxford: Clarendon Press, 1999.

Jackson, Ashley, *The British Empire and the Second World War*, London: Hambledon Continuum, 2006.

Jok Madut Jok, *War and Slavery in Sudan*, Philadelphia, PA: University of Pennsylvania Press, 2015.

Kainerugaba, Muhoozi, *Battles of the Ugandan Resistance: A Tradition of Maneuver*, Kampala: Fountain Publishers, 2010.

Kamongo, Sisingi and Bezuidenhout, Leon, *Shadows in the Sand: A Koevoet Tracker's Story of an Insurgency War*, Johannesburg: 30 Degrees South Publishers, 2011.

Katjavivi, Peter H. *A History of Resistance in Namibia*, London: James Currey, 1988.

Keenan, Jeremy, *The Dying Sahara: US Imperialism and Terror in Africa*, London: Pluto Press, 2013.

Kennes, Erik and Larmer, Miles, *The Katangese Gendarmes and War in Central Africa: Fighting Their Way Home*, Bloomington, IN: Indiana University Press, 2016.

Killingray, David, *Fighting for Britain: African Soldiers in the Second World War*, Rochester, NY: James Currey, 2010.

Laband, John, (Ed.) *Daily Lives of Civilians in Wartime Africa: From Slavery Days to Rwandan Genocide*, Westport, CT: Greenwood Press, 2007.

Lan, David, *Guns and Rain: Guerrillas and Spirit Mediums in Zimbabwe*, London: James Currey, 1985.

Lawler, Nancy, *Soldiers of Misfortune: Ivoirien Tirailleurs of World War II*, Athens, OH: Ohio University Press, 1992.

Lecocq, Baz, *Disputed Desert: Decolonization, Competing Nationalisms and Tuareg Rebellions in Northern Mali*, Leiden: Brill Academic Publishers, 2010.

Lemarchand, Rene, *Burundi: Ethnic Conflict and Genocide*, Cambridge: Cambridge University Press, 1994.

Lemarchand, Rene, *The Dynamics of Violence in Central Africa*, Philadelphia, PA: University of Pennsylvania Press, 2008.

Leys, Colin and Saul, John, *Namibia's Liberation Struggle: The Two Edged Sword*, London: James Currey, 1995.

Levitt, Jeremy I. *The Evolution of Deadly Conflict in Liberia*, Durham. NC: Carolina Academic Press, 2005.

Lewis, Ioan, *Understanding Somalia and Somaliland*, New York: Columbia University Press, 2008.

Jones, Steward Lloyd and Costa Pinto, Antonio (Eds.), *The Last Empire: Thirty Years of Portuguese Decolonization*, Bristol, UK: Intellect Books, 2003.

Lloyd, Alan, *The Drums of Kumasi: The Story of the Ashanti Wars*, London; Longmans, 1964.

Lunn, Joe, *Memories of the Maelstrom: A Senegalese Oral History of the First World War*, Portsmouth, NH: Heinemann, 1999.

McGregor, Andrew, *A Military History of Modern Egypt; from the Ottoman Conquest to the Ramadan War*, Westport, CT: Praeger Security International, 2006.

McLynn, Frank, *The Burma Campaign: Disaster into Triumph, 1942–45*, New Haven, CT: Yale University Press, 2011.

Mamdani, Mahmood, *When Victims Become Killers: Colonialism, Nativism and the Genocide in Rwanda*, Princeton, NJ: Princeton University Press, 2001.

Marcus, Harold, *A History of Ethiopia*, Berkeley, CA: University of California Press, 2002.

Marks, Shula, *Reluctant Rebellion: The 1906–08 Disturbances in Natal*, Oxford: Clarendon Press, 1970.

Martin, David and Johnson, Phyllis, *The Struggle for Zimbabwe*, New York: Monthly Review, 1981.

Martinez, Luis, *The Algerian Civil War 1990–1998*, New York: Columbia University Press, 2000.

Mays, Terry M. *Africa's First Peacekeeping Operation: The OAU in Chad 1981–82*, Westport, CT: Praeger, 2002.

Melvern, Linda, *Conspiracy to Murder: The Rwanda Genocide*, London: Verso, 2006.

Miners, N.J. *The Nigerian Army 1956–66*, London: Methuen, 1971.

Minter, William, *Apartheid's Contras: An Inquiry into the Roots of War in Angola and Mozambique*, London: Zed Books, 1994.

Moorcroft, Paul and McLaughlin, Peter, *The Rhodesian War: A Military History*, London: Pen and Sword, 2008.

Moyd, Michelle, *Violent Intermediaries: African Soldiers, Conquest and Everyday Colonialism in German East Africa*, Athens, OH: Ohio University Press, 2014.

Mwase, G. *Strike a Blow and Die*, Cambridge, MA: Harvard University Press, 1967.

Namakalu, Oswin, *Armed Liberation Struggle: Some Accounts of PLAN's Combat Operations*, Windhoek, Namibia: Gamsberg MacMillan, 2004.

Nasson, Bill, *Springboks on the Somme: South Africa and the Great War, 1914–1918*, Johannesburg: Penguin, 2007.

Nasson, Bill, *The South African War 1899–1902*, London: Hodder Arnold, 1999.

Nasson, Bill, *World War One and the People of South Africa*, Cape Town: Tafelberg, 2014.

Negash, Tekaste and Tronvoll, Kjetil, *Brothers at War: Making Sense of the Eritrean-Ethiopian War*, Oxford: James Currey, 2000.

Newitt, Malyn, *A History of Mozambique*, London: Hurst, 1995.

Nhongo-Simbanegavi, Josephine, *For Better or Worse: Women and ZANLA in Zimbabwe's Liberation Struggle*, Harare: Weaver Press, 2000.

Njoku, Raphael C. *The History of Somalia*, Santa Barbara, CA: Greenwood, 2013.

Nolutshungu, Sam, *The Limits of Anarchy: Intervention and State Formation in Chad*, Charlottesville, VA: University of Virginia Press, 1995.

Nwabara, S.W., *Iboland: A Century of Contact with Britain, 1860–1960*, Atlantic Highlands, NJ: Humanities Press, 1978.

Obasanjo, Olusegun, *My Command: An Account of the Nigerian Civil War 1967–70*, Ibadan, Nigeria: Heinemann, 1980.

Odom, Thomas P. "Shaba II: The French and Belgian Intervention in Zaire in 1978," Fort Leavenworth, Kansas: US Army Command and General Staff College, Combat Studies Institute, 1993.

Omissi, David E. *Air Power and Colonial Control: The Royal Air Force, 1919–1939*, Manchester, UK: Manchester University Press, 1990.

Orpen, Neil, *East Africa and Abyssinian Campaigns: South African Forces in World War II, Vol. I*, Cape Town: Purnell, 1968.

Orpen, Neil, *Victory in Italy, South African Forces: World War II*, Cape Town: Purnell, 1975.

Othen, Christopher, *Katanga, 1960–63: Mercenaries, Spires and the African Nation that Waged War on the World*, Stroud, UK: The History Press, 2015.

Pakenham, Thomas, *The Boer War*, London: Weidenfeld and Nicholson, 1979.

Page, Malcolm, *KAR: A History of the King's African Rifles*, London: Leo Cooper, 1998.

Page, Melvin, *The Chiwaya War: Malawians and the First World War*, Boulder, CO: Westview Press, 2000.

Paice, Edward, *Tip and Run: The Untold Tragedy of the Great War in Africa*, London: Weidenfeld and Nicolson, 2007.

Pankhurst, Richard, *The Ethiopians: A History*, Oxford; Blackwell Publishing, 2001.

Parsons, Timothy H. *The African Rank-and-File: Social Implications of Colonial Military Service in the King's African Rifles, 1902–1964*, Portsmouth, NH: Heinemann, 1999.

Parsons, Timothy H. *The 1964 Army Mutinies and the Making of Modern East Africa*, Westport, CT: Praeger Publishers, 2003.

Pennell, C.R. *Morocco: From Empire to Independence*, Oxford: One World, 2009.

Pollack, Kenneth, *Arabs at War: Military Effectiveness, 1948–1991*, Lincoln, NE: University of Nebraska Press, 2002.

Pollack, Peter, *The Last Hot Battle of the Cold War: South Africa vs. Cuba in the Angolan Civil War*, Oxford: Casemate, 2013.

Pretorius, Fransjohan, *Historical Dictionary of the Anglo-Boer War 1899–1902*, Plymouth, UK: Scarecrow Press, 2009.

Pretorius, Fransjohan, *Life on Commando During the Anglo-Boer War 1899–1902*, Cape Town: Human and Russeau, 1999.

Prunier, Gerard, *Africa's World War: Congo, the Rwanda Genocide and the Making of a Continental Catastrophe*, Oxford: Oxford University Press, 2009.

Prunier, Gerard, *The Rwanda Crisis: History of a Genocide*, New York: Columbia University Press, 1995.

Randrianja, Solofo and Ellis, Stephen, *Madagascar: A Short History*, Chicago, IL: University of Chicago Press, 2009.

Ranger, T.O. *The African Voice in Southern Rhodesia*, London: Heinemann, 1970.

Ranger, T.O. and Bhebhe, N. (Eds.) *Soldiers in Zimbabwe's Liberation War*, London: James Currey, 1995.

Reid, Richard, *Frontiers of Violence in North-East Africa: Genealogies of Conflict Since 1800*, Oxford: Oxford University Press, 2011.

Reid, Richard, *Warfare in African History*, Cambridge: Cambridge University Press, 2012.

Reno, William, *Warfare in Independent Africa*, Cambridge: Cambridge University Press, 2011.

Reyntjens, Filip, *The Great African War: Congo and Regional Geopolitics, 1996–2006*, Cambridge: Cambridge University Press, 2009.

Rotberg, Robert and Mazrui, Ali, (Eds.) *Protest and Power in Black Africa*, New York: Oxford University Press, 1970.

Roumani, Maurice, *The Jews of Libya: Coexistence, Persecution, Resettlement*, Eastbourne, UK: Sussex Academic Press, 2008.

Rouvez, Alain, *Disconsolate Empires: French, British and Belgian Military Involvement in Post-Colonial Sub-Saharan Africa*, Lanham, MD: University Press of America, 1994.

Rupiya, Martin, (Ed.), *Evolutions and Revolutions: A Contemporary History of Militaries in Southern Africa*, Pretoria: Institute for Security Studies, 2005.

Rusagara, Frank, *Resilience of a Nation: A History of the Military in Rwanda*, Kigali: Fountain Publishers, 2009.

Rutherford, Kenneth, *Humanitarianism Under Fire: The US and UN Intervention in Somalia*, Sterling, VA: Kumarian Press, 2008.

Sarkin, Jeremy, *Germany's Genocide of the Herero: Kaiser Wilhelm II, His General, His Settlers, His Soldiers*, Cape Town: University of Cape Town Press, 2010.

Samson, Anne, *World War One in Africa: The Forgotten Conflict Among the European Powers*, London: I.B. Tauris, 2013.

Saul, Mahir and Royer, Patrick, *West African Challenge to Empire: Culture and History in the Volta-Bani Anti-Colonial War*, Athens, OH: Ohio University Press, 2001.

Scheck, Raffael, *Hitler's African Victims: The German Army Massacres of Black French Soldiers in 1940*, Cambridge: Cambridge University Press, 2006.

Schmitt, Deborah Ann, *The Bechuanaland Pioneers and Gunners*, Westport, CT: Praeger, 2006.

Scholtz, Leopold, *The SADF in the Border War, 1966–1989*, Cape Town: Tafelberg, 2013.

Seegers, Annette, *The Military in the Making of Modern South Africa*, London: I.B. Tauris, 1996.

Shepperson, G. and Price, T. *Independent African: John Chilembwe and the Origins, Setting and Significance of the Nyasaland Native Rising of 1915*, Edinburgh, UK: Edinburgh University Press, 1958.

Shillington, Kevin, *History of Africa*, New York: St. Martin's Press, 1995.

Shirreff, David, *Barefeet and Bandoliers: Wingate, Sandford, the Patriots and the Part they Played in the Liberation of Ethiopia*, Barnsley, UK: Pen and Sword, 2009.

Shubin, Vladimir, *The Hot Cold War: The USSR in Southern Africa*, London: Pluto Press, 2008.

Simons, Geoffrey Leslie, *Libya: The Struggle for Survival*, New York: Saint Martin's Press, 1993.

Sibanda, Eliakim *The Zimbabwe African People's Union, 1961–1987*, Trenton, NJ: Africa World Press, 2005.

Simpson, Thula, *Umkhonto we Sizwe: The ANC's Armed Struggle*, Cape Town: Penguin, 2016.

Siollun, Max, *Oil, Politics and Violence: Nigeria's Military Coup Culture, 1966–76*, New York: Algora Publishing, 2009.

Smith, Colin, *England's Last War Against France: Fighting Vichy 1940–42*, London: Weidenfeld and Nicolson, 2009.

Smith, Iain, *The Origins of the South African War 1899–1902*, London: Longman, 1996.

Stapleton, Timothy J. *A History of Genocide in Africa*, Santa Barbara, CA: Praeger Security International, 2017.

Stapleton, Timothy J. *A Military History of Africa*, 3 vols., Santa Barbara, CA: Praeger Security International, 2013.

Stapleton, Timothy J. *A Military History of South Africa: From the Dutch-Khoi Wars to the End of Apartheid*, Santa Barbara, CA: Praeger Security International, 2010.

Stapleton, Timothy J. *African Police and Soldiers in Colonial Zimbabwe, 1923–80*, Rochester, NY: University of Rochester Press, 2011.

Stapleton, Timothy J. *No Insignificant Part: The Rhodesia Native Regiment and the East African Campaign of the First World War*, Waterloo, IA: Wilfrid Laurier University Press, 2006.

Stapleton, Timothy J. *Warfare and Tracking in Africa, 1952–1990*, London: Routledge, 2016.

Steenkamp, Willem, *South Africa's Border War, 1966–1989*, Gibraltar: Ashanti, 1989.

Sterns, Jason, K. *Dancing in the Glory of Monsters: The Collapse of the Congo and the Great African War*, New York: Public Affairs, 2011.

Stewart, Andrew, *The First Victory: The Second World War and the East Africa Campaign*, New Haven, CT: Yale University Press, 2016.

Stiff, Peter, *The Covert War: Koevoet Operations Namibia, 1979–89*, Alberton, South Africa: Galago, 2004.

Stiff, Peter, *The Silent War: South African Recce Operations, 1969–1994*, Alberton, South Africa: Galago Publishing, 1999.

Strachan, Hew, *The First World War in Africa*, Oxford University Press, 2004.

Straus, Scott, *Making and Unmaking Nations: War, Leadership and Genocide in Modern Africa*. Ithaca, NY: Cornell University Press, 2015.

Straus, Scott, *The Order of Genocide: Race, Power, and War in Rwanda*, Ithaca, NY: Cornell University Press, 2007.

Stremlau, John, *The International Politics of the Nigerian Civil War, 1967–70*, Princeton, NJ: Princeton University Press, 1977.

Stuart, James, *A History of the Zulu Rebellion 1906 and of Dinuzulu's Arrest, Trail and Expatriation*, London: Macmillan, 1913.

Tareke, Gebru, *The Ethiopian Revolution: War in the Horn of Africa*, New Haven, CT: Yale University Press, 2009.

Thomas, Martin, *The French Empire Between the Wars*, Manchester, UK: Manchester University Press, 2005.

Thompson, Paul, *Bambatha at Mpanza: The Making of a Rebel*, privately published, 2004.

Turner, John W. *Continent Ablaze: The Insurgency Wars in Africa 1960 to Present*, Johannesburg: Jonathan Ball, 1998.

Udogu, E. Ike *Liberation Namibia: The Long Diplomatic Struggle between the United Nations and South Africa*, Jefferson, LA: Macfarland, 2012.

Vandervort, Bruce, *To the Fourth Shore: Italy's War for Libya, 1911–12*, Stato maggiore dell'esercito, Ufficio storico, 2012.

Vandervort, Bruce. *Wars of Imperial Conquest in Africa, 1830–1914*, Bloomington, IN: Indiana University Press, 1998.

Van der Waals, W.S. *The Portugal's War in Angola*, Rivonia, South Africa: Ashanti, 1993.

Van Der Waag, Ian, *A Military History of Modern South Africa*, Cape Town: Jonathan Ball, 2015.

Villafana, Frank, *Cold War in the Congo: The Confrontation of Cuban Military Forces, 1960–67*, New Brunswick, NJ: Transaction Publishers, 2012.

Vines, Alex, *Angola Unravels: The Rise and Fall of the Lusaka Peace Process*, New York: Human Rights Watch, 1999.

Wallace, Marion, *A History of Namibia: From the Beginning to 1990*, New York: Columbia University Press, 2011.

Wallis, Andrew, *Silent Accomplice: The Untold Story of France's Role in the Rwandan Genocide*, London: I.B. Tauris, 2006.

War Office, *The Abyssinian Campaigns; The Official Story of the Conquest of Italian East Africa*, London: Ministry of Information, 1942.

Watson, Bruce Allen, *Exit Rommel: The Tunisian Campaign 1942–43*, Mechanicsburg, PA: Stackpole Books, 1999.

Watt, Nigel, *Burundi: The Biography of a Small African Country*, London: Hurst, 2008.

Weigert, Stephen, *Angola: A Modern Military History, 1961–2002*, New York: Palgrave, 2011.

Willis, Michael, *Power and Politics in the Maghreb: Algeria, Tunisia and Morocco from Independence to the Arab Spring*, London: C. Hurst, 2012.

Willis, Michael, *The Islamist Challenge in Algeria: A Political History*, New York: New York University Press, 1997.

Wood, J.R.T. *Counter-Strike from the Sky: The Rhodesian All-Arms Fireforce in the Bush 1974–1980*, Johannesburg: 30 Degrees South Publishers, 2009.

Wright, John, *A History of Libya*, London: C. Hurst and Co., 2012.

Zewde, Bahru, *A History of Modern Ethiopia, 1855–1991*, Oxford: James Currey, 2009.

Articles and Chapters

Atangana, Martin R. "French Capitalism and Nationalism in Cameroon," *African Studies Review*, 40(1) (April 1997), 83–111.

Becker, Felicitas, "Traders, 'Big Men' and Prophets: Political Continuity and Crisis in the Maji Maji Rebellion in Southeast Tanzania," *Journal of African History*, 45 (2004), 1–22.

Blacker, John, "The Demography of Mau Mau: Fertility and Mortality in Kenya in the 1950s: A Demographer's Viewpoint," *African Affairs*, 106 (2007), 205–227.

Chappell, Stephen, "Air Power in the Mau Mau Conflict: The Government's Chief Weapon," *The RUSI Journal*, February–March 2011, 156(1), 64–70.

Costa Pinto, Antonio, "The Transition to Democracy and Portugal's Decolonization," in Stewart Lloyd Jones and Antonio Costa Pinto (Eds.), *The Last Empire: Thirty Years of Portuguese Decolonization*, Bristol, UK: Intellect Books, 2003.

Davenport, T.R.H. "The South African Rebellion of 1914," *English Historical Review*, 78 (1963), 73–94.

Esterhuyse, Abel and Jordaan, Evert, "The South African Defence Force and Counter-insurgency, 1966–1990," in Deane-Peter Baker and Evert Jordaan (Eds.), *South Africa and Contemporary Counterinsurgency; Roots, Practises and Prospects*, Claremount, South Africa: International Publishers, 2010, 104–127.

Engelbrecht, C.L. and MacKenzie, W.J. "Operation Rose: The Only Amphibious Landing by South African Forces at War," *South African Military History Journal*, 2(1), 1971.

Fedorowich, Ken, "Sleeping with the Lion? The Loyal Afrikaner and the South African Rebellion of 1914–15," *South African Historical Journal*, 49 (2003), 71–95.

Hodges, G.W.T. "African Manpower Statistics for the British Forces in East Africa, 1914–18," *Journal of African History*, 19(1) (1978), 101–116.

Iliffe, John, "The Organization of the Maji Maji Rebellion," *Journal of African History*, VIII, 3 (1967), 495–512.

Jackson, Ashley, "Bechuanaland, the Caprivi Strip and the First World War," *War and Society* 19, No. 2 (October 2001), 109–142.

Joseph, Richard A. "Ruben Um Nyobe and the 'Kamerun' Rebellion," *African Affairs*, 73(293) (October 1974), 428–448.

Killingray, David, "African Civilians in the Era of the Second World War, 1935–50," in Laband, John, (Ed.) *Daily Lives of Civilians in Wartime Africa: From Slavery Days to Rwandan Genocide*, Westport, CT: Greenwood Press, 2007, 139–167.

Lata, Leenco, "The Ethiopia–Eritrea War," *Review of African Political Economy*, 30 (September 2003), 369–388.

Lodge, Tom, "Soldiers of the Storm: A Profile of the Azanian People's Liberation Army," in Jakkie Cilliers and Markus Reichardt, (Eds.) *About Turn: The Transformation of the South African Military and Intelligence*, Halfway House: IDP, 1995, 105–117.

Maaba, Brown Bavusile, "The PAC's War Against the State, 1960–63," in *The Road to Democracy in South Africa Vo. 1 (1960–70)* South African Democracy Education Trust, Cape Town: Zebra Press, 2004, 257–297.

Magubane, Bernard, Bonner, Philip, Sithole, Jabulani, Delius, Peter, Cherry, Janet, Gibbs. Pat and April, Thomzama, "The Turn to Armed Struggle," in *The Road to Democracy in South Africa Vo. 1 (1960–70)* South African Democracy Education Trust, Cape Town: Zebra Press, 2004, 53–145.

Monson, Jamie, "Relocating Maji Maji: The Politics of Alliance and Authority in the Southern Highlands of Tanzania, 1870–1917" *Journal of African History*, 39 (1998), 95–120.

Ngoga, Pascal, "Uganda: The National Resistance Army," in C. Clapham (Ed.), *African Guerrillas*, Bloomington, IN: Indiana University Press, 1998, 91–106.

O'Toole, Thomas, "The 1928–31 Gbaya Insurrection in Ubangui-Shari: Messianic Movement of Village Self-Defence?" *Canadian Journal of African Studies*, 18(2) (1984), 329–344.

Stapleton, Tim, "Views of the First World War in Southern Rhodesia (Zimbabwe) 1914–1918," *War and Society*, 20(1) (May 2002), 23–44.

Sunseri, Thaddeus, "Statist Narratives and Maji Maji Ellipses," *The International Journal of African Historical Studies*, 33(3) (2000), 567–584.

Swart, Sandra, "A Boer and His Gun and His Wife Are Three Things Always Together: Republican Masculinity and the 1914 Rebellion," *Journal of Southern African Studies*, 24(2) (1998), 737–751.

Tareke, Gebru, "The Ethiopian-Somalia War of 1977 Revisited," *International Journal of African Historical Studies*, 3(3), 2009, 635–667.

Thomas, Roger G. "The 1916 Bongo Riots and Their Background: Aspects of Colonial Administration and African Response in Eastern Upper Ghana," *Journal of African History*, 24 (1983), 57–75.

Thompson, Paul S. "The Zulu Rebellion of 1906: The Collusion of Bambatha and Dinuzulu," *International Journal of African Historical Studies*, 36(3), 2003, 533–557.

Twaddle, Michael with Lucile Rabearimanana and Isaria Kimambo, "The Struggle for Political Sovereignty in Eastern Africa, 1945 to Independence," in Mazrui, Ali (Ed.) *General History of Africa, VIII: Africa since 1935*, Berkeley, CA: University of California Press, 1993, 221–248.

Van Der Waag, Ian, "The Battle of Sandfontein, 26 September 1914: South African Military Reform and the German South West Africa Campaign, 1914–15," *First World War Studies*, 4(2), 2013, 141–165.

Webb, Stewart Tristan, "Mali's Rebels: Making Sense of the National Movement for the Liberation of Azawad Insurgency," in Romaniuk, S.N. and Webb, S.T.

(Eds.), *Insurgency and Counter-insurgency in Modern War*, London: CRC Press, 2016, 135–144.

Wessels, Andre, "South Africa and the War Against Japan," *South African Military History Journal*, 10(3), 1996.

Willan, B.P. "The South African Native Labour Contingent, 1916–1918," *The Journal of African History*, 19(1) (1978), 61–86.

Williams, Rocky, "Integration or Absorption: The Creation of the South African National Defence Force, 1993–1999," *African Security Review*, 11(2), 2002, 17–25.

Williams, Rocky, "The Other Armies: A Brief Historical Overview of Umkhonto we Sizwe (MK) 1961–1994," *South African Military History Journal*, 11(5), June 2000.

Wood, J.R.T. "Countering the Chimurenga: The Rhodesian Counterinsurgency Campaign 1962–80," in Marston, D. and Malkasian, C. (Eds.) *Counterinsurgency in Modern Warfare*, (New York: Osprey Publishing, 2008), 185–202.

Yorke, Edmund, "The Spectre of a Second Chilembwe: Government, Missions and Social Control in Wartime Northern Rhodesia, 1914–1918," *Journal of African History*, 31 (1990), 373–391.

Index